A Treatise on Prayer
from the Heart

Jean Pierre Caussade, S.J.

A Treatise on Prayer from the Heart

*A Christian Mystical Tradition
Recovered for All*

Translated, edited, and introduced by
Robert M. McKeon

THE INSTITUTE OF JESUIT SOURCES
Saint Louis

**Number 17 in Series I: Jesuit Primary Sources
in English Translation**

BV
215
.C3913
1998

Library of Congress Card Catalog Number 98-70159
ISBN: paperback: 1-880810-31-X

CONTENTS

Introduction to

*A Treatise on Prayer
from the Heart*

INTRODUCTION

~~~~~~
~~~~~~

Why Caussade's *Prayer from the Heart* Today?

A conversation I had several years ago with a colleague ran along these lines:

"I've given up on the Catholic Church."

"Why?"

"I am drawn to interior silence and prayer coming from within, not reciting prayers such as the Hail Mary over and over again or listening to long sermons. I finally found what I was looking for in Zen Meditation."

"But look! Aren't you aware of the great mystics, such as the Carmelites St. John of the Cross and St. Teresa of Avila?"

"No, but so what! What little mystical tradition there is in Catholicism or, for that matter, in Christianity is the exclusive province of monks and nuns who have retired from the world. A real mystical tradition accessible and possible for laypeople isn't found in Catholicism."

Saddened, I ended the conversation. As a matter of fact, my own search for God extending over some twenty years confirmed that there was much truth in what my interlocutor was saying. However, I knew that within the teachings of the Church is a constant call to deep union with God. At times the Church seemed to adopt an anti-mystical posture, but it never entirely lost a tradition of interior silence as the step and sign of progressive union with God. We must never forget what the apostle Paul tells us in Eph. 3:17–20:

> Having been rooted and founded solidly on charity, let Christ dwell in your hearts through faith, in order that you be fully able to grasp, with all the holy ones, the breadth and length and height and depth of Christ's love, and know the love that originates from Christ and that thrusts beyond our knowledge, in order that you may be filled in everything with the plenitude of God. [Praise] to [God] who has dominion over all and is able to accomplish far beyond what we ask or know according to the power that is working within us.[1]

Nor should we overlook what Vatican II tells us: "[T]he pilgrim Church on earth looks at God, from whom she has received everything, until she is brought finally to see Him as He is, face to face."[2]

Yes, we are all called to contemplation and mystical union with God. But how do we proceed, especially those laypeople among us who lead full, active lives? Has anyone written an accessible guide book on prayer like Francis de Sales's *Introduction to the Devout Life*? The answer is a resounding yes! Jean Pierre Caussade's *Treatise on Prayer from the Heart*, written around 1735, leads the reader step by step into deep mystical prayer. He answers our thirst for prayer by showing a simple and direct path to prayer.

---

[1] Translated from the Greek rather than from the Vulgate.

[2] *Dogmatic Constitution on Divine Revelation (Dei verbum)*, in *The Documents of Vatican II*, ed. Walter M. Abbott, S.J. (New York: Guild Press, America Press, Association Press; Angelus Book, 1966), no. 7, last three lines (p. 115); for the Church as the people of God, see *Dogmatic Constitution on the Church (Lumen gentium)*, chap. 2.

The Main Themes of Caussade's
Prayer from the Heart

True prayer has to spring from our center, from the heart, as Caussade says. The word "heart" has multiple meanings, but they all convey the idea that the heart lies deep at the center of our being and gives form to our actions. "For where your treasure is, there your heart is."[3] In everyday language we associate the heart with the affective, emotional side of our makeup. Heart-struck, heartache, sweetheart, coldhearted, heart-forsaken, brokenhearted, and similar expressions all describe our feelings. Caussade links these to the heart as the source of prayer, but he has more in mind: the heart is also conceived of as having a knowledge component. The heart is the central faculty of our being, and consequently it is neither pure feeling nor pure intellect; it stands under these and gives them the specific character each has in each one of us.

Caussade brings to the fore the biblical meaning of the heart and the Homeric sense of the gut. Caussade is not alone in this view; for instance, Blaise Pascal, the seventeenth-century French intellectual and religious figure, wrote, "The heart has reasons that reason [pure intellect] doesn't know at all."[4] He is contrasting the reasoning process that goes on in the mind alone with the one that occurs in the heart. Reasoning in the heart that springs from the inner unity of our being does not separate mind from feelings or feelings from the mind as does pure reason or pure affectivity. Accepting the Augustinian view, Caussade emphasizes that Christ resides in the heart and that it is the

---

[3] Luke 12:34 and Matt. 6:21.

[4] "Le coeur a ses raisons que la raison ne connaît point" (*Pensées*, no. 423 [no. 277 in the Brunschvicg edition]); see Jean Laporte, *Le Coeur et la raison selon Pascal*; Henri Bremond, *Histoire littéraire du sentiment religieux en France*, 6:457; Louis Lafuma, "L'Ordre de l'esprit et l'ordre du coeur selon Pascal."

place where Christ communicates with us.[5] What Caussade called prayer from the heart his contemporaries called contemplation. Thus, the spiritual faculty of contemplation is the heart, not the physical heart beating in us but an immaterial faculty, just as reason is not the brain but the faculty of thought.

A heart-charged prayer is not one filled with strong feelings but one springing from our deepest self. Feelings issue from our sensibility, not from our deep center. At the start of question 2, chapter 5, of his *Prayer from the Heart,* Caussade distinguishes affective prayer, that of the feelings, from prayer from the heart. In question 1, chapter 9, under no. 3, Caussade distinguishes three faculties in the soul: imagination, mind, and heart. Is the heart the will? Yes and no. In one sense, without doubt, the heart could be identified with the will, because the heart is the center of love, an attraction to whatever our will seeks. Love of God springs from the heart. But, on the other hand, God speaks to us in the heart where we know him. God just doesn't attract us but also informs us about himself. Thus, the heart should properly be considered the central faculty that works through the will and the intellect.

The German philosopher Immanuel Kant distinguished two realms: what appears to us, the phenomenal world, and what lies under appearances, the noumenal world. According to him, we can only reason about what appears to us, because thought is always carried out in images. We cannot have real concepts of the reality that stands under what appears to us; all we can know is that there is such a reality. Since our minds are embodied in and function through the material world, we cannot truly know the immaterial or spiritual world. The self that underlies us he calls the transcendental self: this we know we have but do not know directly. This transcendental self, I would

---

[5] See St. Augustine, *Homilies on St. John's Epistle,* 3.13, and *Sermons,* 102.2. These passages are quoted by Mary T. Clark in her edition of *Augustine of Hippo: Selected Writings,* 45.

argue, corresponds to what Caussade means by the heart, our true center that we all know we have but do not experience directly. There God sees us spiritually, but we can only stand blindly before him.

But since prayer should spring from the heart, our center, how should we dispose ourselves to assure that the heart really is present to God and consequently becomes the source of prayer? Those who have practiced so-called Ignatian meditation or any form of mental prayer know well that inevitably we can end up listening to our own chatter and talking to and with ourselves rather than with God. These kinds of prayers over time can easily prevent us from listening to God. Still, these forms of prayer are important and are necessary to a balanced spiritual life, just as skillful speech is for social life. We have to listen, however; we have to pause in our conversations if we are to converse. Otherwise, we engage in a monologue such as we find in Ionesco's play *The Bald Soprano*.

Caussade advises us to enter into inner silence by what he calls attentive pauses. With practice these pauses can extend to as long as half an hour. He warns us not to become discouraged by distractions and urges us to practice inner asceticism, which leads to purity. Note well the meaning of purity: it is something unmixed, uncontaminated by foreign elements. He urges us to seek four levels or kinds of purity: that of conscience, of heart, of mind, and of action. Purity of conscience corresponds to a firm resolution to walk with God and not to give up at our failures. After every fall we should pick ourselves up, ask for forgiveness, and continue on our path. Caussade's advice here reminds me of what a tennis pro once told me: "Forget your bad shots; note them and then continue the game without holding onto them and letting them distract you from then on." Shunryu Suzuki uses the following metaphor to describe this detachment: "No Trace: when you do something, you should burn yourself completely, like a good bonfire, leaving no trace of yourself."[6] Hence, full detachment, which implies letting go of our ways and letting God manage our lives, corresponds to purity of conscience.

In purity of heart, we have our heart fully centered on God and freed from the allurement of things. Attachment to objects easily leads us to rest in a pleasurable passion coloring and setting the stage for everything we do. Buñuel's film *The Strange Object of Desire* offers a clear illustration of how passion can so color our perception that reality escapes us. Purity of mind implies a quiet mind. Those who have tried to find interior silence know that our minds are always wandering and jabbering like monkeys in a tree,[7] or a huge pen filled with quacking ducklings that stop quacking whenever one whistles. Reciting a mantra such as "Maranatha" quiets the mind down, silences the jabberings and quackings. In aiming at purity of mind, we must distinguish random wanderings from those following the same patterns. Random ones should be dropped and forgotten; but those that repeat similar patterns reveal areas where we have not as yet really let go, where we need to find new ways of thinking and feeling. Finally, when we practice purity of action, we act only out of love for God, who manifests his will in the good impulses that spring from our heart.

These four forms of purity can be summarized thus: Single-mindedly we must follow God. This path of Caussade, so briefly outlined here, requires asceticism, for we must abandon our own views on how things ought to be and give up control over our inner lives. We must never forget that God wants to be the master of our lives; he knows best. God, not we, is the artist-painter; we mustn't

---

[6] Shunryu Suzuki, *Zen Mind, Beginner's Mind,* 62.

[7] In the Buddhist tradition the mind is often compared to a monkey.

interfere with his work.[8] Caussade's idea of giving in to God by letting the present moment govern our lives finds full development in his classic, *The Sacrament of the Present Moment,* known to many readers under the title *Abandonment to Divine Providence,* an edition unfortunately marred by serious defects.[9]

Now that I have briefly laid out the gist of *Prayer from the Heart,* let us examine why it is true to say that this book presents a Christian mystical tradition recovered for all.

Background to Caussade's *Prayer from the Heart*

During the seventeenth century, France witnessed a blossoming of mysticism. Mysticism simply means experiencing God. It was the age of the great mystical saints, Francis de Sales and Jane Frances Frémyot de Chantal; of the French Jesuit school of spiritual direction; of the lay mysticism of Mme Guyon; and of the bishop-writer Fénelon. It grew out of the Flemish school found in Benedict Canfield, out of the Spanish Jesuit school exemplified by Ignatius of Loyola and Baltasar Álvarez, and out of the Spanish Carmel, notably in Teresa of Avila and John of the Cross. But for all of these schools the acknowledged master and authority was St. Augustine.

Issuing out of the Flemish tradition, Benedict Canfield's *Règle de perfection* (1609) expresses well the abstract

---

[8] See St. John of the Cross, *The Living Flame of Love,* in *Collected Works,* no. 42 of the second redaction (no. 37 of the first), 625f.

[9] The English translations made before 1966 (e.g., that of John Beevers) are based on the editions of Fr. Henri Ramière, which were published during the second half of the nineteenth century. Unfortunately, Ramière's editions differ significantly from the manuscript on which he worked. Michel Olphe-Galliard's edition of 1966 follows the manuscript and consequently is much more reliable than Ramière's; an English translation of it by Kitty Muggeridge was published in 1981 under the title *The Sacrament of the Present Moment.*

voluntaristic school of mysticism.[10] "Abstract" here means independent of every form of knowledge: the mystic leaves behind all thought to achieve pure union of will with the godhead. In this school, union implies the loss of the self through fusion with the divine; the humanity of Christ is put aside and the three Persons of the Trinity tend to merge into an undifferentiated godhead. On the other hand, Cardinal Bérulle, founder of the Oratorians, emphasizes Christ and his suffering humanity.[11] The conflict between these two views greatly colored the seventeenth-century controversy on quietism, of which we will speak later. Since the views of Canfield minimized the role of Christ and implied a direct, enduring, essential union with God in this life, those who followed his inspiration were hard put to defend their orthodoxy, especially against the charge that they were guaranteeing eternal salvation to those who had mystical experience, no matter what of their subsequent lives might turn out to be. The reader of Caussade will discover that our author carefully distances himself from Canfield's fusionist view of mystical union.

St. Ignatius of Loyola's *Spiritual Exercises* formed and still forms the backbone of Jesuit training and spirituality. These exercises aim to use the imagination (the memory) to place ourselves within the events of the life of Christ or the reality of the divine order of the world, and then to use the mind (the understanding) to reflect on what we are imagining, in order to infuse our active life with the will of the Lord. Finally, they strive to motivate the will to carry out the activities that the Lord wants us to undertake. Thus, for Ignatius of Loyola, prayer forms the foundation of the active life. But in the *Exercises* little place may seem to be given to interior silence; the closest we come is found in "the second method of prayer [which] consists in contem-

---

[10] The designation "abstract voluntaristic school" comes from Louis Cognet, *Crépuscule des mystiques;* see especially pp. 26–34.

[11] See Louis Cognet, "Bérulle et la théologie de l'Incarnation."

plating the meaning of each word of a prayer." Ignatius gives this as his second rule:

> If one is contemplating [that is to say, doing mental prayer on] the Our Father and finds in one or two words matter which yields thought, relish, and consolation, one should not be anxious to move forward, even if the whole hour is consumed on what is being found. At the end of the hour the rest of the prayer will be recited in the customary way.[12]

In practice, a well-formed Jesuit spiritual director will not deter a directee from following an inner movement from mental prayer to silence if discernment shows that this comes from God. St. Ignatius of Loyola's rules for the discernment of spirits, which are given at the end of the *Exercises,* require attention to the will of God and outline the differences between the solicitations of the good angel and those of the evil spirit. "In the case of those who are going from good to better, the good angel touches the soul gently, lightly, and sweetly, like a drop of water going into a sponge. The evil spirit touches it sharply, with noise and disturbance, like a drop of water falling onto a stone."[13]

Because prayer life should be judged by the fruits it produces, prayer based on inner silence, while at the same time leading to gentleness and joy, surely comes from God. However, mystical contemplation wasn't always welcomed within the Jesuit order, as the example of Baltasar Álvarez shows. For many years he faithfully tried to follow to the letter the meditation rules of the *Exercises,* but under the inspiration of the Holy Spirit "by intervals he stopped speaking within himself to be present to God."[14] Because of

---

[12] *The Spiritual Exercises of Saint Ignatius,* ed. and trans. George E. Ganss, S.J., no. 254 (p. 99).

[13] Seventh rule for the Second Week, no. 335 (pp. 127f.).

[14] "Voilà ce que je [Álvarez] pense de ce qui se passe en moi, et de la manière d'oraison, et de cesser les discours par intervalles pour la présence de Dieu" (Here is how I interpret what happens in me both about the method of prayer and about leaving off conversation

his reputation and influence, he was instructed to prepare for the head of the Society of Jesus a report on his prayer. But since Everard Mercurian, who was then superior general, feared that contemplation would turn Jesuits from the active life required by the order, he was suspicious of Álvarez's prayer of recollected silence, so in 1578 he enjoined him to stop practicing and teaching it; furthermore, he banned it from the entire order. Later, however, a new Father General, Claudio Aquaviva, recognized that contemplation would enhance the active apostolate of the order and lifted the ban in 1599.

A few years later, Louis de La Puente published Baltasar Álvarez's biography, which includes the report Álvarez sent to the superior of his order and a defense of his prayer of silence. Moreover, in this biography appear references to the Scriptures, the Fathers of the Church, and medieval Schoolmen, which underpinned many polemic works concerning quietism at the end of the seventeenth century. Caussade probably read this biography in its 1618 French translation by René Gaulthier, for I find echoes of Álvarez's report in Caussade, especially with the idea of "attentive pauses."[15]

The French Jesuit school of spiritual direction resembles the Spanish Jesuit school in many ways, because the Jesuit order played an important role in fostering the Catholic Reformation in France, where its members conducted elite schools, advised notables, and gave spiritual direction.

---

for intervals for the sake of the presence of God). These lines are found in Louis de La Puente, *La Vie du père Baltasar Álvares,* chap. 13, sec. 2, next-to-last paragraph [p. 139]). See Paul Dudon, "Les Leçons d'oraison du père Balthazar Alvarez."

[15] Álvarez's report is published in chap. 13 of de La Puente's biography. The Jesuit Roman censors of Caussade's *Spiritual Dialogues,* a reworking of the *Treatise on Prayer from the Heart,* recognized the link to Álvarez, whose biography they cite when they criticize Caussade's notion of attentive pauses. See "La révision romaine," in Caussade, *Traité sur l'oraison du cœur, Instruction spirituelles,* 379.

Spiritual direction imparted by the Jesuits followed two
imperatives: the teaching of prayer and the discernment of
God's will in the lives of the directees. Clearly St. Ignatius
of Loyola's *Exercises* constituted a systematic approach to
achieving these two objectives. In France Fr. Louis Lallemant, his two disciples (Fr. Jean Rigoleu and Fr. Jean
Joseph Surin), and Fr. François Guilloré are the best
known of the French Jesuit school of spirituality. This
school promoted contemplation as the way to stand humbly
before the Holy Spirit, who resides at the center of the
human soul. The aim of prayer was to withdraw into one's
center to rest in God's presence, to discern his will, and to
carry it out. The life of prayer required discipline and mortification, for devotees have to die to themselves if they
want to make a place for God. For instance, Lallemant
outlined seven principles of the spiritual life:

1. to know our goal: only God can make us truly happy;
2. to pursue the ideal of perfection: specifically as outlined by the rules and procedures of the Jesuit order;
3. to purify the heart: what we should purify ourselves
   of; purity of action and purity of mind;
4. to be docile to the promptings of the Holy Spirit:
   working with the gifts and fruits of the Holy Spirit;
5. to lead an interior life of inner quiet: the only true
   source of peace;
6. to be united with our Lord by knowledge of his life
   and teachings, by love, and by imitation of his virtues;
7. to follow the three steps of the spiritual life: Ignatian
   meditation, affective prayer, and contemplation.

Lallemant aimed at teaching spiritual directors how
to lead their directees into contemplation. His approach is
much more pedagogic than that of a Teresa of Avila or a
Francis de Sales. His *Doctrine spirituelle,* from which this list
is taken, was composed from the c   rse notes taken by his

student Jean Rigoleu and fulfills exactly Lallemant's aim of teaching spiritual directors. We find here, therefore, a real school of spirituality whose curriculum grew out of the *Exercises* and relied on the example of Baltasar Álvarez.

Caussade's *Prayer from the Heart,* on the contrary, reflects the pedagogical concern of the French Jesuit school, but has a different audience in view and a different purpose. Our author is writing for directees who haven't found guides or directors willing or able to unveil to them the possibility of contemplative prayer, to prepare them for it, to recognize when God is calling them to it, and to help them to cooperate with this calling. Through his writings Caussade becomes a spiritual director ready to guide anyone who takes the time to consult him by reading his books and following the advice contained therein. The question-and-answer approach of his treatise reflects this objective, for it doesn't read like a catechism; instead, it presents the questions that directees would ask their directors and the answers they would give. We don't have to wait to meet a qualified spiritual guide to start on the journey, for Caussade is there to guide us through his writings.

We can be quite certain that the Jesuit school influenced Caussade, for the fourteen-year formation undergone by a Jesuit scholastic was designed with the sole objective of molding him into a Jesuit. But when we turn to consider the influence that the Spanish mystics or the Salesian school exerted on him, we become less certain. Not that they didn't have any influence, for they constituted a major part of the climate of seventeenth- and eighteenth-century French spirituality. Caussade, who eulogizes John of the Cross (beatified, but not canonized until after the mid-eighteenth century), cites him a few times as an authority; however, he cites Teresa of Avila (canonized in 1622) almost thirty times, and Francis de Sales (canonized in 1665) about twenty times. Since Teresa of Avila and Francis de Sales were highly regarded and considered orthodox authorities, Caussade draws abundantly and freely on their writings to back up the main themes he is developing.

Those, especially the Jansenists, who attacked the contemplative experiences of their contemporaries, could not directly attack the teachings of these saints without undermining their own credibility and orthodoxy. When the question arose whether the prayer of inner quietude inevitably led to illusions, Caussade called on Teresa of Avila to certify the worth of this prayer. He drew on her and on Francis de Sales to justify his argument that contemplation, prayer from the heart, is an appropriate path, one that could lead its followers to full spiritual development and intimate union with God. All deeds appearing good to the mind had to pass St. Francis de Sales's litmus test: They kept peace and gentleness in the soul and did not lead to inner turmoil and disturbance.

When explaining the advantages of "prayer from the heart," Caussade tells his reader to look at the writings of Teresa of Avila, Jane Frances de Chantal, John of the Cross, Lallemant, Rigoleu, and Surin. In *Prayer from the Heart,* he specifically recommends the following authorities to his readers:

Henri-Marie Boudon, archdeacon of Evreux (1624–1702), *Les Saintes Voies de la croix*

François Guilloré, *Les Progrès de a vie spirituelle selon les diférents états de l'âme*

Thomas à Kempis, *The Imitation of Christ*

Lorenzo Scupoli, *The Spiritual Combat*

Jean-Joseph Surin, *Catéchisme spirituel,* vol. 1

In his letters he refers his directees to the following works:

Francis de Sales, "De benignité et patience envers soi-même," found in Jean-Pierre Camus's *L'Esprit de saint François de Sales,* tome 6, part 18, chap. 13, sections. 20 and 21 (pp. 474–76)

Francis de Sales, *Les Epistres du bienheureux Messire François de Sales, évesque et Prince de Genève*

François Guilloré, *Les Progrès de la vie spirituelle selon les diférents états de l'âme* (a work he particularly likes)

Jane Frances de Chantal, *Lettres,* that is, *Les Épistres spirituelles,* ed. Marie-Aimée de Blomay

Jean-Joseph Languet, *Traité de la confiance en la Miséricorde de Dieu*

Robert Morel, *De l'espérance chrétienne et de la confiance en Dieu*

Lorenzo Scupoli, *Treatise on Peace of Soul,* found at the end of *The Spiritual Combat*

Throughout his writings he refers very often to St. Paul, Teresa of Avila, Jane Frances de Chantal, Francis de Sales, St. Augustine, and Jacques-Bénigne Bossuet; in addition, in his letters he refers often to François de Salignac Fénelon, but he doesn't mention him directly in *Prayer from the Heart.*

To argue that contemplation should be the usual prayer of the members of the Order of the Visitation of the Blessed Virgin Mary, Caussade calls on St. Jane Frances de Chantal, the order's founder, already declared blessed but not canonized until after the mid-eighteenth century. Her response to article 28 of the rules of her order has a discussion about prayer in which we can find many themes developed by Caussade: simplicity of heart, attentive pauses, dryness as an important step on the path, purity of heart, and abandonment to God.[16]

Just what does the spiritual climate of his age teach Caussade? Many of his contemporaries were dazzled by the word "contemplation," which they identified with extraordinary phenomena such as ecstasies, visions, and levitations. But as Caussade knew, these people erred, for contemplation rarely brings with it anything extraordinary. Indeed,

---

[16] Jane Frances Frémyot de Chantal, "Réponse sur l'article 28, des retraites" (Response to article 28 on retreats), *Vive Jésus réponses . . . sur les règles, constitutions et coustumier,* 500–515.

many were called to contemplation and experienced it un-
aware of what it was they were experiencing. Unfortunately, when they spoke to a priest about their experiences, they
received such bad advice as

- Interior silence is idleness; consequently make every
  effort to do Ignatian meditation and avoid silence.

- Interior silence is dangerous, for it leads to illusions,
  especially from evil spirits.

- Practicing interior silence inflates the ego; it is presumptuous, because only exceptionally holy people
  are called to inner silence.

- Interior silence constitutes self-induced bliss, an inner
  illumination that turns us away from doing what
  God wants us to do.

Such poor advice led some people to turn away from
the interior silence to which God was calling them. It is
true, as Caussade knew, that initially we do, in fact, exercise
control over our own spiritual life through our practices of
meditation, good resolutions, and good deeds. But as God
draws us into deeper prayer, we have to put behind us our
ways of doing things and turn the control of our spiritual
life over to God. Practicing interior silence by Caussadean
attentive pauses fosters detachment and teaches us to align
our will with God's. As is the case with any spiritual activity, we must judge it by the fruits it brings, such as interior
peace and joy, greater willingness to respond to the immediate calls of charity and obedience, and diminished attachment to our own vision of how things ought to be. Thus,
attentive pauses seemed to Caussade to be a superior way
to avoid nourishing self-love, just as they did to St. Francis
de Sales, who wrote as follows to St. Jane de Chantal:

> . . . a great gentleness and willingness to yield in every-
> thing that isn't sin or an occasion of sin; it's a flexible
> disposition able gracefully to do the virtuous or charitable
> thing. For example: try interrupting the meditations of
> someone who is very attached to her spiritual exercises and
> you will see her upset, flustered, taken aback. A person

who has this true freedom will leave her prayer, unruffled, gracious toward the person who has unexpectedly disturbed her, for to her it's all the same—serving God by meditating or serving Him by responding to her neighbor. Both are the will of God, but helping the neighbor is necessary at that particular moment. We have occasion to practice this freedom whenever things don't go the way we'd like them to; for anyone who is not attached to her own ways will not get impatient when things go otherwise. . . . The will of God is indicated in two ways: through necessity or charity.[17]

This prayer from the heart, which occurs on a deep level within the suprasensible world, purges us bit by bit of our egoism; consequently, by freeing us from our own selfish satisfactions, it forms an advantageous way of receiving divine help to acquire humility. It suffers from no greater dangers than any other form of prayer—indeed, it is less dangerous. Illusions arise in meditation as much as they do anywhere else, but in the prayer from the heart we are distancing ourselves from inner activity, which implies that we should be less drawn to illusions. The practice of unattachment gives us the best training against distractions: we learn to ignore them. Unattachment prevents us from grasping at consolations.

Dryness, continuous distractions, and strong temptations do not at all imply that we are on the wrong path and that God doesn't support what we are doing; on the contrary, they are signs of spiritual progress. God sends us trials to purge us; he teaches us to put our confidence in his love and to renounce our own ways. When we fall, we must, without agitation or panic, get up, ask for forgiveness, and continue on our path. Our weaknesses help us find God's greatness.

How can we avoid the subtle gerrymandering of our egoism? For instance, how can we discern whether the

---

[17] See Francis de Sales, *Oeuvres,* 12:352–70 (letter no. 234), translated in *Letters of Spiritual Direction,* 138f.

decision to fast strengthens our egoism and attachment to our own will or, as it should, purges our selfishness? Using the expressions of Shunryu Suzuki, is it "little mind" or "big mind" that commands?[18] André Louf asks whether the superego, the idealized self, or false gods are ruling our lives rather than the Lord.[19] The clergy of the sixteenth and seventeenth centuries worried that perhaps illusions were ruling the faithful. Caussade argues that we can escape the danger of illusions by following the advice he gives in his *Prayer from the Heart,* especially in chapter 3, where he discusses whether there are abuses and errors to fear from the prayer from the heart and how we can avoid them by detaching ourselves from all inner feelings and anything that seems extraordinary.

If we are to understand the immediate background that influenced Caussade, we need to enter upon a brief discussion of Mme Guyon (1648–1717) and the controversy she stirred up regarding inner quietness. Along the way, we will suggest that the reaction to her mysticism directly reveals the place of laywomen within the official organization of the post-Reformation Roman Catholic Church. The clerical state was viewed as superior to that of the lay state.[20] The duties of a bishop elevated him to a superior state, those of priest, to a lower state, those of religious, to a still-lower state; on the very lowest rung of all, the laity found themselves. Laypeople who didn't consecrate themselves by vows of chastity, obedience, and poverty led intrinsically less perfect lives, which were continuously tainted by the norms of the world. Thus their competence in worldly matters excluded any similar competence in spiritual matters. They dealt with spiritual matters only

---

[18] *Zen Mind,* 90–92.

[19] André Louf, *Tuning In to Grace: The Quest for God,* chap. 7.

[20] See for instance Thomas Aquinas, *Summa Theologica,* IIa–IIæ, q. 184, arts. 4 (Whether whoever is perfect is in the state of perfection) and 5 (Whether religious and prelates are in the state of perfection).

privately and tangentially. They might achieve high degrees of personal sanctity, but on account of their state, they were not called to or authorized to teach about spiritual matters. Bishops were the guardians and teachers of spiritual matters; others could do so only insofar as their bishop authorized them. Thus a Mme Guyon could practice her mystical life, but she shouldn't propagate and teach it without the permission of her bishop. Even she acknowledged this principle, for she asked her bishop, Bossuet, to examine her writings so that he could certify their orthodoxy.

Unfortunately for Mme Guyon, Bossuet—like the Jansenist Pierre Nicole and the head of the Carthusians, Innocent Le Masson—were biased against laypeople, especially women, in religious matters. The scholar Marie-Louise Gondal writes:

> If she had been a princess, she [Mme Guyon] would have attracted their [Bossuet, Nicole, Le Masson] flattery. If a nun, she couldn't be very dangerous. If a saint, she would serve at their beckoning. But as a laywoman, she was a threat they couldn't control. It was necessary to keep this voice from being heard and necessary to destroy [in the words of Le Masson] a venom which takes over the heart unnoticeably.[21]

Bossuet in the introduction to his *Instructions sur les estats d'oraison* clearly espouses an antifeminist viewpoint.[22]

Two other points need emphasis if we are to understand the lay mysticism of Mme Guyon: the nature of her spiritual path and her relationship with King Louis XIV's wife, Mme de Maintenon. At the young age of about eleven or twelve, Mme Guyon was drawn to the Visitation order, read the works of St. Francis de Sales and the biography of Mme de Chantal, and entered into the prayer of quietude. She rapidly attained such strong mystical experiences that she would forget to do the tasks assigned to her

---

[21] Translated from Marie-Louise Gondal, *Madame Guyon*, 74.
[22] See the introduction of the 1697 edition, 7f.

at home; as a result, her mother-in-law and her husband tried to keep her from falling into mystical states. She described her life at this time as "a more intense mystical absorption in spite of my family's hostility."[23] As her autobiography suggests, she started more or less at the summit of mystical experiences rather than at the bottom, where she would have prepared herself by incessantly working at acquiring deep piety, in order to be ready for a possible mystical experience of God, She might never have actually enjoyed this experience, however, because she might never have acquired true piety. The path of her mysticism differed greatly from what was usual among her contemporaries: people traditionally struggled with prayer and mortification to achieve the state of great detachment that must precede any mystical experience. The mystical experience seemed to be a reward for those select few who were able to achieve the heights of asceticism and piety.

To her contemporaries, Mme Guyon's spiritual life seemed to reflect illusion rather than the working of God's hand. Later, after the start of her intense mystical life, she experienced long periods of dryness and practiced mortifications—some reasonable, such as not getting upset or angry, but some downright unreasonable, such as licking spittle up off the ground.[24] As her life unfolded, especially after she was ordered by Mme de Maintenon to leave Saint-Cyr and committed to prison a few years later, she practiced great asceticism by accepting with good grace the oppression she was suffering.[25]

In 1688 Mme Guyon's young cousin, Mme de La Maisonfort, introduced her to Mme de Maintenon, who was trying to set up a convent at Saint-Cyr and planned to have Mme de La Maisonfort, who was an ardent supporter

---

[23] The title of chap. 12 of the first part of her autobiography ("Vie de Madame Guyon," in *Les Cahiers de la Tour Saint-Jacques,* vol. 6).

[24] See her autobiography, pt. 1, chap. 10, para. 2 (p. 39).

[25] See especially Mme Guyon's *Récits de captivité inédit.*

of Mme Guyon, be one of the mainstays of the convent. Mme Guyon's views found fertile ground at Saint-Cyr, where many of the nuns enthusiastically followed her teachings on prayer. But problems arose within the convent; for instance, some sisters refused to work, claiming to be in communion with God. Mme de Maintenon asked Mme de La Maisonfort not to forget that Mme Guyon's ideas had already aroused suspicion; accordingly, she urged her to practice discretion when speaking about her cousin, and to recognize that Saint-Cyr should develop its spirituality along lines already customary in other convents. However, Mme de La Maisonfort stubbornly resisted Mme de Maintenon, who finally had to bring in the local ordinary, Godet des Marais, bishop of Chartres. The arrest and imprisonment of Mme Guyon quickly followed.

Was Mme Guyon a victim of human jealousy and prejudice? we may ask. The answer seems to be yes; after all, her *Moyen court,* whose full title reads in translation, *Very Easy Short Way to Pray That All Can Most Easily Practice and through It Achieve in a Short Time Very High Perfection,* was published with the required imprimatur and, in view of our present-day knowledge, did not warrant condemnation. In her view, prayer simply meant turning the heart to God and practicing charity within the heart.[26] Prayer, she held, is the key to perfection for it leads us away from vice to virtue.

The first degree of prayer, she explains in *Moyen court,* is meditative reading in which the mind fixes on a few words or a short text in order to rest in the presence of God. The second degree she calls prayer of simplicity, an expression that she prefers to others, such as contemplation or prayer of faith or of rest. Those who practice the prayer of simplicity turn their affections to God and very gently keep the fire of affection burning, being careful not to extinguish the flame by too strong an impulse. The next

---

[26] *Moyen court,* in *Opuscules spirituels,* 9.

degree of prayer she calls prayer of simple presence of God or active contemplation, which sounds much like Baltasar Álvarez's notion of prayer. But in Guyon's view, to move from affective prayer to active contemplation, the soul passes through purgation by dryness, abandonment to God's will, and suffering in order to achieve conversion. The final degree of prayer is that of infused prayer. The heart, which is the center where love and charity engulf the will, is the soul's spiritual appetitive faculty. Guyon is, therefore, transforming affectivity or the feeling of love into a spiritual activity in which the feeling remains but becomes rooted in, fed by, and guided by the spiritual.

Prayer, therefore, leads to transfiguration in which the spiritual captures the material and divinizes the person. Here, depending on how Mme Guyon is understood, we can find grounds for unorthodoxy. If we read her as expressing her perception of her experiences, then she can only be accused of perhaps badly expressing herself. On the other hand, if we interpret her as telling exactly what the mystical experience is, then she can be reproached for implying that salvation has already been achieved here on earth, because the transfiguration she implies could be understood as an enduring state. If this were the case, the enlightened person would then be guaranteed salvation. It is this very reading that led Bossuet and others to attack her with such violence; recall Le Masson's description of her as venom.

Fortunately, not all saw her in such a negative light. Fénelon, archbishop of Cambrai and tutor to the King's grandsons, perceived the validity of her experiences, although he did find that at times she expressed herself too rashly.[27] She helped him when his prayer life was at an impasse. From her he discovered that it wasn't necessary to

[27] For a brief sketch on François de Salignac de la Mothe Fénelon, see "Reflections on the Character and Genius of Fénelon" by Thomas Merton. This is the introduction to Fénelon, *Letters of Love and Counsel.*

think when praying and that dryness in prayer constituted a positive development, not a regression. Since before God mankind and the world were nothing, devotees should melt into God, recognize God's fullness, and love him in a fully disinterested way by accepting whatever he sends and by abandoning their own desires and ways. When Mme Guyon was under attack, Fénelon refused to enter the fray against her. He agreed that some of her expressions were exceptionable, but he refused to malign her. His refusal resulted in his banishment from court and exile to Cambrai, where he finished his days.

Fénelon had extensive spiritual correspondence with important people, selections of which were published anonymously during his lifetime. But in 1718, shortly after his death, his nephew published a selection of his uncle's spiritual letters and writings entitled *Oeuvres spirituelles,* which offered reflections and advice on the spiritual life, treating, for example, voluntary faults, sadness, or confidence in God. Caussade most likely read it, for many themes found in Fénelon can be found in Caussade. For instance, Fénelon's statement "There isn't any penance more bitter than the state of pure faith sustained without any feelings"[28] is echoed by Caussade when he develops recommendations for those advanced in prayer from the heart, especially when he warns his readers against the dangerous temptation to fear that faith is lost because they no longer feel anything.

The above discussion of Mme Guyon already reveals one of the major factors that intervened to break the seventeenth-century mystical tradition, namely, the condemnation of quietism and its consequences. Interestingly, the Catholic reform in France turned about two axes—quietism and Jansenism. Both movements saw the need for reform, but they sought reform from very different perspectives. The Jansenists had an antimystical bias; for them, God assumed

---

[28] Fénelon, *Oeuvres* (Pléiade ed.), 612.

only the extraordinary person into the mystical experience. All or virtually all of those claiming mystical experiences were suffering from illusions. These illusions took birth in the so-called mystics' method of prayer, inner silence. To the inner life the Jansenist applied literally the well-known adage: An idle mind is the devil's workshop.

Although Caussade and the Jansenist Pierre Nicole both agree that God resides deep in the heart and that Augustine is the master of the Church Fathers, they have opposite views on the basic orientation of the heart where prayer takes place. Both clearly understand Augustine's futile struggle to do what he knew he should do. But Nicole's pessimistic view builds on Jansenius's interpretation of the relationship between grace and human will, in which grace is *delectatio,* that is, pleasure, and causes the will to act. But since grace, which attracts us to God, is a force or weight different from the will itself, it acts as an intervening force exterior to the will, by which God, so to speak, tries to force us to do what is good. Thus, within us two weights exert their influence—our own weight of human pleasure and God's intervening weight of grace.

In contrast, however, Caussade's view remains firmly attached to a strict interpretation of St. Augustine: Grace allows us to see that true delectation, pleasure, consists in loving God, not running after inferior things.[29] Hence, when we are graced, we spontaneously follow the path of love that God wants us to follow. Grace is the light allowing us to see spontaneously that God is our true good and giving us the strength to accomplish the good. Thus, Caussade sees as good the inner spontaneity of a graced person standing in silence before God. In Nicole's view, however, this person would never know whether a spontaneous movement is good or not, for he or she doesn't know whether God's grace was strong enough to overcome the

---

[29] See Etienne Gilson, *Introduction à l'étude de Saint Augustine,* 204–16, especially 210 n. 4.

will's spontaneous attraction for the most immediate and accessible pleasure. In Nicole's view and that of any Jansenist, the heart can never enduringly turn towards God and what he wills; if we are to do good, grace has to intervene at each moment and overcome our penchant for the pleasures of merely human goods. Only by multiplying deeds that we think are good can we have any hope of being really on the road to salvation.

Thus, the Jansenist sees the human being as almost fundamentally depraved. Only special intervention by God can give us any righteousness, but this intervention is only manifested by what we do. Consequently, as long as we continually direct our inward feelings and thoughts and outwardly act in full conformity with God's law, we can be certain that God is working in us and that we are on the road to salvation. It follows that the faithful must pay careful attention to the least thought, because any deviant thought suggests that we have fallen from God's graces. In Jansenism the superego reigns supreme.

But for Augustine, and surely for Caussade, grace is a light that reveals to us the truth to which we are spontaneously attracted because of its inherent goodness. Hence, a grace-filled heart has a steady orientation towards the truth; it suffices to let this graced inner orientation manifest itself, follow the inner prompting of the Spirit, and accept the events imposed on us at the present moment.

In contrast to the Jansenist, if I may be so bold as to suggest, the quietist drugs the superego into a state of stupor and effectively kills it. For once the faithful have reached the quietistic mystical state, their satori, as the Buddhist might say, they no longer have to concern themselves with sin, against which they have been inoculated, because now they are permanently divinized. Such an unorthodox view was understandably enough condemned in 1687 by Pope Innocent XI's brief *Cælestis Pastor,* which listed some sixty-eight heretical propositions of quietism. It is unclear to whose writings and lives these propositions were intended to apply, other than to the Spanish priest Miguel de Molinos. To the French Crown and episcopate, quietism presented the danger of a movement over which they had no control. Furthermore, it was difficult to identify just who was a quietist. Bossuet's violent attacks against what he calls the new mystics read like a textbook case of attacking a straw man. He forcefully assailed views that his opponent did not actually espouse, and thus was able to emerge victorious from a sham battle.

Was poor Mme Guyon a quietist? Was it right for Bossuet to apply the standards of strict logic to writings that were mostly streams of consciousness or poetical expressions? Did she really believe what Bossuet said she believed? She denied that she was a heretic, always arguing that she was ready to submit to the judgment of the Church; but she wasn't ready to lie in order to achieve a compromise with her accusers. In her *Récits de captivité*, she narrates many attempts of her enemies to impugn her character and trip her up with cross-examinations.

Quietism really didn't constitute a movement so much as a state of mind and a lightning rod that drew the Jansenist's bolts. Priests inclined toward Jansenism saw quietism lurking in the least instance of inner quiet. Spiritual writers had to be careful, for the accusation of quietism by an alert Jansenist could raise problems with the local bishop. Hence, it became prudent to maintain a low profile, to talk about the prayer of silence only in private and circulate information about it only in manuscripts destined for the eyes of the few trustworthy souls who weren't prey to Jansenism.

As a consequence of all this, the mystical tradition that flourished at the start of the century slipped from the stage at the end of the seventeenth century. Yes, mysticism persisted into the eighteenth century in persons such as Caussade and his directees or Fr. Pierre de Clorivière, but it had lost its wide appeal. Even though Jansenism was finally condemned in the eighteenth century, its legacy lived on for a long time, perhaps even until the middle of the twentieth century. As was the case with my interlocutor at the beginning of this introduction, mysticism seemed like something remote from what ordinary Christians could aspire to. Inner peace and intimacy with God, which are achieved through prayer from the heart, just don't fit the pessimistic view of the human being who always remains unsure of where he stands in God's eyes. Perhaps Bossuet said it all: "The Church holds its children in uncertainty so that they are obliged to pray unceasingly for perseverance."[30]

Caussade, like his spiritual predecessors, wanted us to aspire to become mystics, but this view didn't come to the fore again until Vatican II, little more than a quarter of a century ago.

Caussade's Life

L ittle is known about Caussade, other than a few details drawn from administrative archives and the occasional comments he makes about himself in his letters.[31] He was born March 7, 1675, in the Quercy region of France, whose regional center is Cahors, about one hundred miles east of Bordeaux, and died in Toulouse on December 8, 1751. His full name was Jean Pierre Thomas Caussade; none of the eighteenth-century sources puts a hyphen between Jean and Pierre; furthermore, the particle "de" was

---

[30] *Instructions sur les états d'oraison,* bk. 5, chap. 37, para. 1 (p. 175).

[31] For biography see Jacques Gagey's dissertation, *"Le Traité, où l'on découvre la vraie science de la perfection du salut et la tradition spirituelle caussadienne. Histoire critique et théologique,"* 40–56, 612–14; Paul Dudon, "Note sur les éditions du p. de Caussade"; Jacques Le Brun, "Quelques documents relatifs au père de Caussade conservés aux Archives de Meurthe-et-Moselle"; the following works by Olphe-Galliard: biographical information in "Le J.-P. de Caussade, directeur d'âmes," 398f.; *La Théologie mystique en france au XVIII siècle,* 7–11; his edition of Caussade's *Lettres spirituelles,* 9–15.

not attached to his name until the regent of the Duchy of Lorraine added it in 1734, when the priest was almost sixty. After studying philosophy for two years and law for one, he entered the Jesuit order in 1693 when he was eighteen years old. After two years of novitiate at Toulouse, he taught grammar for two years at Auch, then the following year at Aurillac. We have no information about the next year, but the year after that he taught metaphysics at Rodez, then humanities and rhetoric at Saint-Flour. The year following he taught the same subjects at Mauriac, and finally at Albi. Thus, in a period of eight academic years (1695 through the summer of 1703), he taught in at least six different places.

His master of novices had expressed the hope that he was endowed with good sense ("prudentia spe magna"); but his superior for the next two years rated him as having little good sense for his age ("prudentia parva pro ætate"), and four years later at Saint-Flour, his superior credited him with hardly any good sense ("prudentia vix ulla")! But in spite of his apparent loss of good sense, he was allowed to advance to the study of theology at Toulouse for four years (1703–7). During his second year of theology, he was described as intellectually undistinguished ("sapientia sæpe indiscreta"). In 1705 he was ordained to the priesthood and did his tertiary year at Toulouse in 1707–8. His order did not give up on Caussade as a teacher, posting him to teaching assignments for the next seven years: one year at Aurillac teaching grammar, two years at Perpignan teaching physics, and finally four years at Toulouse, where he taught logic the first year, physics the second, logic the third, and physics the fourth, all the while preparing his doctorate in theology, which he received in 1715, at the end of his fourth year at Toulouse. In 1711 his superior at Toulouse characterized him as above average in intelligence ("sapientia plus quam mediocris") and of common virtue ("virtus communis").

Why so many different assignments? Was he an unsuccessful teacher? Did he fit in well with his fellow Jesuits?

Starting in 1715, for the next five years he held the position of prefect of studies in three different Jesuit colleges (one year at Rodez, the next at Montauban, and finally the next three at Auch). After 1720 we find no record of his having any more academic duties.

But he continues to serve only for short periods in any one place: three years at Clermont-Ferrand, one at Saint-Flour, where he was described as sometimes lacking good sense ("prudentia indiscreta aliquando") and one at Le Puy. From 1725 to 1739, he had assignments outside his province, except for two years. First he went to northern France in the Champagne region and then, in 1730, to Nancy, where he started his work of spiritual direction on behalf of the Sisters of the Visitation. He was called back to his province after the first year, but returned to Nancy two years later in 1733 and remained there until 1739. It is surely during these last six years that he pursued his apostolate of spiritual direction and developed his teachings on prayer and abandonment to divine Providence. But his superiors certainly did not seem to hold him in high regard; in 1739 the label of "lacking good sense" was again attributed to him, and he was described as "inclined to melancholy, yet cheerful."[32] In 1740 he was posted back to Toulouse, where he had first entered the Society. For the next three years, he was rector of the college at Perpignan, and for the following three years rector at Albi. Finally in 1746, he was missioned definitively to Toulouse, where until the last year of his life he served as director of the seminary "des clercs."

The period 1730–39 seems to have been the only time when Caussade had any truly enduring influence.

---

[32] Quoted by Olphe-Galliard, *La Théologie mystique*, 8: "aliquando indiscreta" and "biliosus et hilaris."

During this time he worked with the sisters of the Order of the Visitation of the Blessed Virgin Mary, who held him in high regard and who made copies and compilations of his letters and writings.[33]

Caussade's Writings

C aussade's letters,[34] mostly written to the sisters at Nancy, reveal a very spiritual person who advocated fully abandoning oneself to the daily events of life, for God reveals his will in these events. His fellow Jesuits seemed not to have held him in great esteem, for he writes, "I know that they find my spiritual direction a bit too simple-minded."[35]

Caussade's manuscript writings, none of which are in autograph, but rather are copies made by the Sisters of the Visitation, fall into three clusters:

1. His correspondence

2. *Treatise in Which One Finds the True Doctrine of the Perfection of Salvation*

---

[33] See Gagey, *"Le Traité,"* 48f nn. 20–21. Marie-Anne-Thérèse de Rosen wrote about Caussade, "He told us how wonderful is prayer, which you know well is his speciality" (ibid.).

[34] The Sisters of the Visitation burned his autograph letters (see Caussade, *Lettres spirituelles,* 1:44). However, there are a few samples of his handwriting (see Le Brun, "Quelques documents relatifs au Père de Caussade").

[35] "Je sais qu'on trouve ma conduite un peu trop simple, mais n'importe! Cette sainte simplicité que le monde abhorre, je la trouve si charmante que je ne penserai pas même à m'en corriger" (I know that they find my spiritual direction a bit too simple-minded, but so what! This holy simplicity that the world abhors I find so charming that I don't even think of correcting myself of it") (*Lettres spirituelles,* 1:66). Olphe-Galliard holds that there is a hint in his letters that he had to leave Nancy for a year because of some sort of scandal, but we know little of what it might have been, and Gagey rejects this view as pure invention by Olphe-Galliard (*"Le Traite,"* 46 n. 13).

3. *Treatise on Prayer from the Heart*

The themes developed in both of his treatises form the framework and basis for the spiritual direction he gives in his correspondence; furthermore, they contain passages and ideas drawn from his correspondence. *The Sacrament of the Present Moment* (as the 1966 edition of *Abandon à la Providence Divine* is called) reveals notions already present in his correspondence; if it was not actually written by Caussade, at the very least it was produced by the Sisters of the Visitation at Nancy on the basis of his letters.[36] Consequently, we infer that Caussade wrote the two treatises and that his letters furnished draft elements for these treatises.

Although Mother Marie-Anne-Thérèse de Rosen, in her introduction to the *Treatise in Which One Finds the True Doctrine of the Perfection of Salvation,* states that it was composed from letters written by Caussade, Gagey argues the contrary.

The *Perfection of Salvation* was first published in 1861 by Fr. Henri Ramière under the title *Abandon à la providence divine.* During the nineteenth century Ramière's original edition went through nine later editions, each differing from the other by the addition of different letters written by Caussade. None of these editions gave us the *Perfection of Salvation* as Caussade wrote it; instead, Ramière modified Caussade's text to ensure that no hint of quietism could be found in it. This edition is well known to the English reading world under the title *Abandonment to Divine Providence.* In 1966 Michel Olphe-Galliard published the unexpurgated text of the *Perfection of Salvation* under the title *Abandon à la providence divine.* In 1981 Kitty Muggeridge translated

---

[36] In "Le Père Jean-Pierre de Caussade et Madame Guyon," *Bulletin de littérature écclésiastique* of l'Institut catholique de Toulouse (82 [Jan. 1981]: 25–54), Olphe-Galliard argues that chap. 1 of *L'Abandon* is a letter of Caussade, but that the rest of the treatise is by Mme Guyon. For further details see Gagey, *"Le Traite."*

this definitive edition and published it under the title *The Sacrament of the Present Moment*. It remains in print.

Olphe-Galliard in 1962 and 1964 published the *Lettres spirituelles* of Caussade. His primary source was the manuscripts preserved at the Visitation in Nancy. Several years ago a manuscript notebook of Caussade's letters turned up. It features a rich lode of material formerly unknown to scholars.[37]

The Treatise on Prayer from the Heart exists in manuscript form at the Bibliothèque des Fontaines in Chantilly and was published by Olphe-Galliard in 1979, although by that time his eyesight was failing. An exact manuscript copy of chapter 11 is found at the Bibliothèque Publique in Nancy and was published by Le Brun.[38] In both manuscripts the same word is written in as a correction to the copy; thus, it appears that both manuscripts were copied from a common text at the same time with the intention of circulating them within the convent where the copies were made and among those outside who would be sympathetic to Caussade's teaching. When Caussade's *Prayer from the Heart* was to be published, steps were taken to ensure that its orthodoxy could withstand every suspicion, and especially that no charge of quietism could be lodged against it.

A draft most likely by Caussade[39] entitled *Spiritual Dialogues on Different Kinds of Prayer, Based on a Methodical and Rational Analysis of the Thought and Doctrine of M. Bossuet, Bishop of Meaux* was submitted in 1737 to two

---

[37] These letters are in the possession of Fr. Paul Veyron, S.J., and a photocopy of them is on file at the Bibliothèque des Fontaines in Chantilly. Mlle Brunet-Jailly of the Société de Jésus Christ, whose motherhouse is in Lyon, is writing a thesis on them under the direction of Jean Mesnard. Gagey also drew on these letters.

[38] "Texte inédits du Père de Caussade publiés par Jacques Le Brun."

[39] The copyright given in Paris in 1743 names Caussade as the author; see F. Cavallera, "Caussade, auteur des *Instructions spirituelles.*"

Jesuit censors at the Collegium Romanum.[40] No copies of this draft have been found, but we know from the censors' report that it contained two dialogues on prayer. This implies that already the original *Prayer from the Heart* had been substantially revised and changed, especially as regards making the heart the central faculty of prayer. Without doubt, Caussade's practical mystical advice was purged and transformed into a theological treatise on mystical prayer. The revised version of his original writing loses its director-to-directee thrust, to become another intellectual exposition on prayer destined for the perusal of theologians. Yet in spite of Caussade's reworking of *Prayer from the Heart,* the censors found material of which they disapproved, such as the importance attributed to attentive pauses. They argued that one should persist in doing Ignatian meditation. Yet on the whole they approved of *Spiritual Dialogues* in its draft form. Interestingly, they considered Bossuet a poor authority on prayer and consequently recommended that the author of the *Spiritual Dialogues* should be careful not to give offense to the memory of Fénelon, and should suggest no hint of attacking such a great prelate:

> Everyone knows that he [Bossuet] hadn't learned from his own personal experience nor from that of other people and . . . that throughout his life he was busier with polemic theology than with mystical theology. . . . It wouldn't be proper . . . for any hint . . . of attacking the reputation of [the archbishop of Cambrai, Fénelon] . . . so celebrated for his piety and knowledge . . . [to appear].[41]

Finally, in a postscript they admonish the author to state at the beginning of the book that the prayer of silence is only for those whom God calls to a higher level of prayer. Again, even among men somewhat sympathetic to Caussade's teaching, we find reservations about the accessi-

---

[40] See the appendix, "La Révision romaine," in Caussade, *Traité sur l'oraison du coeur,* 374–86.

[41] Ibid., 382f.

bility of the prayer of silence to the ordinary person. Such a
view implies that contemplation is not the natural development of the action of sanctifying grace, but a special calling
by God.

Finally, to publish Caussade's treatise, his colleague,
the theologian Fr. Paul-Gabriel Antoine, was called on to
revise what Caussade had written and claim authorship for
himself. Permission to publish was given to Fr. Antoine in
1737. In 1741 the *Instructions spirituelles en forme de dialogues sur les divers états d'oraison suivant la doctrine de M.
Bossuet, évêque de Meaux* was published in Perpignan at
Jean-Baptiste Reynier by Fr. Paul-Gabriel Antoine.[42] Con-
temporary sources attribute authorship of it to Caussade.[43]
The first part of the *Instructions* differs completely from
Prayer from the Heart, but the second part reworks it by
developing the arguments of *Prayer from the Heart,* even in
some places using the same words. The reworking seems to
have as its objective, on the one hand, polishing the writing
of *Prayer from the Heart* and, on the other hand, removing
from it any suspicion of quietism by placing it under the
mantle of Bossuet, the well-known opponent of quietism. It
is difficult to distinguish exactly what changes Fr. Antoine
brought to what Caussade thought and wrote, but the great
difference in approach between the manuscript of *Prayer
from the Heart* and the second part of the *Instructions* suggests strongly that *Prayer from the Heart* reflects truly what
Caussade thought. Thus I confidently assert that the manu-

---

[42] See pp. 64f. of Paul Dudon, "Note sur les éditions du P. de
Caussade." The *Instructions* was published by Bremond under the title
Bossuet, maître d'oraison; it was republished in 1891 by Ludovic de
Besse, and this edition was reproduced by Canon Bussenot in 1892
and 1895 and published in English in 1931 under title of Jean Pierre
de Caussade, *On Prayer: Spiritual Instructions on the Various States of
Prayer according to the Doctrine of Bossuet, Bishop of Meaux,* trans. Algar
Thorold; a truncated edition of only the second part was published in
Perpignan in 1758 and several times thereafter; this forms the second
part of the Olphe-Galliard edition of *Prayer from the Heart* and is
called *Spiritual Instructions (Instructions spirituelles).*

[43] See Cavallera, "Caussade, auteur des *Instructions spirituelles.*"

script work that I am publishing represents the thought of Caussade quite accurately and shows that contemplative prayer formed an integral part of Catholic tradition.

Today we understand that all believers are called to contemplation; for instance, a document published by the Congregation for the Doctrine of the Faith, *Several Aspects of Christian Meditation,* reminds the reader that in baptism we receive the power of contemplation.[44] Thus the tradition of mysticism that Caussade brings us through his *Prayer from the Heart* now receives official endorsement and is a tradition recovered for all.

Conventions Adopted and Editions Cited

T he folio numbers of the manuscript are given in square brackets. French proper names have usually not been anglicized, but some have been, especially those more familiar to anglophones in their anglicized form. Citations from the Bible, especially from the Psalms, are given according to the old Vulgate, which was built on St. Jerome's translation from the *Septuagint.* The official Vulgate adapted by the Council of Trent in 1546 was the Bible published under Clement VIII in 1502. In 1945 a new translation of the Psalms became part of the Vulgate and replaced the old translation of them to which Caussade referred. Thus, to understand Caussade's references to the Scriptures, I use the Latin of Clement VIII's edition and the Douay Rheims version for the English translation (that of Richard Challoner, done between 1749 and 1752). All quotations from French writings have been translated by me. In citing works that Caussade could have read, I have cited from editions that he could have consulted. Later editions, especially some made in the nineteenth century, have so-called corrections made to them that often simply reflect the nineteenth-century view of what should be the true and orthodox interpretation of spiritual matters.

---

[44] See *Quelques aspects de la méditation chrétienne. Lettre aux évêques de l'église catholique* (Paris: Tequie, 1989), section 21.

A Treatise on Prayer
from the Heart

Written by a
Reverend Jesuit Father
Doctor in Theology

[PRAYER FROM THE HEART]*

Q: [1] What do we really mean by this prayer?¹

A: This prayer most necessarily springs from the heart, otherwise no merit at all can be found in it or any other prayer.² We call it fully heart-charged to distinguish it

---

* Brackets around chapter titles indicate that the text enclosed is found in the Olphe-Galliard printed edition but not in the original manuscript from which this translation was made.

¹ Madame Guyon writes, "L'oraison n'est autre chose que l'application du coeur à Dieu, et l'exercice intérieur de l'amour" (Prayer is nothing other than the application of the heart to God and the interior exercise of love) (*Moyen court*, in *Opuscules spirituels*, 9). She continues: "Il faut un coeur pour aimer. . . . Cette oraison n'est point l'oraison de la tête. . . . Ce n'est pas une oraison de seule pensée; parce que l'esprit de l'homme est si borné, que s'il pense à une chose il ne peut penser à l'autre. . . . Rien ne peut interrompre l'oraison du coeur que les affections déréglées" (To love we need a heart. . . . This prayer is not at all a prayer from the head. . . . It is not a prayer of only thought; because the mind of man is so limited that if he thinks of one thing he cannot think of another. . . . Nothing other than unregulated affections can interrupt prayer from the heart), 11.

² Jane de Chantal writes, "Il n'y a que le coeur qui soit absolument nécessaire à l'oraison, et comme sans cette partie tout le rest n'est qu'une vaine apparence, aussi avec elle seule nous ne manquons jamais de rien" (Only the heart is absolutely necessary for prayer; and just as without this faculty all the rest is only vain appearance, so also with it alone, we never lack anything at all) ("Petit traité sur l'oraison," *Oeuvres* 3:263, or *Doctrine spirituelle*, 187). St. Augustine tells us, "My heart [is] where I am whatever I am"; i.e., the heart is one's

from vocal prayer, in which the heart expresses itself
through the mouth, and from prayer of affection, in which
the heart expresses itself with interior speech, pronounced
interiorly as it would be pronounced aloud if we wanted
others to hear what we are saying in our hearts. [2][3] In
exact terms, this fully heart-charged prayer is carried out in
the heart by unsigned acts,[4] which are unexpressed even
interiorly, but truly practiced in the depths of the heart; or,
as the great bishop of Meaux [Bossuet] says, by simple,
unexamined, direct acts;[5] or again, by an effective and ac-

---

center (*Confessions*, X, iii, 4 [p. 181 in Chadwick's World Classics
edition]). He also writes, "You have made us for yourself and our
heart is restless until it rests in you" (ibid, I, i, 1 [p. 3]).

[3] Numbers in brackets, for example, this [2], indicate the page
of the manuscript on which is found the text that follows.

[4] In Scholastic philosophy, a sign is a word attached to a
concept and serves to describe or suggest the concept. An act is any
activity, whether of the mind or of the heart or of the body. Thus an
unsigned act is an activity that is not manifested by a word or action.
We intuitively know it is occurring, but we know nothing about it
other than that it is happening and that in some cases it stirs us to
further action. Baltasar Álvarez writes about the prayer of silence: "Il
n'y a point de discours ordinaire, il y a des demandes, et durant que
nostre Seigneur accoise l'ame, tout est exercice de virtue avec demande, non en l'acte signifié, ains en l'acte practiqueé, comme disent les
Theologiens; car que ne demande point une ame qui se taist en la
presence de Dieu, avec foy qu'en se presentant devant luy, son coeur?"
(There is not at all ordinary conversation; there are requests. But
while our Lord is calming the soul, all is exercise of virtue with request, not in a signed act but in the practiced act, as the theologians
say; for what does a soul silent in God's presence ask with faith other
than to present to him his heart?) (La Puente, *La Vie du père Baltasar
Alvares*, 137f.).

[5] Writing cautiously, Caussade is suggesting that Bossuet is
talking about prayer from the heart, but he isn't. He is instead concerned with prayer in general and contemplation in particular. Furthermore, Mme Guyon uses the words "direct et non réfléchi" (direct
and unexamined) (*Moyen court*, 22, no. 6 [p. 62]) for the soul that is
fully turned to God through the practice of prayer, an outpouring of
the heart in the presence of God (*Moyen court*, 20, no. 1 [p. 47]).

tual turning of the heart towards God and every person loved by God.

Let us give an example to better establish and make understood a truth that depends upon a clear understanding of all that we have to say here. A mother who tenderly loves her son, in looking at him or thinking of him, even for a long time, will have actual love for him in her heart during all this time, in actuality not shown by signed, expressed acts, which she can't make, but by simple direct acts really practiced in her heart, or, if you wish, by the same [3] continual act prolonged during the whole time she looks at him or thinks of him.[6] All this is carried out so actually and so freely for every object for which the heart has affection that if this object is evil, we really sin the

---

Rather than by unreflected or "unconsidered," I have translated "non réfléchi" by "unexamined," a term that accurately reflects Bossuet's meaning of "un acte réfléchi," which consists in examining, considering, watching, anticipating, and evaluating what we have done, are doing, and are about to do. A direct act occurs without reflection; spontaneity or intuitivity characterizes it. Bk. 5 of Bossuet's *Instruction sur les états d'oraison* is entitled "Des actes directs et refléchis, apperceus et non apperceus, etc." (On direct and reflected acts, perceived and not perceived, etc.); however, when he writes, "parmi les reflexions il y en a de si delicates, qu'elles échappent à l'esprit" (among reflected acts there are some that are so delicate that they escape the mind's attention) (V, xii [p. 143]; similarly xvii [p. 148]), he in reality is accepting the notion of unreflected prayer and only contends that this state of unreflection is transitory (V, viii [p. 137]).

[6] Fénelon writes: "Un père tendre ne pense pas toujours distinctement à son fils; mille objets entrâinent son imagination et son esprit, mais ces distractions n'interrompent jamais l'amour paternel; à quelque heure que son fils revienne dans son esprit, il l'aime, et il sent au fond de son coeur qu'il n'a pas cessé un seul moment de l'aimer, quoiqui'il ait cessé de penser à lui" (A tender father is not always thinking about his son; thousands of objects entice his imagination and mind, but these distractions never interrupt his paternal love; whenever the thought of his son returns to his mind, he loves him and he feels in the bottom of his heart that he has not ceased loving him for an instant, although he stopped thinking of him" (*Oeuvres* 1:611, Pléiade ed.).

whole time we spend paying attention to it or entertaining it with the heart's simple dispositions; it is in no way disavowed, but desired and consented to by these simple tendencies of the heart to which we voluntarily adhere. Thus we sin not by signed acts expressed interiorly which we are careful to avoid; rather, we want to be able to hide these interior secret iniquities from ourselves; but nevertheless we sin by acts truly carried out in the heart or by a subsisting, [4] persevering act, one and the same, which bears the stamp of even more passion, malice, and perversity of the heart.

Q: How are these notions applied to this topic?

A: Nothing is easier, for it doesn't require more to be worthy than to be unworthy; God doesn't have a fuller awareness of the evil practiced in the heart by these direct unsigned acts than the good accomplished in prayer by simple acts of the same kind; God tends more to reward than to punish. Draw this conclusion: before God, all acts executed only in the heart are as much for good as they are for evil, except in a directly opposite way.

Q: I easily understand all this for objects perceived by the senses, but not for [5] insensible ones that do not make as much of an impression, since they are not at all able to stir our passions.

A: Isn't grace stronger, or at least more effective, than the passions? Since grace gives us real power to overcome them, then why aren't we able to do good in the heart by means of this grace, just as we are able to do evil by means of nature's perversities? Did the saints pursue the love of God, crosses, and humiliations less than sinners do the love of the world, their pleasures, and their fame?

Q: Doesn't this statement merely show that it is easier to be attracted to objects of the senses than to insensible ones?

A: We are not concerned here with the ease of attraction for some or with the difficulty for others, but precisely with what happens during fully heart-charged prayer [6] from acts that are practiced but not at all signed.

Q: But how can we do this prayer and assure ourselves
that we are doing it?

A: Most virtuous people—and even sinners, once deeply
moved—could very easily do it, at least intermittently, if they knew this prayer well; for if,[7] in the course of
their meditation, reading, vocal prayer, and so forth, they
feel the heart touched in a holy way by some kind of pious
stirring, the fear of God, love, regret for the past, or the
desire to do better in the future, then what prevents them
from yielding to these simple stirrings, from resting in
them to give themselves the leisure to penetrate right down
to the bottom of their souls; and then, if necessary, after
renewed stimulation of similar feelings, what prevents them
again from halting, from yielding in the same manner,
trying to hold onto all these simple but edifying impressions as long as possible?

Q: What good or what advantage comes from it?

A: [7] 1. We could give space to the sweet impressions
of grace that we too often choke off or interrupt
with our many inner agitations or our usual inner routines.

    2. We could continue prayer longer and more easily.
With the help of grace, we could do what divine Providence has done with food for the body, and find flavor and
pleasure in prayer. Thus, we ourselves could transform
prayer, the most necessary thing in the world, into something easy and agreeable.

Q: But how do we recognize these simple, unexamined,
and unperceived direct acts of the heart, to assure
ourselves that we are really doing this kind of prayer?

A: If we let ourselves be a little self-attentive, these unexamined and consequently unperceived acts are in
themselves in a sense felt, as the philosophers have said. It
is only by feeling and awareness, as the Schoolmen say, that
we know our soul, its workings, and its ways of [8] acting
which are revealed in these acts. We recognize so well, in
spite of ourselves, these simple acts when unreservedly

---

[7] The word "if" is missing from Olphe-Galliard's edition.

practiced for evil. For if in giving alms or in practicing some other virtue, there arises in my heart a simple movement of vanity or self-satisfaction that I do not immediately reject, because I have allowed myself to be led by its pernicious sweetness, right away I feel that I am doing evil and that this unsigned act of the heart fully spoils the good deed. Those who have some tenderness of conscience don't fail to accuse themselves of this simple movement, as well as of its duration, although they had only adhered to it in their hearts.

Q: Now I am beginning to understand a bit what a fully heart-charged prayer is; it is, you say, a prayer from the heart and of the whole heart, because God clearly sees all that goes on in the heart.

A: He wants only the heart. It is from the heart, as he himself says, that both good and evil come; all the goodness and malice of ours acts have no other source.[8] Furthermore, the ensuing acts, which differ from the simple acts of giving assent, in themselves add exactly nothing, [9] as theologians assert.

Q: But do you want to reduce every prayer to this kind?

A: Not at all, as you see, for we need the others to do this one well. Indeed, how could the heart produce pious movements and good desires, much less sustain itself in them, if it isn't moved, touched, and excited?[9] How, without special grace, will it be moved unless by medita-

---

[8] "Quæ autem procedunt de ore, de corde exeunt, et ea coinquinant hominem. De corde enim exeunt cogitationes malæ, homicidia, adulteria, fornicationes, furta, falsa testimonia, blasphemiæ. Hæc sunt, quæ coinquinant hominem; non lotis autem manibus manducare non coinquinat hominem" ("But the things which proceed out of the mouth, come forth from the heart, and those things defile a man. For from the heart come forth evil thoughts, murders, adulteries, fornications, thefts, false testimonies, blasphemies. These are the things that defile a man. But to eat with unwashed hands doth not defile a man") (Matt. 15:18-20).

[9] The Olphe-Galliard edition substitutes "explicité" (made clear) for "excité" (excited), which is in the manuscript.

tion, reading, by various reflected-upon and discursive acts that ought to place the heart in motion, in action, and reheat it when it finds itself cooled off?

Q: Then why speak so much about the acts of this kind of prayer if it presupposes the others as first prompters?

A: 1. Because the prompter prayers do not at all presuppose these prayers from the heart, and because too often one engages in them without the heart entering into them in the least, even though such engagement is essential. On this we must insist here.[10]

2. We want to draw many people from a very common [10] and very harmful error, namely, believing that they aren't praying or meditating well unless they incessantly make reflections and acts expressed interiorly or exteriorly. In some this gives birth to excessive eagerness that troubles them rather than filling them with the peace in which God abides and works, as Scriptures tells us.[11] In others this error gives birth to distaste, boredom, and discouragement in prayer the instant they feel the cessation of what the majority calls acts, although the unsigned acts about which we are speaking still subsist in the heart, which was moved and touched, and can easily continue to subsist there if we knew well how to recognize them, to rest there with them, to entertain them with simple attention, and to be content with them, because they properly constitute and are the best kind of prayer. Even acts represented and expressed interiorly are nothing before God except by virtue of these direct unsigned acts, because acts take birth in the heart before they can be represented in any way.

3. Without an exact understanding of these direct unsigned acts about which we are talking, we couldn't reach a good understanding of the different ways in which the

---

[10] The word "here" is missing from Olphe-Galliard's edition.

[11] "Et factus est in pace locus ejus: et habitatio ejus in Sion" ("And his place is in peace: and his abode in Zion") (Ps. 75:3). All Psalms are quoted from and cited according to the old Vulgate.

ancient and modern authors speak [11] about fully heart-charged prayer. Of all the kinds of prayer, it is

a. the most perfect because it is the simplest

b. the most natural for the human heart, for which it is the pure language

c. the most efficacious in itself since it alone, to speak exactly, redresses the heart and turns it to God

d. the most powerful with respect to God because it goes straight to God's heart free from and beyond all expressions

These are the interior sighs of which St. Paul speaks,[12] the groans ineffable even to him who sends them heavenward without words, neither spoken exteriorly nor interiorly, words being too weak to express the simple language of the heart. All human beings agree with this. After they have tried to witness mutually their gratitude or friendship, they add, "I wish you could see the feelings in my heart." But God sees what humans can neither see nor express as they wish. He hears whatever we say, even in the very preparing of our hearts: "Your ears hear the preparing of their heart," in the words of the prophet;[13] [12] that is to say, he hears the very first movement of a heart which stirs itself to form a simple desire, according to the beautiful expression of the great bishop of Meaux [Bossuet].[14]

---

[12] "Similiter autem et Spiritus adiuvat infirmitatem nostram; nam quid oremus, sicut oportet, nescimus, sed ipse Spiritus interpellat gemitibus inenarrabilibus" ("Likewise the Spirit also helpeth our infirmity; for we know not what we should pray for as we ought; but the Spirit himself asketh for us with unspeakable groanings") (Rom. 8:26).

[13] "[Desiderium pauperum exaudivit Dominus;] præparationem cordis eorum audivit auris tua" ("[The Lord hath heard the desire of the poor;] thy ear hath heard the preparation of their heart") (Ps. 10 according to the Hebrew [second half of Ps. 9]:17).

[14] Bossuet, *Instruction sur les états d'oraison,* V, xxiv (pp. 155f.); Bossuet starts xxiv with "Desiderium pauperum, as in n. 13.

Chapter 2

Different Names Given to This Kind of Prayer

Q: What are the different expressions various writers use to describe this kind of prayer?[1]

A: To clearly understand the answer to this question, first of all it is necessary to know what happens when people of prayer rest in these unsigned acts of which we were just speaking. They develop a kind of habit and discover after a while such ease of attraction and benefit that they no longer speak the pure language of the heart to God intermittently and for a few instants, but very often almost for the full time of prayer. For them a well-pondered[2] word of the Scriptures, a single representation of one of the mysteries, a certain remembrance of God or[3]

---

[1] Like Baltasar Álvarez (see chap. 13 of La Puente's biography), Caussade lists various names for prayer from the heart and links them to the various appellations that his contemporaries used to describe contemplation, especially the acquired variety. He and the Jansenists, such as Pierre Nicole, share the view that the heart is central. Nicole writes, "Les mouvements du coeur, dans lesquels consiste la veritable prière" (True prayer consists in movements of the heart) (*Traité de l'oraison*, bk. 1, chap. 3, first sentence [p. 12]). But they do differ in the fundamental orientation that the heart can take.

[2] The Olphe-Galliard edition has "posée" (placed), whereas the manuscript reads "pesée" (pondered).

[3] The Olphe-Galliard edition reads "and," but the manuscript has "or."

Jesus Christ—any of these are enough to touch, to put into movement, and to occupy the heart piously with this fully heart-charged prayer during a half hour and sometimes a full hour. This prayer will always grow better and better, as explained by the writers who have spoken of it, using and attaching to it different names, all of which basically express one and the same thing: [13] a prayer entirely from the heart.

1. Many call it a prayer of rest in God.[4] It is anything but idleness, as many people imagine, because the mind and the heart do not rest the way the body does when it ceases to act.[5] On the contrary, they continue their action, but in a gentler way that charms our soul. Thus, when a miser lets his mind and his heart—his thoughts and affections—rest in his treasure, or the profane lover in the object of his passion, or any others in what they love, none of them in their resting stop acting at all. They are in no way idle, but very wickedly occupied during all of that pernicious repose of their minds and hearts. Why? All of them willfully hold their thoughts and their affections firmly fixed on the object of their affection. They plant there in their center only what, according to St. Paul, is truly idolatry of the heart.[6]

---

[4] Jean Joseph Surin calls the prayer of simple rest in God ordinary contemplation, which is "un simple repos de l'âme, dans lequel elle goûte et connaît les choses divines, sans qu'elle ait peine à se tenir en la présence de Dieu, et à considérer avec affection les choses célèstes" (a simple rest of the soul, in which it tastes and knows divine things without having difficulty in holding itself in God's presence and in considering heavenly matters affectionately) (*Caté-chisme spirituel,* 10).

[5] La Puente, in *Vie du père Baltasar Alvares,* chap. 40, sec. 1, para. 1 (pp. 455–57), argues that prayer in which the soul is not speaking or thinking is not idleness.

[6] Caussade combines "Quorum finis interitus, quorum deus venter et gloria in confusione ipsorum, qui terrena sapiunt" ("Whose end is destruction; whose god is their belly; and whose glory is in their shame; who mind earthly things" (Phil. 3:19); "Scitis quoniam, cum gentes essetis, ad simulacra muta, prout ducebamini, euntes"

Likewise, when by meditation, spiritual reading, prayer, and hundreds of other exercises a soul grows accustomed to thinking about God through attending interiorly to him, should we wonder that during the time of prayer anything that awakens in the soul the sweet memory of past impressions stops and fixes [14] all its thoughts and affections there where its treasure lies,[7] there where it has already placed its heart? But here we find true rest in God, during which we adore and love him actually in spirit and in truth, using the words of Jesus Christ,[8]—not, it is true, by multi-

---

("You know that when you were heathens, you went to dumb idols, according as you were led" (1 Cor. 12:2); "Ipsi enim de nobis annuntiant qualem introitum habuerimus ad vos, et quomodo conversi estis ad Deum a simulacris servire Deo vivo et vero" ("For they themselves relate of us, what manner of entering in we had unto you; and how you turned to God from idols, to serve the living and true God") (1 Thess. 1:9); "Quia, cum cognovissent Deum, non sicut Deum glorificaverunt aut gratias egerunt, sed evanuerunt in cogitationibus suis, et obscuratum est insipiens cor eorum. Dicentes se esse sapientes, stulti facti sunt, et mutaverunt gloriam incorruptibilis Dei in similitudinem imaginis corruptibilis hominis et volucrum et quadrupedum et serpentium. Propter quod tradidit illos Deus in concupiscentiis cordis eorum in immunditiam, ut ignominia afficiant corpora sua in semetipsis, qui commutaverunt veritatem Dei in mendacio et coluerunt et servierunt creaturæ potius quam creatori, qui est bendictus in sæcula. Amen" ("Because that, when they knew God, they have not glorified him as God, or given thanks; but became vain in their thoughts, and their foolish hearts were darkened. For professing themselves to be wise, they became fools. And they changed the glory of the incorruptible God into the likeness of the image of a corruptible man, and of birds, and of four-footed beasts, and of creeping things. Wherefore God gave them up to the desires of their heart unto uncleanness to dishonor their own bodies among themselves. Who changed the truth of God into a lie and worshipped and served the creature rather than the Creator, who is blessed for ever. Amen") (Rom. 1:21–25).

[7] "Ubi enim est thesaurus tuus, ibi est et cor tuum" ("For where thy treasure is, there is thy heart also") (Matt. 6:21).

[8] "Sed venit hora et nunc est, quando veri adoratores adorabunt patrem in spiritu et veritate; nam et Pater tales quærit, qui adorent eum" ("But the hour cometh, and now is, when true adorers shall

ple acts, not even interiorly expressed, but by simple pro-
longation and continuation of the same fully heart-charged
act. This act, which is simply practiced in the bosom of the
heart, subsists and perseveres as long as divine rest endures.
If the corruption of nature can operate in the soul that long
and pernicious resting of which we have spoken, should we
be surprised that habit, which is second nature, when
joined with grace, which is much stronger, can bring about
this holy resting which we are describing, and in so doing
merely following a good many excellent authors, ancient
and modern?

2. Many call it prayer of faith,[9] of the presence of
God,[10] of simple gazing.[11] Just as I can gaze at material
objects with the eyes of the body, and spiritual things with
the eyes of the mind, so can I also gaze at divine things,
and even at God, with the eyes of faith. If this gaze lasts
only an instant, [15] it is merely a passing good deed; but

---

adore the Father in spirit and truth. For the Father also seeketh such
to adore him") (John 4:23).

[9] Louis Lallemant recommends "la voie de la foi" (the path of
faith) because "l'on y marche plus dans la pauvreté spirituelle et dans
l'humilité" (we walk more in the state of spiritual poverty and in that
of humility) (*Doctrine spirituelle,* pt. 5, chap. 4, art. 2 [p. 268]).

[10] La Puente, in *Vie du père Baltasar Alvares,* chap. 14. sec. 1,
para. 2 [pp. 142], calls Álvarez's prayer that of "la présence de Dieu"
(the presence of God). According to Lallemant, we enter into contemplation through the gift of the presence of God (*Doctrine spirituelle,* pt.
7, chap. 4, art. 2 [pp. 343f.).

[11] Surin calls contemplation "un simple regard de l'âme avec
amour, par lequel, sans aucun travail, elle pénètre les choses divines" (a
straightforward loving gaze of the soul, by which, without effort, it
penetrates divine matters) (*Catechisme spirituel,* 10). André Baiole calls
it "un regard amoureux de Dieu . . . un entretient de l'âme avec Dieu
. . . qui comprend un simple regard du costé de l'entendement, et un
acte d'amour du costé de la volonté" (a loving gaze on God . . . a
conversation of the soul with God . . . which comports a straightforward gaze from the understanding and an act of love from the will")
(*De la vie intérieure,* bk. 3, chap. 4 [p. 356]).

if, by special grace[12] or by faithfulness to ordinary grace,[13] I
have acquired the habit and the ability to hold myself in
this loving gaze and to maintain it during a considerable
time—a quarter of an hour, for example—then this will be
a quarter of an hour spent in this fully heart-charged
prayer, which here we call that of pure faith or of simple
gazing. If, then, with growing habit and grace, this loving
gaze, this heart-charged recollection of God, became almost
continuous, then I would be practicing literally what God
himself ordered his servant Abraham: "Walk continually in
my presence and you will be perfect."[14]

3. Others call it prayer of simple recollection,[15] which is
practiced in this way: one of the persons of whom we are
speaking [a woman, let us say], after entering into prayer
according to her custom, and feeling as though her soul
had gone out from herself—not at all by distinct strides, as
St. Augustine says,[16] but by thoughts and affections then

---

[12] When Caussade wrote, this was called infused contemplation.

[13] When Caussade wrote, some called this acquired contemplation, but this expression was, in the minds of people like Bossuet,
linked with quietism.

[14] "Postquam vero nonaginata et novem annorum esse cœper-
at, apparuit ei Dominus, dicitque ad eum, Ego Deus omnipotens;
ambula coram me, et esto perfectus" ("And after he began to be
ninety and nine years old, the Lord appeared to him: and said unto
him: I am the Almighty God: walk before me, and be perfect") (Gen.
17:1).

[15] Teresa of Avila discusses prayer of quiet or recollection in
her *Way of Perfection,* chaps. 29 and 31; she calls the second degree of
prayer one of "quietude and recollection" (*Life,* chap. 15, par. 1); in
describing Baltasar Álvarez's prayer, La Puente writes, "Cette oraison
s'appelle aussi de quiétude, ou recollection intérieure" (This prayer is
also called prayer of quietude or interior recollection) (*Vie du père
Baltasar Alvares,* chap. 14, sec. 1, para. 3 [pp. 142f.]).

[16] "Non enim pedibus aut spatiis locorum itur abs te" ("One
does not go far away from you by walking or by any movement
through space") (*Confessions,* I, xviii (28) [p. 20 in Chadwick ed.]) and
"Ecce intus eras et ego foris" ("And see, you were within and I was in
the external world") (*Confessions,* X, xxvii (38) [p. 201 in Chadwick ed.]).

found spread out and, as it were, dispersed over sensible
objects—immediately tried to bring her thoughts and affections back into herself, and her mind, so to speak, folded
up on itself, as St. Francis de Sales says,[17] almost like a snail
returning into its shell, according to the expression [16] of
St. Teresa.[18] This was done for the purpose of attaching
herself to God, who resides in the center of her soul, in the
most intimate place of her substance, which is her living
temple, as the Apostle says.[19] If this recollection lasts only
an instant, it is simply a good act, but if it lasts a considerable time, either from habit acquired by ordinary grace or
by a certain special attraction, it is then truly a fully heart-
charged prayer that receives the name "simple recollection."

4. Others call it prayer of silence,[20] as when St. Augustine says: "Let my soul be silent to itself to listen to its
God, to admire."[21] If this profound interior silence comes
from respect and admiration, or if it is accompanied by
these emotions, as is almost always the case in the presence

---

[17] *Traité de l'amour de Dieu,* VI, vii (*Oeuvres* 4:326–30 [Pléi-
ade ed., 628–32]).

[18] *Interior Castle,* IV: 3, 3.

[19] "Nescitis quia templum Dei estis et Spiritus Dei habitat in
vobis?" ("Know you not, that you are the temple of God, and that the
Spirit of God dwelleth in you?") (1 Cor. 3:16).

[20] This expression comes from La Puente, *Vie du père Baltasar
Alvares,* chap. 14, sec. 1, para. 4 [pp. 143–45], who calls Álvarez's
prayer "oraison de silence" (prayer of silence). In chap. 3, resp. 2,
Caussade says the words "oraison de silence, de repos, de quiétude"
(prayer of silence, of rest, of quietude) frighten people, as they fright-
ened Mercurian when he enjoined Álvarez to cease any prayer of this
nature.

[21] Caussade seems to be summarizing the main point of the
contemplative experience St. Augustine had in the company of his
mother at Ostia (*Confessions,* IX, x (25) [pp. 171f. in Chadwick ed.]).
Augustine writes "Cum in silentio fortiter quærerem, magnæ voces
erant ad misericordiam tuam, tacitæ contritones animi mei" ("As in
silence I vigorously pursued my quest, inarticulate sufferings of my
heart were loudly pleading for your mercy") (ibid., VII, vii, (11) [p.
120]).

of the princes of this world, it is then, so they say, not only true prayer but the most worthy homage to God. Indeed what can ashes, dust, a worm say to God? Even the princes of this world are generally pleased to see themselves honored by this respectful silence. It is often the best way to court them, because it flatters them all the more.

5. St. Teresa calls it prayer of heavenly tastes,[22] that is to say, where we taste [17] God according to the advice of the prophet who says: "Gustate et videte,"[23] taste and see, but not see and then taste. Why? Because God makes himself known much more by the heart, which tastes and which loves, than by the mind, which ponders and reasons. As it is by means of tasting God that we come to love him more, so it is by means of tasting[24] the world and its pleasures that we inevitably attach ourselves to them more strongly. Consequently, we see simple souls, uninstructed, without insight, having much greater thoughts and sentiments about God than minds most sublime in their specu-

---

[22] "The experiences that I call spiritual delight in God *[gustos Deos]*, that I termed elsewhere the prayer of quiet" (*Interior Castle* [IV, 2, para. 2], in *Collected Works*, 2:323); Rodriguez and Kavanaugh translate "gustos" by "spiritual delights." One should read chaps. 1 and 2 to get a developed view of the difference Teresa makes between "consolations" (feelings) and "spiritual delights." Caussade's reference to Teresa clearly shows that the heart is not a faculty of affection or feeling. Ignatius of Loyola writes, "For what fills and satisfies the soul consists, not in knowing much, but in our understanding the realities profoundly and in savoring them interiorly" (*Exercises,* no. 2, [p. 22 in Ganss's translation]). The *Dictionnaire de Spiritualité,* vol. 6, cols. 626–44, s.v. "goûts spirituels" (spiritual delights), concludes: "Il est difficile, sinon impossible, de dire exactement ce qu'est le goût spirituel" (It is difficult if not impossible to say exactly what is meant by spiritual delights).

[23] "Gustate, et videte quoniam suavis est Dominus: beatus vir, qui sperat in eo" (O taste, and see that the Lord is sweet: blessed is the man that hopeth in him") (Ps. 33:9).

[24] The words "God that we come to love him more, so it is by means of tasting," which appear in the manuscript, do not appear in the Olphe-Galliard edition.

lations. But can the way to taste God be to try to look for him continually in every pious exercise without ever wanting to stop to rest and be in silence, in order to give ourselves the leisure to taste the sweetness of his perfumes, which cause us to run and fly along the path of his commandments, as the Spouse says in the Songs: "We run [after you] in the fragrance of your perfumes"?[25] But those who, as soon as they sense these celestial bouquets, these divine tastings, halt there in order to collect them, not so much for the sweetness as for the fruits of the virtues that should take birth from them—those truly do the fully heart-charged prayer of tastes, of which St. Teresa speaks. [18]

Q: Couldn't you with a few examples give a better understanding of what you have just said?

A: Nothing is easier for those who have had some experience of it. But for others, it is as though we were speaking of a rare fruit that they have never tasted; we could skillfully represent for them the shape and color but not the odor and taste, because matters of purely sensible experience can only be well understood by experience itself. To compensate for this, Hugh of St. Victor has[26] imagined nothing better than to have a soul who is actually doing this prayer speak, so that these ripened and expressed feelings could pass right into the heart or mind of those who still don't yet have the least experience of it. Here, therefore, is how Hugh of St. Victor, so[27] famous in this matter, has a man speak while undergoing the secret charms of divine recollection: "Who is it who touches and satisfies me with such sweetness and vehemence that I

---

[25] "In odorem curremus unguentorum tuorum!" ("We will run [after thee] to the odor of thy ointments") (Songs 1:3). In the old Vulgate "curremus" ("we will run") comes first; in Olphe-Galliard edition it comes last; and in the manuscript it appears between "odorem" ("odor") and "unguentorum" ("of thy ointments").

[26] The Olphe-Galliard edition reads "couldn't" rather than "didn't," thus departing from the manuscript. [In this edition the word in question is translated as "has"—ED.].

[27] The word "so" is omitted in the Olphe-Galliard edition.

begin in some way to alienate myself from myself? I feel myself carried away but without knowing where; my conscience rejoices, my heart inflames, I lose the memory of my troubles, my desires remain satisfied, [19] as if with loving arms I embrace inside of me I don't know what; I work with all the forces of [my heart] to hold onto it and never lose it. My soul struggles and fights not to be deprived of what it wants to embrace incessantly, but perhaps my beloved is there. I beg him to tell me who he is [and to speak clearly to me]; to attain this I beg him not to leave but to make here a permanent home. Truly, my soul, there is your beloved who comes to your abode, hidden, invisible [to charm you, to carry you off]."[28]

---

[28] The words in square brackets do not appear in Hugh of St. Victor and consequently are additions by Caussade; the Hugh of St. Victor quotation is from *De arrha animæ* (Treatise on the foretastes of the soul joined to God) and is found on p. 204 of Roger Baron, *Science et sagesse chez Hugues de St.-Victor,* and in J.-P. Migne, *Patrologiæ cursus latinæ,* 176:97. The text reads: "[Anima:] Quid est illud dulce, quod in ejus recordatione aliquando me tangere solet, et tam vehementer atque suaviter afficere, ut jam tota quodammodo a memetipsa abalienari, et nescio quo abstrahi incipiam? . . . Exhilaratur conscientia, in oblivionem venit omnis præteritorum dolorum miseria, . . . cor illuminatur, desideria jucundantur, . . . quasi quiddam amplexibus amoris intus teneo, et nescio quid illud sit, et tamen illud semper retinere, et nunquam perdere toto adnisu laboro. Luctatur quodammodo delectabiliter animus, ne recedat ab eo, quod semper amplecti desiderat. . . . Nunquid ille est dilectus meus? Quæso, dic mihi, ut sciam an ille est, [ut si denuo ad me venerit,] obsecrem eum ne recedat, sed semper permaneat. [Homo:] Vere ille est dilectus tuus, qui visitat te, sed venit invisibilis, venit occultus, [venit incomprehensibilis.] . . . [venit . . . sed ut trahat affectum]" ([The Soul:] What is this delightful thing that is accustomed to touch me now and then when I recall it, and to move me so powerfully and sweetly that I begin to be entirely set apart and snatched away from myself in some unknown way? . . . I am aware that I am filled with joy, into forgetfulness goes every distress at past sorrows . . . the heart is illuminated, my desires are gladdened. . . . as with embraces of love, I grasp something within me in the embrace of love, but I know not what it is, and yet I labor with total effort to hold onto it always and to lose it

Q: Isn't that only what we call mystical language, that is to say, secret and mysterious?

A: If I weren't afraid of profaning an expression accepted by the Scriptures and the Fathers, I would be willing to say that the language of profane lovers is even more secret and mysterious. However, all too many young people understand this language only from the corruption of their hearts and savor it in those books where the feelings of profane love have been pushed to an extravagant excess. As a result, we have been constrained to introduce some moderation in what follows in order not to rebuff even the worldly from reading [the sort of] material in which the idle today almost with impunity find their greatest delight. I say "almost with impunity," for whereas people burst with very intense zeal against just one book suspected, often inappropriately, of being dangerous or excessive concerning matters [20] of devotion, where and how do they speak against the great number of books that corrupt morals and tamper with the faith? Why does this happen? In matters of piety, people have become so sensitive that a shadow frightens or startles their minds; but today in matters of the corruption of faith and morals, they are so accustomed to everything that almost nothing appears astonishing, scandalous, or outrageous any more. So they look upon these developments with tranquility.

Q: Moreover, couldn't this come about because, if we wish to encourage or to restrain a certain zeal,[29] it suffices to

---

never. Enjoyably, in a way, my mind wrestles, lest what it desires to embrace forever should depart from it. . . . Is it my beloved? Please tell me that I may know whether it is, [that if once more he should come to me,] I may beg him not to leave but to remain always. [The Man:] Truly this is your beloved who visits you, but he comes invisible, he comes hidden, [he comes incomprehensible.] . . . [he comes . . . but in order to draw out your affection]). See also Roger Baron, "L'Influence de Hugues de St.-Victor," in *Recherches de théologie*.

[29] The Olphe-Galliard edition has "souls" instead of the manuscript's "zeal."

know that there are many things to handle and to fear on the one side and nothing on the other?

A: So it follows, at least, that we should convince ourselves of the prodigious and holy difference between the readings which people believe they should distrust, although these only teach obedience, humility, and dependence, and the rest, which people believe they ought to tolerate, although these inspire only totally contrary feelings.

Q: Aren't there directors who, when consulted on this kind of prayer, prohibit it even for good souls who are beginning to experience it or feel a great attraction for it?

A: Without doubt there are, and this generally happens because these unlearned souls err by explaining their interior state very badly to those whom they consult. They might say, for example, that [21] often for them either during prayer, Mass, or after Communion no acts are made even for a long time. "Thus it is idleness, a pure waste of time," they are correctly told, given their explanation; but if, better educated or more attentive to their interior state, they were to say, as Mme de Chantal formerly did in an almost similar case, "My Father, I can no longer meditate or make ordinary prayers or even reflect on the mysteries which the Church celebrates and which I hear preached; I feel, however, in my mind a simple remembrance of these mysteries, and in my heart certain sweet, soothing, delicate, and very deep affections," directors would answer them in the way of the saint of Geneva [de Sales]: "My daughter, everyone must meditate and pray according to his inclination; this is the way the Church, preachers, and [spiritual] books understand it."[30]

----

[30] Here Caussade paraphrases the following passage from Henri de Maupas du Tour: "Souvent j'en ai esté en peine: tous les Predicateurs et les bons livres enseignent, qu'il faut mediter les bénéfices et mystère de nostre Seigneur: cependant l'âme qui est en l'estat ci-dessus, ne le peut en façon quelconque en cette manière: mais il me semble qu'elle le fait en une façon très excellente, qui est un simple souvenir et représentation fort delicate des mystères avec des affections très douces et savoureuses. . . . [Response:] Que l'âme s'arrest au

Q: Couldn't we help good souls a little to explain them-
       selves better, just as for quite different subjects we often
help sinners and the worldly with some questions?

A: Not only can we, but I even believe that we should,
       saying therefore to them: "But during the time of which
you are speaking, for want of your ordinary acts, do you feel
your mind deep down most disengaged from things of the
earth, fully engaged with God, or tending [22] towards God?
Do you feel your heart filled with a certain taste for God, or
with great peace and inner[31] tranquillity in the presence of
God? Furthermore, during the day, do you find yourself less
dissipated and more courageous in avoiding evil and practicing
good?" According to their answers, we may send them away
either fully consoled and strengthened or better instructed and
undeceived.

Q: Aren't there many writers, especially among the an-
       cients, who speak about this prayer using only the ex-
pression "contemplation"?

A: This is true, and today it causes a sort of scandal, not
       from what it is, but because it is badly apprehended by
some minds who, since they are dazzled just by the word
"contemplation" without understanding it well, first imagine all
that we can say or think about the greatest saints in such matters; that is to say, for them prayer is

---

mystère en la façon d'oraison que Dieu lui a donnée: car les Prédica-
teurs et Pères spirituels ne l'entendent pas autrement" (Often I was in
difficulty; all preachers and good books teach that we must meditate
on the benefits and mysteries of our Lord; however the soul which is
in the state [described] above can not pray in this manner in any way
at all: but it seems to me that it is doing it in an excellent way, which
is a simple remembrance and very delicate representation of the Mysteries with very sweet and delectable affections. . . . [Answer:] Let the
soul fasten on the mystery of the way of prayer that God has given it:
for preachers and spiritual fathers do not understand it otherwise) (*La
vie de . . . Jeanne Françoise Frémiot . . . ,* pt. 2, chap. 8, ques. 7 [pp.
196f.]).

     [31] The Olphe-Galliard edition omits "interieure," which ap-
pears in the manuscript.

1. infused and fully passive contemplation
2. in an eminent degree
3. accompanied with extraordinary gifts: visions, raptures, ecstasies
4. given in accord with their state
5. in a most prefect way

And in fact it is nothing less than that in relation to the great souls in general, because in such souls it is

1. only a simple, active recollection that we acquire with ordinary grace
2. or else a mixed recollection, that is to say, an active [23] part and an infused part
3. given not by disposition but quite transiently
4. in a very low degree
5. without ever having anything extraordinary appear
6. practiced for a long time with all the imperfections of beginners

And that's how the virtuous Mother de Chantal, whom I can well cite from Msgr. de Meaux, ought to be understood, when, in a book addressed to her whole order,[32] she says in formal terms that, the more she advances in age and experience, the more she remains convinced that God wants to lead and indeed leads, not only a few, not even many, but almost all of the Daughters of the Visitation by this holy[33] prayer that,

---

[32] See Jane Frances Frémyot de Chantal, *Vive Jésus réponses,* 517. The "Réponse sur l'article 28, des retraites," 500–515, contains an excellent discussion about prayer that is prepared for by mortification and recollection all day. It requires simplicity of heart; novices should start with meditation, but as they advance they should practice what Caussade calls attentive pauses (505). Suffering dryness is a key act of abandonment to God. The last stage of prayer is that of simple surrender to God. Great purity of heart is needed. We see that Caussade's *Prayer of the Heart* reflects the teaching of St. Jane de Chantal.

[33] The Olphe-Galliard edition substitutes "simple" for the manuscript's "sainte."

following the example of St. Francis de Sales, she calls simple handing over.[34] This is nothing other than a pure act of total abandonment, but the soul continues, sustains, and perseveres in it for a long enough time to merit its being called not a simple act but a prayer. We should use the same perspective to interpret certain directors of various religious orders and of the ecclesiastical state when they say that a few of the many people whom they direct, some of them even seculars, advance a great deal toward perfecting their state—in a fairly short time and even easily—by this simple prayer of recollection and rest in God.

Q: Do you want to reduce all to this unadorned prayer of simplicity, as others call it?[35] [24]

A: Not at all, no more than those who speak of mental prayer, who surely don't claim that we should do nothing else except meditate; there is a time for everything, as the famous bishop of Meaux [Bossuet] says, drawing on Fr. Baltasar Álvarez:[36] according to the occasion and the inclination of

---

[34] "Regard" (looking) corrected to "remise" (handing over), written in the same hand as the rest of the manuscript. "Notre bienheureux père [de Sales] la nommait oraison de simple remise en Dieu" (Our blessed father [de Sales] called it prayer of simple surrender to God) (*Vive Jésus réponses,* 508); she adds that this kind of prayer is strongly opposed by those whom God leads by the road of discourse (509).

[35] Mme Guyon writes: "Le second dégré [d'oraison] est apellé par quelques uns contemplation, oraison de foi, et de repos; et d'autres lui donnent le nom d'oraison de simplicité; et c'est de ce dernier terme dont il se faut servir ici, étant plus propre que celui de contemplation, que signifie une oraison plus avancée que celle dont je parle" (The second degree of prayer is called by some contemplation, prayer of faith and of rest, and others call it prayer of simplicity; and it is this last expression that must be used here, for it is more appropriate than that of contemplation, which signifies a more advanced prayer than I am speaking about here) (*Moyen court,* chap. 4, art, 1 [p. 19], in *Opuscules spirituels*).

[36] Caussade is paraphrasing Bossuet, *Instruction sur les états d'oraison,* VII, x (pp. 243f.). Bossuet cites from La Puente, *Vie du père Baltasar Alvares,* chap. 40, sec. 1, para. 2 (pp. 457f), but changes the

any and everyone, there is a time for reading, self-examination, vocal prayer, and intentional acts articulated as much in the mouth as in the heart; but quite certainly and most remarkably, no one knows better how to do all these as needed than the practioners of this prayer, because they have more of this interior spirit, which is like the heart and soul of every pious exercise.

Q: Do the Scriptures and the Fathers speak of this prayer?

A: The Prophets, the Psalms, and the Old and the New Testaments speak of it in numerous places, but in a brief and shrouded way, as are many other truths that tradition and the Fathers have explained to us. St. Denis, disciple of the Apostles,[37] and after him, the majority of the Fathers of the Church and the most famous spiritual writers speak of it worthily; it suffices to read about it in the learned treatise [by Fr. Nicolas of Jesus Mary with notes by Fr. James of Jesus] added to the marvelous book of the most blessed John of the Cross,[38] where we shall understand fully from its innumerable citations the true meaning of I know not how many hidden and mysterious expressions, which consequently are called [25] mystical, but which can only surprise those who are not at all acquainted with them either from experience or from study.

---

order of what La Puente writes.

[37] Pseudo-Dionysius, an unknown author of the sixth century whose writings were thought to have been those of Dionysius the Areopagite, mentioned in Acts 17, and later thought to be those of the ninth-century St. Denis of Paris. These writings had a great influence on mysticism and its study. Great medieval authorities such as Bonaventure and Aquinas consulted and studied them, as did John of the Cross and Teresa of Avila in the sixteenth century.

[38] The French translation of the works of St. John of the Cross includes a 268–page clarification by Fr. Nicolas of Jesus Mary and fifty-five pages of remarks by Fr. James of Jesus. These additions form an extensive justification of what St. John of the Cross writes. The authors draw on traditional theologians, especially Thomas Aquinas, and on philosophers, mostly Plato. They also make frequent reference to Teresa of Avila. Mystical theology, like every art or science, has its own proper language; but it is not purely speculative, for it builds on experience.

Chapter 3

[ABUSES AND ERRORS TO FEAR FROM THIS PRAYER]

Q: Aren't there abuses and errors to fear from this prayer?

A: Where are there none? The great misery of man is to abuse everything: such abuse exists in vocal prayer, where, even according to the avowal of those who make it almost their exclusive practice, the mind and the heart have frequently such a small part;[1] such abuse, such waste of time in meditation, where, after many years of such a holy and sanctifying exercise, we find much too often the same faults and passions; such abuse, such errors manifest themselves in devotion of all kinds, because so many people have so badly understood and practiced devotion that today even upright people suffer with pain when they are called devout, which by itself, so they say, is taken amiss in the world but which God wants to remain the way it is; such abuse appears in the reception of the sacraments, since many draw from them so little fruit that directors complain about this, preachers reproach us, and the most upright public is sometimes scandalized by it; finally,[2] such abuse,

---

[1] For problems with vocal prayer see Fr. François Guilloré, "Les illusions des prières vocales et des pratiques" (Illusions in vocal prayer and in practices), *Oeuvres spirituelles*, 670–75.

[2] The Olphe-Galliard edition has "encore" (still) instead of the manuscript's "enfin" (finally).

such errors abound as regards confidence in God [and] devotion to the holy Virgin, which are so often preached to us but which, as is generally recognized, many sinners [26] and the worldly make not a matter of justifiable confidence but of veritable presumption; thus they are persuaded to put off conversion indefinitely and to live all the more undisturbed in their disorders.

Therefore, it is always necessary to fear error and abuse even in the most holy matters. In fact, we can only avoid them by this wise fear; furthermore, it is a principle for everything concerning salvation that we must never separate fear from[3] confidence: one without the other is despair or fatal presumption. But from fear of abuse, we should never throw ourselves into the other extreme, which would mean abolishing what we are abusing, for, according to St. Augustine,[4] when we reject every abuse, we must still retain and recommend the good that we were abusing; otherwise there would remain nothing good that had not already been abolished. Therefore, we would have the right

---

[3] The Olphe-Galliard edition drops "for everything concerning salvation that we must never separate fear from," which is found in the manuscript, and instead reads "principle of confidence."

[4] See Augustine's discussion of Matt. 13:24–30, especially: "Quibus veritas ipsa respondet non ita hominem constitutum esse in hac vita, ut certus esse possit, qualis quisque futurus sit postea cujus in presentia cernit errorem, vel quid etiam error ejus conferat ad profectum bonorum; et ideo non esse tales auferendos de hac vita, ne cum malos interficere conatur bonos interficiat, quod forte futuri sunt, aut bonis obsit, quibus et inviti forte utiles sunt" (Truth itself replies that in this life man is not so constituted that he can be sure what sort of person everyone in whom he sees error will afterwards become, or what his error might even contribute to the progress of the good people; and so such persons should not be removed from this life, lest in trying to kill bad persons, one kill the good persons that perhaps they will turn out to be, or work against the good people for whom, even against their will, they are perhaps useful) (ques. 12 in "Quæstionum XVI in Matthæum," lines 150–157 [pp 130f.] in *Aurelii Augustini Opera*, pt. VIII, 3, in Corpus Christianorum, series latina, vol. 44 B.

to censure every man who, using as a pretext the abuses and errors that are introduced[5] into devotion to the Holy Virgin, confidence in God, the reception of the sacraments, and the exercise of prayer, would never speak unless it was against these abuses, deploring them. Would people be any less blamable if, under pretext of these abuses or of what could crop up during this prayer, they would never speak unless it was against these abuses? This is especially true today, when it is known to all that, to avoid one extreme, they have fallen into the opposite fault and have gone to such excess that they have [either] almost abolished knowledge of this prayer or so much disfigured the [27] true idea of it that if someone speaks openly against it, they are neither scandalized, nor surprised, but they are quite shocked if someone should speak favorably of it with the intention of reestablishing it among pious people.[6]

Q: But isn't there greater reason to fear abuses here than in any other religious practice?

A: Here we find the most plausible ruse that the enemy of salvation uses today to exterminate, if it were possible, even the name of this prayer, which has in all ages appeared to him to be the most apt to destroy his reign and to reestablish that of Jesus Christ. Consequently, it is proper to examine well if this prejudice, which has become all too common, is well founded. According to St. Teresa,[7] no sooner did people begin to discuss mental prayer openly during her time than the very name of this practice (then fairly new)[8] led people on all sides to cry out: "What do we

---

[5] Reading "mellent" (mixed) [here translated "introduced into"—ED.], not "mettent" (put), as Olphe-Galliard does (72).

[6] For a study of antimysticism in the eighteenth century, see Louis Cognet, *Crépuscule des mystiques;* Henk Hillenaar, *Fénelon et les jésuites;* and Henri Bremond, "Pierre Nicole ou l'anti-mystique" (Peter Nicole or antimysticism), in *Histoire Littéraie du sentiment religieux,* vol. 4, chap. 11 (pp. 472–588).

[7] *The Way of Perfection,* chap. 21, paras. 2, 7, and 8.

[8] The manuscript reads "then fairly new," whereas the Olphe-

have to do with this prayer; it's filled with pitfalls, perils, and illusions; so many people are led astray by it." But for her part, the saint cried out, "Such blindness! such folly! an infinity of people are lost for want of prayer, and, if someone were deluded by prayer through his own fault, a scarecrow is made out of it for us. Ah! my dear daughters," she added, "be very careful [28] never to be caught in this diabolical trap." It is only by dint of hearing about mental prayer that the name and the prayer itself have become so common that, without the authority of St. Teresa, perhaps we would not have believed that in her time many intelligent and virtuous people could have fallen into such an unreasonable bias. But the common enemy, who prowls about continuously like a roaring lion, as St. Peter says,[9] had precisely only to change cannons, since when they but hear someone mention the prayer of silence, rest, or quietude, people today are no less alarmed and likewise sacrifice all to error and illusion.

But why? Because a miserable gang of quietists (I say miserable on account of the small number of these detestable hypocrites) will have profaned both the name and the prayer itself; but the consequence of such profanation is less to fear because it is more visible, more coarse. People no longer dare to speak of this divine prayer or read the authors who deal with it, not even those who are cited by the great bishop of Meaux [Bossuet], the prelate least subject to suspicion in all the world when he writes about this material. If there appears an excellent spiritual book [29] in which they find a word or an expression that they don't at first understand well or that would appear to have some likeness to these condemned errors,[10] it's enough; a panicky

---

Galliard edition has "fairly new."

[9] "Sobrii estote, et vigilate. Adversarius vester diabolus tamquam leo rugiens circuit quærens quem devoret" ("Be sober and watch: because your adversary the devil, as a roaring lion, goeth about seeking whom he may devour") (1 Pet. 5:8).

[10] Those of quietism, which can be found listed at the end of

terror seizes certain spirits, [and] this book is condemned, rejected, and forbidden.[11] And also, of what use is it that everywhere there are many people more enlightened [and] better educated—either by certain readings or by their own proper experience or that of others—if this demon of human respect shuts their mouths under the pretext of some scandal or other, because they will be, so they say, criticized right away, censured,[12] and rendered suspect to the ignorant horde?

Q: Then what harm occurs?

A: What harm? In this way and by various traps, the enemy of salvation has very rapidly arrived at the goal of stealing what has always passed for the greatest treasure of the spiritual life from any number of good souls. In this way—in spite of the good intentions and the wise precautions of the bishop of Meaux [Bossuet] carefully to disentangle those whom he calls the true mystics, that is to say, the truly spiritual, from the false, the good prayer of the former from the errors of the latter—these souls confuse all and likewise condemn all.[13] In this way, according to the expression of Jesus Christ,[14] [30] every day they pull up the good grain with the weeds.

And why do they continue to do so? Some people find it much easier and quicker to condemn than to go to the trouble of examining and taking advice; but those who, by their profession, should go to the trouble, how do they

---

Bossuet's *Instructions sur les états de l'oraison.*

[11] Caussade may be referring to Fénelon, *Explication des maximes des saints sur la vie intérieure,* condemned in 1699.

[12] The Olphe-Galliard edition drops "censurés" (censured), which is in the manuscript.

[13] Thus Bossuet's *Instructions sur les états de l'oraison* seems to have failed in its purpose, or perhaps we find here in Caussade a trace of irony.

[14] "Et ait: Non; ne forte colligentes zizania eradicetis simul cum eis triticum" ("And he said: No, lest perhaps gathering up the cockle, you root up the wheat also together with it") (Matt. 13:29).

excuse themselves? Alas! Whereas with very praiseworthy zeal, they wear themselves out studying and working to try to draw sinners and worldly people from the road of perdition, they don't want to do anything to equip themselves to help and to lead good souls along the painful and obscure paths of perfection—these good souls, chosen from among the best, as they say, just one of whom, as our masters say, could with time give more glory to God than one hundred other mediocre people. Undoubtedly this work and these concerns are hidden and obscure; none of these lead to a sure reputation but to [something] much better; for the merit will surely be much greater since there is greater purity of intention.

Q: Why is it that you find bad today what people found good not even thirty or forty years ago, when we saw mature men [who were] very well informed, sometimes even great preachers, speak against the abuses of this prayer?

A: Well, they did what was right and necessary; but for other times, other precautions, other remedies must be employed. When an abuse whose consequences are feared begins to spread itself, they can hardly do enough to oppose it. But when, following [31] an unfortunate consequence of human misery, in wishing to avoid one extreme we unfortunately fall into the other, then it is most fitting to speak much less of past abuses than of what was almost abolished out of fear of them. Thus they quite wisely used the Fathers of the Church to accommodate themselves to the public needs of the time. Look at how St. Augustine, at grips with the Manicheans, who wished to destroy free will, spoke in favor of freedom and almost not at all of grace; then look at how, in disputing against the Pelagians, who were denying the necessity of grace, he elevated and exalted it so much that you would almost say that grace alone did everything. These two views appear irreconcilable, but they become reconcilable as soon as we recall the diverse circumstances and times during which the great doctor spoke.[15]

Q: But aren't there any secure and easy rules accessible to all, by which all the kinds of abuses and errors in this matter are recognized, forestalled, and destroyed?

A: One especially fits the bill. Jesus Christ himself gave it to us in a few words: "We know the tree by the fruit it bears."[16] Therefore, every prayer that by its practice reforms, changes, and regulates bit by bit conduct, morals, actions, speech, and feelings—in short, all of our exterior and interior acts—is [32] incontestably an excellent prayer. If it doesn't produce these good effects, then for me it becomes questionable; but if by misfortune it produces bad effects, as it does for the quietists, it is evidently an illusion and an abomination. Since every prayer is only a means to practice virtue and to please God, it is necessary, therefore, to judge it by its purpose, which is conduct, and to judge conduct by faith, by the Gospel, by the example of saints.

Q: Applying this rule of Jesus Christ, is it as easy to evaluate this prayer as others?

A: It is much easier, because this prayer, which is the most efficacious of all, ought to reveal itself more quickly by deeds. Consequently, it is unnecessary to wait very long to see its fruits, as directors too easily can do. I would not delay long over people who applied themselves to this simple prayer; for if in the space of only two or three months I didn't perceive some notable change in them, I would consequently be suspicious of the goodness or, to speak more accurately, of the truth of their recollec-

---

[15] For the refutation of Pelagianism by St. Augustine, see Etienne Gilson, *Introduction à l'étude de saint Augustin,* 204–16; Augustine attacks Manicheanism (see ibid., 81–87), not exactly as suggested by Caussade, but by proving the primacy of the spiritual over the material and so ipso facto that of free will over the determinism of the materialistic God of light of Manes.

[16] "Igitur ex fructibus eorum cognoscetis eos" ("Wherefore by their fruits you shall know them") (Matt. 7:20).

tion; and soon afterwards I wouldn't hesitate to treat it as pure imagination. Why? Because everywhere that true recollection is present, the effects and the fruits become palpable and [33] tangible in a fairly short time. It is necessary to remark only that

1. if this recollection is purely active without anything infused (which we know from the difficulty of beginning to do it and continuing it), then it is less efficacious, and so it is necessary to wait a little longer to see its fruits;

2. the making of so prompt and decisive a judgment belongs only to the one who alone knows the interior of the person. Why? Because even when their recollection is mixed and even fully infused, onlookers cannot know

a. whether certain feelings and agitations are not at all the first motions, those that are called indeliberate;[17]

b. whether other offenses that escape to the exterior have been lacking in discernment[18] or have been followed by great interior victories;

c. whether God, to keep those persons in profound humility, does not permit certain woes and weaknesses in which the affections of the heart play no part;

d. whether they aren't suffering interiorly the pain and humiliation of all these without ever getting discouraged in their firm resolve to belong to God without reserve, which St. Francis de Sales places among the heroic virtues;[19]

---

[17] An expression taken from Bossuet; see Littré's dictionary of the French language s.v. "indélibéré."

[18] In French we read literally "not prudence," which in the context of the text means "not learning to discern what leads to God" (see Littré s.v. "Prudence"). "Lacking in discernment" seems the most appropriate translation.

[19] See St. Francis de Sales's teaching on the good use of faults in *Introduction à la vie dévote,* III, vi, para. 3 (*Oeuvres,* 3:153 [Pléiade ed., 146f.]) and in *Traité de l'amour de Dieu,* IX, vii, paras. 4–6 (*Oeuvres,* vol. 5 (vol. 2 of *Traité*): 132f. [Pléiade ed., 779–81]).

e. whether those persons do not find themselves in what are called ordeals, to which, from time to time God submits people of this prayer and during which, [34] St. Teresa says,[20] one appears very different from what one fundamentally is, especially to eyes little enlightened in the ways of the interior.

Q: Don't we still have to fear what they call illusions, which, so it seems to me, you have yet to discuss, at least according to people's ordinary understanding of them?

A: The simple words of Jesus Christ previously referred to can sufficiently cure all such illusions, because usually we recognize all kinds of trees by their fruit, and their fruit by faith and the Gospel.

1. It is certain that, along the simple path of ordinary recollection, even if infused, of which we are speaking, there is never anything extraordinary; it is exactly on this basis that we distinguish it from extraordinary recollection, which is accompanied by visions, revelations, raptures, and so on.[21] Consequently, on this account there are no illusions to fear. In truth this fear is merely a pure phantasm and a vain scarecrow in certain minds that seem to want to know nothing whatever of this matter.

2. To destroy every prejudice of voluntary or involuntary ignorance in this matter, I am willing to assume the most extraordinary experiences that anyone would like to imagine; but still there is no need at all to fear that this leads to illusion in those who follow the rule of Blessed John of the Cross:[22] [35]

a. that they usually reject all that seems extraordinary to them;

---

[20] *The Book of Her Life*, chaps. 28 (12–18), 31 (17–23), and 40 (18–21).

[21] The Olphe-Galliard edition drops the manuscript's "etc."

[22] *The Ascent of Mount Carmel*, II, xvi (6, 10–15), xvii (6–7) and III, xiii (6–9).

b. that they never speak about it under the pretext of examining from where this came;

c. that they never attend to it voluntarily.

This saint says[23] that by these things we are protected from the demon's traps, if he or she is the source of them, since, far from adhering to these [snares], we disdain and reject them; and [we are protected] from the foolish dreams of the imagination, since we never permit ourselves to reflect on them voluntarily[24] in order to occupy ourselves with them and, even less, to tell others about them. And if by good luck these extraordinary things come from God, we lose nothing in rejecting them, since they perform their good effects independent of our cooperation and in spite of all our resistance. God acts, therefore, as master [and] as sovereign, and, according to the expression of St. Teresa,[25] like a giant who wants to lift a straw.

---

[23] *Ibid*, II, xviii (7), xxvii (3–6). As John of the Cross was not canonized until 1726, Caussade surely did not start writing this treatise on prayer before then.

[24] The Olphe-Galliard edition drops "volontairement" (voluntarily), which is in the manuscript.

[25] *Interior Castle*, VI, chap. 5 para. 2.

Chapter 4

HUMILITY HAS TO PRECEDE THIS PRAYER AND IS EXCELLENTLY PRACTICED WHILE DOING IT

Q: This whimsical[1] title surprises me; I don't understand anything, for you speak only of humility, and I have never heard anything else said about this prayer except that it was to be much feared on account of vanity. [36]

A: How little experience do those have who fear vanity[2] from this prayer, either for themselves or for others. With the most magnificent words, let us praise it as much as we want to. Because it is essentially the most humiliating and annihilating of all prayers, it can precisely be called

---

[1] The Olphe-Galliard edition has "seul" (alone) instead of manuscript's "caille" (whimsical).

[2] See Pierre Nicole, *Réfutation des principales erreurs des quiétistes,* where he writes: "Quand il n'y en aurait point d'autre [illusion] que celle d'une vanité secrète qu'elle inspire aux âmes par l'idée qu'elle leur donne qu'elles sont dans un degré de vertu fort élevé, ce serait déjà une très périlleuse tentation, d'autant qu'il leur serait très difficile de se détromper de cette fausse opinion" (When there would be no other illusion than that of a secret vanity that it instills in souls, giving them the idea that they are at a very high level of virtue, this would be already a very dangerous temptation, especially as it would be very difficult to deliver oneself from this false opinion) (189).

■ sublime in the eyes of God but not in the eyes of men, according to what they ordinarily understand;

■ sublime in the same sense as the incomparable knowledge of Jesus Christ, "supereminentem scientiam Iesu Christi" ("the surpassing knowledge of Jesus Christ"), in the words of St. Paul when he explains so magnificently the knowledge of the cross,[3] which ultimately is no more than the practical understanding of the sufferings and humiliations of the God-man, where very few people need to fear vanity and much less to find it;

■ sublime, not because it puffs up the spirit as human knowledge does, as St. Paul tells us,[4] but rather because it brings it low, humiliates it, and annihilates it by the simple regard of the grand totality that is God and the nothingness of the creature;[5]

■ sublime, not because it lifts and enhances the learned and the great geniuses, but rather because it obscures and engulfs us in the holy shadows of faith where we have only a vague, general, [37] and confused notion of God, without form or images or illustrious[6] views, and where in truth we

---

[3] Caussade combines "Scire etiam supereminentem scientiæ charitatem Christi ut impleamini in omnem plenitudinem Dei" ("To know also the charity of Christ which surpasseth all knowledge, that you may be filled unto all the fullness of God") (Eph. 3:19) with "Verbum enim crucis pereuntibus quidem stultitia est, his autem, qui salvi fiunt, id est nobis, virtus Dei est" ("For the word of the cross, to them indeed that perish, is foolishness; but to them that are saved, that is to us, it is the power of God") (1 Cor. 1:18). Interestingly, Thomas Dubay urges the reader to realize that the text of Paul from his letter to the Ephesians is calling us to "the transforming summit" of intimate and thorough union with God (*Fire Within,* 175).

[4] "Scientia inflat, caritas vero ædificat" ("Knowledge puffeth up; but charity edifieth") (1 Cor. 8:1).

[5] See St. John of the Cross, *Ascent of Mount Carmel,* I, 2, 1; also helpful are the articles in *Dictionnaire de Spiritualité* s.v. "Anéantissement" (annihilation) (vol. 1, cols. 560–565) and "Humilité" (vol. 7, pt. 1, cols. 1175–79).

[6] The Olphe-Galliard edition has "distinctes" instead of manu-

feel that we love, but without knowing how, as St. Teresa says,[7] because the object is incomprehensible and will be better understood only insofar as it appears more incomprehensible;

■ sublime, finally, not from the beautiful ideas and the grand knowledge by which we are enriched, but rather, according to the expression of M. de Meaux [Bossuet],[8] because we are impoverished of all natural light, all resulting magnificent knowledge, beautiful thoughts, and rich ideas in order to be fully poor in spirit.

This poverty is nakedness of spirit. Do these obscurities, shadows, and inexplicabilities naturally have what serves to awaken and entertain pride rather than to crush and annihilate it? If someone still doubts, I send him to his own proper experience, for whoever prays can,[9] without changing his usual way and easily without risk, make several attempts during these attentive pauses that we shall further explain in greater detail.[10]

---

script's "distingués" (illustrious).

[7] *Book of Her Life,* chap. 14, paras. 6 and 7; *Way of Perfection,* chap. 31, para. 2.

[8] The expression attributed to Bossuet (*Instruction sur les états d'oraison,* V, xx, 152) is a citation by Bossuet from Cassian's *Conferences,* no. 10, 11: "This formula the mind should go on grasping until it can cast away the wealth and multiplicity of other thoughts, and restrict itself to the poverty of this single verse" (*Western Asceticism,* ed. Owen Chadwick, 243); this translation follows more closely Bossuet than that of the Paulist Press edition of the *Conferences* (136). See John of the Cross, who writes, "To draw near the divine ray [God], the intellect must advance by unknowing rather than by the desire to know, and by blinding itself and remaining in darkness rather than by opening its eyes" (*Ascent of Mount Carmel,* bk. 2, chap. 8, in *Works,* 128).

[9] The Olphe-Galliard edition drops the word "peut" (can) of the manuscript.

[10] In chap. 6.

Q: If this prayer is in itself so humbling, then why do writers who speak of it warn us to guard against vanity? [38]

A: First of all, pride is so natural and so well rooted in us that there is nothing so sanctifying or so humbling that can keep pride from easily slipping in. We can swell up from humiliation, even interiorly glorify ourselves over it, vainly delight in it, and so pride ourselves on having reached the abysses of humiliation and of the practice of humility. Secondly, if in seeking out this kind of prayer, we were following the false ideas that even certain pious people have of it, or the vain desire of some imagined elevation or other, then it is sufficient for us to become either incapable of this prayer and lose attraction for it or fall into illusions.[11]

Q: Then why in particular does this sublimity of prayer enliven the zeal of certain upright people, so that precisely because of its sublimity they are even unable to put up with our mentioning it to anyone at all?

A: At the very least, this still doesn't go as far as it did at the time of St. Teresa,[12] who recounts that many directors, to whom one would speak of this recollection or of this rest in God, would clearly prefer to hear mortal sins. In matters of spirituality and prayer,[13] there are many people [39] who are wedded to their own opinions, just as there are so many others in matters of doctrine or religion whom we rebuke. Just as the latter, without having studied, examined, or read about certain questions, nevertheless dabble by following the current style of speaking about, judging, or deciding about these questions, so the former

---

[11] For the illusions of humility see François Guilloré, "Les illusions de la vie spirituelle," (Illusions of spiritual life) (*Oeuvres spirituelles,* 701–8); he warns us that even interior prayer can lead to illusions (705).

[12] For instance, see *Life,* 13, 14.

[13] The words "of . . . and prayer" are dropped in the Olphe-Galliard edition.

believe that they have the right to want to use the same approach in matters [of prayer] without being any better informed, because they lack practice and study, and have not read certain books for which they themselves admit that they have only contempt and disgust.[14]

Q: Therefore, in the case of these two problems why not keep the wise policy that they follow in all other affairs, namely, to suspend judgment and decisions until they have examined and gained full knowledge of the case, as they say?

A: They don't, because many of them don't believe that they need to examine, consult, or read; furthermore, others even believe that it would be dishonorable[15] to let others think that they would have needed to do so, and that it would be more appropriate and more glorious to make a prompt and unhesitating decision. Moreover, in their favor, we should assume that they entertain no feeling of vanity, [40] because they fear it so much, even concerning the practice of this holy prayer.[16]

---

[14] Perhaps Caussade has in mind Nicole, who wrote that he "ne s'est pas jugé capable de'entrer dans le détail de ces oraisons [those of the new mystics] et de ces états extraordinaires, et il s'est contenté par tout d'inspirer un attachement inviolable à la doctrine de l'Eglise, par laquelle il est certain qu'on les doit examiner, sans prétendre en faire aucune application à personne" (didn't consider himself capable of detailed consideration of the prayer of the new mystics and of these extraordinary states; thus he fully limited himself to inspiration built on an inviolable attachment to the Church's doctrine, on which without doubt we should examine them without trying to apply them to any one person) (*Traité de l'oraison*, preface, last paragraph).

[15] The manuscript reads "peu [little] honorable," not "plus [more] honorable," in contrast to the Olphe-Galliard edition.

[16] Fear of illusions, of losing control, and of not being fully orthodox seemed to play an important role in the opposition to contemplative prayer. The Fénelon-Bossuet controversy and the condemnation of quietism, followed by that of Jansenism, all contributed to a climate in which people were fearful of being accused of unorthodoxy.

Q: What difference, therefore, do you find between this prayer and the so extraordinary and sublime prayer of most saints?

A: Concerning the extraordinary, [as] we have already said,[17] this prayer is not accompanied by extraordinary gifts, as is the prayer of the saints: visions, revelations, ravishments, ecstasies, and so forth. About the sublimity of this prayer and that of the saints, we must think about it along the lines of what we have been saying and [understand] it differently from that prayer. Certain vain spirits who were chasing after sublimity sought after this way of praying; but, once they found nothing in it[18] or less than what they had imagined, they quickly abandoned it and, irritated at having been fooled by their vain pretensions, thereafter spoke of it only with contempt, describing it as pure imagination. Such is the lofty effect of these high, sublime, but false ideas that these vain spirits have put into their own heads, perhaps even following the opinion of some so-called spirituals, who in the same way think and proclaim these ideas instead of saying that here we find the prayer of the humble and that prayer that makes [those that practice it] humble.

Furthermore, there is the same difference between the prayer of the good souls of whom I speak and the prayer of the saints of whom you speak, as there is between all the virtues possessed [41] by the latter in an eminent degree, and by the former in a very low or inferior degree; the same difference that is found between the usual patience of average Christians who try, as we say, to make necessity into a virtue and the extraordinary and fully heroic patience of the saints, who go so far as to place their joy in the cross, in humiliations—to such an extent[, indeed,] as to seek those [as eagerly] as the worldly seek pleasures and

---

[17] At the end of chap. 3.

[18] The manuscript reads "et qui n'y ayant trouvé rien" (they found nothing in it), whereas Olphe-Galliard has "lesquels n'ayant trouvé rien" (finding nothing).

honors. Finally, to get back to my[19] point, there is the same difference as between those who, at their eyes' least glance at God, annihilate themselves and lose themselves in God by the force of being immersed again and again into the immense bosom of the divinity, and those who fix their eyes on God and rest in his presence.

Q: Explain for us these last expressions, which seem to contain a bit of mystical jargon.

A: I beg you to answer me yourself. If I say to you, "Here's a man who immerses himself again and again in debauchery, here's another who is fully overwhelmed in business, lost in his schemes and ambitious projects," don't you understand me? So why, therefore, [42] as soon as these expressions and hundreds of other similar ones are applied to God and to divine things, do they then become mystical, foreign, and incomprehensible? There is so much injustice and contradiction among men and so much ignorance in a subject matter in which they believe themselves learned without understanding either common language well[20] or the expressions in use—a subject matter that, like every art or science, has its proper expressions without anyone taking exception to them.

Q: In spite of all that you have been able to say, I don't know how to keep myself from thinking that there surely is something very profound and very sublime in this prayer, for I recall having heard from one of France's most learned,[21] whose name is well known, that he had read as many as two or three times about the diverse degrees of prayer and union of which St. Teresa speaks, without understanding anything.

---

[19] The manuscript reads "me" in place of Olphe-Galliard's "se."

[20] The Olphe-Galliard edition drops the manuscript's "en bien" (well).

[21] Scholars have been unable so far to determine who this person may be.

A: This shows exactly and still better how we can call
         this prayer sublime. It has a sublimity that, far from
flattering human pride (as does the sublimity of the other
sciences),[22] always confounds it, because to understand this
sublime prayer well and moreover to practice it require an
abasement [43] of the mind and a mistrust of oneself, one's
learning, and one's understanding. It requires us not to be
great in our own eyes from the swelling of veiled arro-
gance, but to be truly small from humility of heart, which
humbles all. Jesus Christ himself wanted us to understand
this when he said, "I thank you, all powerful Father, that it
pleased you to reveal these things to the humble, whereas
you hid them from the wise, the haughty, the enlightened,
the prudent of the world."[23] For this reason, St. Bonaventure, in his thorough treatment of the same subject on
which I am just embarking, forbade his disciples to speak of
it to the unlearned: "Beware lest . . ."[24]

---

[22] The Olphe-Galliard editions writes "oraisons" instead of the
manuscript's "sciences."

[23] Freely quoted from Matt. 11:25 and Luke 10:21.

[24] The manuscript reads, "Cave ne. . . ." The writer Caussade
is referring to is not Bonaventure but Hugh of Balma's *Mystica theologia* (for his biography see *Dictionnaire de spiritualité,* vol. 7, pt. 1, cols.
859–73). The text actually reads: "[Dionysius] ad Timotheum scri-
bens, dicit sic: 'Vide ['Cave' of Caussade's MS] autem ne quis indoc-
torum ista audiat; indoctos dico eos qui secundum philosophiam
mundanam, cognitioni existentium ad obtinendam Dei cognitionem et
veram sapientiam firmiter innituntur, existimantes nihil esse substanti-
aliter super existentia omnia et super ipsum ens. Unde putant se per
investigationem existentium creaturarum sibi connaturalem, compre-
hendere Deum, qui ponit tenebras latibulum suum. . . .' Et hoc est,
quia ista cognitio est totaliter supra mentem, & ubi omnis intellectus
deficit, qui non apprehendit nisi sub ratione veri vel boni. Mystica
vero Theologia, per apicem affectionis docet discipulos veritatis consurgere per amorem, imo quod plus est, nunquam actualiter mens
posset istis motibus consurgere, si aliquid cogitaret consurgens, imo
miserabiliter deprimeretur a sua elevatione affectio; sed potius intellec-
tivam quasi pedisequam subtractam relinquit inferius, & sine sui
obsequio ad dilecti unionem consurgit motibus sursum activis, ab ipsa

eminentius elevata plus distat ab ea, quam ab ortu solis meridies, &
hoc quotiescumque vult de die sive nocte, centies vel millesies, si
corpus posset sustinere. Et quod ita sit, exemplo materiali ad præsens
utar [utor], ut valeas intelligere. Considero motum lapidis, suo pon-
dere naturaliter descendentis ad centrum. Sic per pondus amoris
affectus dispositus in Deum sine omni cogitatione, vel deliberatione
consurgit, veluti in suum centrum se extendens, & motibus istis se
elevat in continuo desiderio, cuius complementum & intuitus quietem
in æterna beatitudine obtinebit, nisi quandoque ad modicum temporis,
sicut est in raptu, divina sublevatione supra seipsum non natura, sed
gratia sublimetur. Sed si hoc non potest percipere doctor speculativus,
vel scholasticus discipulus, audiat ab Apostolo qui fuit principalis
hierarcha sapientiæ, quam nullus sapientium Græcorum intelligere
potuit, quoniam hæc sapientia solum spirituali examinatione cognosci-
tur. De qua loquitur Corinthiis dicens: Spiritus noster spiritui divino
unitus, sentit quæ sunt eius, & hæc sapientia est, quam inter perfectos
loquebatur" (Dionysius writes to Timothy: "See to it [beware], however, that not one of the ignorant hear this; I call the ignorant those
who place their reliance on existing things. [And mocking them he
continues right away:] I call those ignorant who in their view believe
that they can grasp divine matters by their own ingenuity or the
abundance of their knowledge, and furthermore who really believe
that on the basis of their own knowledge can know him who makes
darkness his hiding-place. . . ." This is the case because such knowledge is fully above the mind and where every intellect is insufficient
because it can apprehend only under the activity of reasoning on the
true or the good. As a matter of fact, Mystical Theology teaches the
disciples of truth to rise up by love through the apex of affection; and,
what is more, the mind can in reality in no way rise up with these
movements if in rising it is thinking of something; indeed, affection
would then be miserably pushed down in its ascent. But rather, affection leaves the intellect behind like a servant and, without its help,
rises up by its upwards active motion to union with its loved one; and
elevated far higher than the intellect, the affection is more distant from
the intellect than the noonday sun is from the sun at sunrise. And this
occurs as often as it wants day or night, hundreds or thousands of
times if the body could support it. I now use a material example in
order that you may be able to understand that this is the case. I consider the motion of a stone which from its weight naturally falls to the
center. In this way, affection when disposed by the weight of love rises
up into God without any cogitation or deliberation, as if it were
reaching out to its center, and by these movements it lifts itself in a

Q: But who are those whom you place in the ranks of the unlearned?

A: In spite of this father's very respectable authority and that of St. Denis, disciple of St. Paul,[25] who many centuries before had said the same thing, I believe that it is more appropriate for me[26] to pass over the question in silence. If someone wants to know more, he has only to read the last paragraphs of *The Mystical Theology* of St. Bonaventure, which is only found in the fifth volume of his work called *The Opuscule.*[27]

Q: But aren't you yourself, in writing on this subject [44] going against the interdiction of St. Bonaventure and St. Denis?[28]

---

continuous desire; in eternal beatitude it will receive the fulfillment of this and the rest of its gaze; except whenever for a restricted time, as occurs in a rapture, it may be lifted by divine elevation above itself, not by nature but by grace. But if a speculative doctor or a scholastic disciple is not able to perceive this, let him hear from the Apostle who was the principal hierarch of this wisdom, which none of the Greeks was able to fathom because it is only known by this spiritual examination of which he speaks to the Corinthians [see 1 Cor, 2:6–16], saying, "Our spirit, which is united to the divine spirit, perceives what belongs to it and this is the wisdom of which he was speaking among the perfect") (686c2–687c1, and *Source Chrétienne,* II, 230–33, in which the text is slightly different from that of the seventeenth-century edition). The Pseudo-Dionysius remark is from *The Mystical Theology,* chap. 1, no. 2 (*The Complete Works,* 136); for a similar viewpoint see Evagrius Ponticus, *The Praktikos,* ed. John Eudes Bamberger (14f.).

[25] Pseudo-Dionysius, an unknown sixth-century author whose writings were thought to have been those of Dionysius the Areopagite, mentioned in *Acts* 17, and later thought to be those of the ninth-century St. Denis of Paris; but Caussade doesn't mention Denis of Paris.

[26] The Olphe-Galliard edition writes "s'en" instead of the manuscript's "m'en" (for me).

[27] This is Hugh de Balma's writing in the edition of St. Bonaventure referred to above.

[28] See Pseudo-Dionysus, *The Mystical Theology,* chap. 1, no. 2 (*The Complete Works,* 136).

A: Not at all! (1) Those who are forbidden to speak of
       it are far from reading this text. (2) Here is only a
very small sample or, rather, a prelude and simple beginning of the doctrine of these saintly and wise[29] prominent
figures. (3) What I am writing aims mostly to reclaim many
intelligent and virtuous people from a prejudice, people
whose biases and feelings, in spite of their good intentions,
throw most saintly souls into fears and doubts that prevent
some from following their inclination for this prayer and
many others from being prepared to do it in the way that
we shall soon describe.

Q: Why did you add that of all the prayers this one is
       the most humbling?

A: First of all, it is the prayer of the weak, whom God
       pushes on unceasingly and holds by the hand like
small children; strong and courageous souls, says St.
Teresa,[30] don't need this to make them progress in virtue.
[45] Secondly, in the other kinds of prayer, we act with
grace on our own initiative: we think, we reflect, we reason, we become attached—in a word, we appear[31] to act by

---

[29] The Olphe-Galliard edition writes "dévots" (pious) instead
of the manuscript's "scavans" (wise).

[30] Teresa in her autobiography (chap. 11, paras. 13f.) explains
that determined strong beginners who persist are making real progress, because they are building on a solid foundation. But a weak
person who possesses little fortitude like herself is led by the gifts of
consolation acquired in prayer of recollection. Earlier (chap. 11, paras.
4 and 11) she adds that the courage to persevere comes from the Lord
and he rewards this person greatly after she has learned what little
she's worth. Later (chap. 15, para. 14–15) she explains that prayer of
quietude or recollection has as its fruit true humility, because we learn
that good doesn't come from us but only from God. So, she continues, no effort of ours brings us true humility and "in his goodness he
has held me by his hand so that I might not turn back" (chap. 21,
para. 11 [p. 143]).

[31] The Olphe-Galliard edition writes "constamment" (we
steadfastly act) in place of the manuscript's "sensiblement" (we appear
to act).

means of all the powers of our own soul. Insofar as we
believe we have succeeded in our actions, we feel very
pleased and very satisfied with ourselves. In St. Francis de
Sales's view, our miserable satisfactions do not add up to
God's satisfaction.[32] In contrast to the other kinds of prayer
where our mind and will are tied to their usual ways of
working, the Holy Spirit works and does all within us in
such a profound and hidden way that we hardly perceive
our minds freely cooperating, because they do so with
direct but unreflected and unperceived acts, of which M. de
Meaux [Bossuet] speaks.[33] Thus we are inclined to believe
that we have done nothing: we fear having been idle, we
complain to our directors, we consult and often harass
them; and if, at other times, especially in the beginnings,
these interior actions manifest themselves very sensibly, we
feel very good, although at the same time we realize that
they do not spring from our own resources, since they are
something so strange and so commanding that it is impossible to attribute them to [46] ourselves, as St. Teresa
says.[34] Thus, with God we can without doubt delight in
them but not boast about them, any more than can a poor
person who has just received lavish alms.

Hence, in everything that they do, say, or think,
people who are accustomed to this prayer discover well and
perceive what comes from their own depths and what is
foreign and borrowed. By virtue of this they come to a
conviction of heart so intimate and so habitual that, without effort and from an unquestionable inner feeling which
wards off every reflection, they immediately ascribe to God
every good deed. Why? They almost never have those first
movements of vain complacency that, without cease, be-
siege and harass most devout people in whom, according to

---

[32] *Introduction to the Devout Life,* IV, xiv, 5, *Treatise on the Love of God,* IX, x (Pléiade ed., 170–2 and 788f.).

[33] In bk. 5 of *Instruction sur les états d'oraison.*

[34] *Spiritual Testimonies,* 54, in *Collected Works,* 5:347f., and *Way of Perfection,* chap. 31, paras. 2 and 10.

their own avowal, these vain complacencies often spoil and corrupt all the good that they appropriate to themselves, revealing abundant secret self-love that is as natural and maybe as frequent as breathing, were it not for special grace and extraordinary vigilance. [47]

Q: This way seems interesting to me and so unusual[35] that I implore you, if you can, to explain it to me in greater detail: How are this profound humility and total mistrust of one's self above all inherent in this holy recollection?

A: First it happens in a simple thought or, rather, in a simple sentiment of that sovereign Majesty which absorbs and engulfs all. Then we see ourselves or, rather, feel ourselves like a mere dot in that immensity, or like a small worm crawling on several grains of dust. Therefore, human beings are no more than mere shadows of beings; everything seems annihilated before him who is and so calls himself.[36] Expressing this same sentiment, King David called out that, even without knowing it, he had been reduced to nothing.[37] Why? This happens much less by distinct ideas than by a hidden and obscure sentiment, almost like printing on paper in a very short time and in the obscurity of a printing shop [48] all that is wanted, which we then read in daylight. Likewise, not during the obscurity of this prayer but afterwards in various occasions, these sentiments and confused ideas develop through knowledge of and insights into the present time [in the minds of] people who, it must be added, are simple and without instruction.

By the way, from this we can infer the source from which the saints drew with such facility, promptitude, and abundance the most admirable of all that they left us in

---

[35] The Olphe-Galliard edition has "si peu connue" (so little known) in place of the manuscript's "si peu commune" (so unusual).

[36] "Dixit Deus ad Moysen: EGO SUM QUI SUM" ("God said to Moses: I AM WHO AM") (Exod. 3:14).

[37] "Et ego ad nihilum redactus sum, et nescivi" ("And I am brought to nothing, and I knew not") (Ps. 72:22).

their divine writings, which only follow and reveal the plenitude that they received in prayer. This plenitude, however, was usually neither the matter nor the subject of their writings, contrary to what a not inconsiderable number of people imagine.[38]

---

[38] The Jansenist Nicole argued that those who read books on mysticism would imagine that the same things were happening to them. He writes: "Ces personnes ayant ouï parler dans quelques livres spirituels de vie intérieure, d'opérations divines, de recueillement, de pur amour, se laissent surprendre par l'éclat des ces mots, et conçoivent un désir présomptueux d'éprouver l'état qu'ils voient décrit dans ces livres, non par un amour véritable de la justice, mais par un orgueil secrèt que leur fait désire d'être grands et élévés dans la grâce, et qui n'est pas moins dangereux que celui qui leur ferait désirer d'être grands et élévés dans le monde. Ainsi ils se forment des idées à leur mode de tout ces états divins, que l'on ne conçoit jamais bien sans les avoir éprouvés. Ils en font l'objet de leurs spéculations et de leurs raisonnements. Ils en apprennent les principes par mémoire comme ceux d'une autre science. Ils arrangent en mille manières ces mot et ces idées extraordinaires, dont ils se sont emplis l'esprit. Ils s'échouffent l'imagination pour les comprendre: et la faiblesse de leur esprit jointe à l'impression du démon que s'y mêle, leur persuade beintôt qu'ils les comprennent, et qu'ils les éprouvent. Rien n'est plus dangereux et plus irrémediable que cette sorte d'illusion: parce qu'il est presque impossible d'en retirer ceux qui y sont engagés" (These people after reading in some spiritual books on the interior life about divine operations, recollection, and pure love, let themselves be taken in by the sound of these words and conceive a presumptuous desire to undergo the state that they find described in these books, which is not based on true love for justice but on a secret pride that leads them to desire to be great and elevated in grace and that is no less dangerous than desiring to be great and elevated in the world. Thus they construct ideas of these divine states according to their own fashion, states that one does not really understand without undergoing them. They make them the object of their speculations and their cogitations. They memorize the principles like those who memorize the principles of another science. They arrange in thousands of ways these words and extraordinary ideas with which they have filled the mind. They heat up the imagination in order to understand them. Finally the weakness of their minds joined to the influence of the devil, who mixes in, soon persuades them that they understand them and that they are experiencing them.

Second, on other occasions this divine recollection takes place in the deep abyss of our misery, weakness, powerlessness for any good, and perversion and corruption of heart that render each of us capable of the same disorders, excesses, [and] abominations, from which spring contempt, hate, and holy[39] horror of ourselves, a mistrust so strong and so pressing that we actually seem drawn to all kinds [49] of crimes and about to commit them. From this there arises, not in the mind but in the heart, that conviction so rare and at the same time so inherent in this holy recollection that a wise person only needs a touch of this deep and humble self-knowledge. This conviction suffices to judge that the person out of whom similar sentiments well forth has drawn them from this prayer and walks without doubt in this path of great self-denial. So also it very often suffices—after perceiving in another a slight wisp of pride, self-sufficiency, self-esteem, or a certain air of vanity even[40] in talking about spiritual matters, or perceiving a scoffing, fault-finding, and carping mind—to judge not only fully the contrary but, furthermore, that such a person is incapable of this prayer.

Nothing is more dangerous and irremediable than this kind of illusion because it is almost impossible to remove it from those tied up by it) (*Imaginaires et les visionaires,* 29f.). He expresses a similar view in "De quelle sorte [d'pensé] l'imagination nous fait tomber en divèrses illusions" (The kind of thinking the imagination leads us to fall into in different illusions) (*Traité de l'oraison,* bk. 1, chap. 8 [pp. 40–47]). Without doubt one can very easily delude oneself into believing that one is receiving extraordinary communications from God. This possibility of delusion led Nicole to conclude that such reading should be avoided. On the other hand, as we see, Caussade advises us to put aside all such inner stirrings and to read mystical books for their content, the call to submission to God, not for their packaging, the description of extraordinary phenomena.

[39] The Olphe-Galliard edition omits the manuscript's "sainte."

[40] The words "a certain air of vanity even" are dropped by the Olphe-Galliard edition.

Until I see persons of this kind work with all their force to fight off these failings, which, as light as we want to suppose them, are directly opposed to this prayer of simplicity, I would willingly give a name still more humbling if the expression I have in mind, fully consecrated as it is by the Scriptures, would not repel all those who have never discovered the lowly feelings that we draw out of ourselves[41] in the exercise of this prayer. The king-prophet understood it well when he said to God, "I have become before you like a beast of burden, and it is [50] on account of this that I remain always in your presence."[42]

Therefore, this prayer is truly the prayer of small folk and the humble, whom it renders always smaller and humbler,[43] incessantly diminishing them both before God and themselves. This virtue alone so greatly reveals the presence of the spirit of Jesus Christ that the Church has constantly determined the different degrees of prayer primarily by this solid humility of heart that I understand, not as consisting only in a blind submission of the spirit to all its decisions, but as more, namely, a perfect submission in all and everywhere, always avoiding anything that can possibly offend and displease God.

---

[41] The manuscript reads "draw out of ourselves," whereas the Olphe-Galliard edition shows "have of ourselves."

[42] "Ut jumentum factus sum apud te: et ego semper tecum" ("I am become as a beast before thee: and I am always with thee") (Ps. 72:23).

[43] The Olphe-Galliard edition drops the manuscript's "whom it renders always smaller and humbler."

Chapter 5

THE ADVANTAGE OF THIS PRAYER

Q: Is this prayer necessary?

A: In general, prayer is necessary to obtain grace, without which there is no salvation; but no kind of prayer in particular is necessary, except in a certain sense prayer from the heart, because the heart should animate every prayer. Without the heart, mental prayer would merely[1] be pure mental entertainment and vocal prayer only the empty sounding of words. Just as God took to task his chosen nation when he said through one of his prophets, "These people glorify me with their lips, but [51] their heart is far from me."[2] Consequently, purely heart-charged prayer, which is made by acts not at all signed but simply[3] carried out in the depths of the heart during prayer of recollection, silence, and rest in God—this prayer, I say,

---

[1] The Olphe-Galliard edition reads "only a little" rather than "only," as found in the manuscript.

[2] "Et dixit Dominus: Eo quod appropinquat populus iste ore suo, et labiis suis glorificat me, cor autem eius longe est a me, et timuerunt me mandato hominum et doctrinis" ("And the Lord said: Forasmuch as this people draw near me with their mouth, and with their lips glorify me, but their heart is far from me, and they have feared me with the commandment and doctrines of men") (Isa. 29:13)

[3] The Olphe-Galliard edition has "only" in the place of the manuscript's "simply."

must be placed among the many other practices and exercises about which people lecture to us without end, stressing their utility and importance in proportion to their salutary effects.[4]

Q: Drawing on this principle, how should we rank this prayer, at least among the other kinds of prayer?

A: Here are the opinions of the most famous writers and the familiar comparisons that many use to explain it:[5]

■ By means of meditation we go to God slowly and with effort like those who go on foot;

■ By means of affective prayer we go more quickly and with less effort like those who go on horseback;

■ By means of prayer of simple recollection we go very quickly and with little effort, like those who go on a good boat with a favorable wind.

---

[4] Bremond, in *La Vie chrétienne sous l'Ancien Régime* and *La Prière et le prières de l'Ancien Régime,* vols. 9 and 10 of *Histoire du sentiment religieux en France,* discusses the many practices and exercises of spiritual activities that could easily fully fill one's day and leave no time for prayer from the heart, a prayer in which one practices attentive pauses.

[5] The comparison is a composite drawn from Surin, *Catéchisme spirituel* (12f. in the 1693 Paris edition or 13f. in the 1730 Lyon edition); but Surin is describing what he calls "ordinary contemplation," which is looking on and resting in God; here he isn't using the expression "prayer from the heart." The same comparison applied to contemplation is also found in the 1979 Paris edition of Lallemant's *Doctrine spirituelle.* See there his principle 4 (chap. 3, art. 2, sect. 2 [p. 188]) and principle 7 (chap. 4, art. 1, sect. 4 [p. 342]). The analogy is already in Teresa of Avila, *The Way of Perfection,* chap. 28, para. 5, in her *Collected Works,* 2:141f. De Sales uses the image of sailing in writing to Jane de Chantal about prayer of rest (Françoise-Madeleine de Chaugy, *Jeanne de Chantal, Vie et ses oeuvres,* 1:499). Mme Guyon uses it to explain the development of prayer as we acquire experience (*Moyen court,* chap. 22, nos. 7–9 [pp. 63–65]). Rigoleu also uses the sailing downwind metaphor (see below, no. 4, footnote 11, from the response to the next question).

Q: Does this view tally with experience?

A: Writers and the most respected confessors assure us
that it does:

1. St. Teresa who, even during the time when they
doubted the truth of her recollection because, as she says,
they saw her [52] still so imperfect, gave no reply except[6]
"I know what I was not long ago; now I feel that what I
have become came from this divine help."[7]

2. The venerable Mother de Chantal, in speaking about
changing her confessor and going to the holy bishop of
Geneva, who straightaway understood her inclination and
ordered her to surrender herself to it, exclaimed, "My God,
it seemed to me that all of a sudden there occurred a holy
and happy reorientation throughout my interior."[8]

3. Blessed John of the Cross presupposes [this view]
and stresses it in almost all his writings, and this authority
alone is better than a thousand others. One of the most
illustrious lights of France, M. Bossuet,[9] cites him in his
famous book against the quietists in about the same vein as

---

[6] "Si non" (except) is omitted by the Olphe-Galliard edition.

[7] The manuscript reads "ce divin secours" (this divine help)
not "discours" (discourse), as in the Olphe-Galliard edition. This
paraphrases what she wrote in her *Life,* chap. 13, paras. 88f. Teresa
explains that imperfections are normal and that it is the Lord who
takes them away (*Life,* chap. 7, paras 17f., and chap. 11); the same
theme is found in her *Spiritual Testimonies,* no. 1 para. 8, (pp. 28f.);
no. 2, para. 5; no. 59, paras. 3–12, in *Collected Works,* 1:312f., 317–
19, 355–58).

[8] Jane de Chantal wrote: "O Dieu! que ce jour me fut heureux! Il me sembla que mon âme changeait de face et sortait de la
captivité intèrieure où les avis de mon premier directeur m'avaient
tenue jusqu'alors" (O God! How this day made me happy! It seemed
that my soul changed direction and exited from the interior captivity
in which the advice of my first confessor held me until then) (de
Chaugy, *De Chantal, la vie et les oeuvres,* 1:63).

[9] Bossuet calls John of the Cross "ce sublime contemplatif"
(this sublime contemplative) (*Instructions,* VII, ix [p. 241]).

Schoolmen cite St. Thomas or the other Fathers of the
Church.

4. As to confessors, I shall only cite three of the best
known, in my view, by their writings: Father Louis Lallemant,[10] Father Rigoleu,[11] and Father Surin.[12] They declare
that they have known people who by means of the help of
this simple prayer have advanced more in a few months

---

[10] Louis Lallemant writes: "Car alors notre Seigneur donnera à
une âme, par une seule oraison, une vertu et même plusieurs vertus,
dans un plus haut degré qu'on ne les acquerrait en plusieurs années
par ces moyens extérieurs" (For therefore our Lord will give to a soul
in one prayer a virtue and even many virtues in a higher degree than
we can acquire them after years of exterior effort) (*Doctrine spirituelle,*
principle 2, [chap, 4, art. 1 (p. 115)]).

[11] Pierre Champion (1633–1701) writes about Jean Rigoleu:
"Le dessein qu'il formait sur [une personne voulant se mettre sous sa
conduite] était de la conduire à une vie vraiment intérieure. . . . Il
disait souvent que quand on s'est une bonne fois livré au Saint Esprit,
et que l'on march sous sa conduite, on va comme un navire qui a le
vent en poupe, et qui vogue à pleines voiles, et que l'on avance plus en
un jour, qu'on ne faisait auparavant en une année entière" (The plan
he had for [a person who wanted to be under his direction] was to
lead her to a truly interior life. . . . He often said that when we have
once and for all given ourselves over to the Holy Spirit and walk
under his direction, we sail like a boat running downwind with full
sail and that we make more progress in one day than we made formerly during a whole year) (*La Vie et la doctrine spirituelle du père L.
Lallemant,* 37f.); and Rigoleu himself writes to Marie de S. Scholas-
tique: "Quand Dieu fait tout dans une âme, il y fait bien de l'ouvrage
en peu de temps. Mais il y a si peu de personnes qui se disposent à
cette oraison [de simple recueillement]" (When God does all in a soul,
he accomplishes a lot in a short time. But so few people open themselves to this prayer [of simple recollection]) (*ibid.,* Letter 11, p.
403f.)

[12] See Surin, *Catéchisme,* "Comment se fait la troisième partie
du recueillement, qui est le bon emploi du coeur?" (How is the third
part of recollection achieved? what is the good use of the heart?) (vol.
2, part 8, chap. 1, last response [pp. 375–78]); he writes as well about
the benefits of responding positively to God's call to sweet rest (ibid.,
1:105).

than during fifteen or twenty years by means of all their [53] other exercises of piety.

5. Furthermore, many important remarks have been made that will serve to confirm all that I have just said:

a. There are practically no saints who haven't practiced this prayer, but most of them have done so in such an extraordinary way or to such an eminent and perfect degree that we won't discuss them here.

b. Most of the holy but not yet beatified people of the last century whose biographies have been written also have practiced this prayer in different degrees. Furthermore, as it appears, it is above all[13] by this powerful help that they so quickly rose to the highest perfection.[14]

c. Among the holy souls of our century who belong to religious orders or the ecclesiastical state, who practice celibacy, or who simply live in the world, we find that those who stand out the most among [these] virtuous persons also practice this prayer; each does so according to his or her own degree and manner, in either the purely active or the mixed life, sometimes on a more or less temporary basis; but their[15] virtues seemed to grow in proportion to their fidelity to this prayer.[16] Moreover, their prayer grows,

---

[13] "Above all" is omitted by Olphe-Galliard.

[14] Caussade's *Lettres spirituelles* suggest the following:

Pierre Champion, *La Vie du père Jean Rigoleu de la Compagnie de Jésus*
———, *La Vie et la doctrine spirituelle du père L. Lallemant*
Jean Crasset, *Vie de Madame Heylot*
Guillaume Daubenton, *La Vie du bienheureux Jean-François Regis*
Jean-Joseph Languet, *La Vie de la vénérable Mère Marguerite-Marie [Alacoque]*
Jean Maillard, *Le Triomphe de la pauvreté et des humiliations, ou la vie de Mlle de Bellère du Tronchay, appelée communément Soeur Louise, avec ses lettres*
Jean-Baptiste Saint-Jure, *La Vie de Monsieur de Renty*

[15] Olphe-Galliard reads "their" instead of the manuscript's "whose." [This present edition, however, retains "their."—ED.]

[16] Olphe-Galliard reads "practice" instead of the manuscript's

improves, and becomes simple insofar as they practice radical self-denial more faithfully, [54] especially by total abandonment to God in all sorts of contradictions, humiliations, and interior and exterior crosses.[17]

d. Sometimes we hear those most experienced in the practice of spiritual direction complain, for the most part, of the little progress of a great number of people who, after having attained mediocre virtue, remain there all their lives. But, as they also assert, if the prayer in question comes to be used, immediately the direction of these same people becomes more easy and efficacious, and the directors see them advance and make great strides while expending much less effort.[18]

e. Furthermore, we perceive that in most genuine and unequivocal conversions—either from vice[19] to grace, or from the lack of devotion to piety, or from piety to fervor, or from fervor to a perfect life, or from a perfect life to a supernatural and divine life—we perceive[, I repeat,] that in most of these solid, durable, and edifying conversions, the purely heart-charged prayer of simple recollection appears to be, to a considerable extent, the secret spring and the greatest driving power of all that forges good, whether exteriorly [55] or interiorly.[20]

Q: Can you give some examples?

A: Among the many that have come to my attention, I shall cite only one that has given opportunity for

---

"oraison" (prayer).

[17] See Caussade's *Lettres,* 1:91–93 (same as 312–14), 134f., 189f., 314f.; 2:120–122, 185–90, 253–55.

[18] Caussade surely is thinking of his own experience, for example, with Sister Anne-Marguerite Boudet de la Bellière; see his letter to her published in *Lettres,* 2:108–13.

[19] Olphe-Galliard substitutes "vide" (empty) for the manuscript's "vice."

[20] Here we see clearly that Caussade's prayer from the heart is contemplation.

two very useful thoughts, so it seems to me. Speaking one day with one of those great sinners whose conversion had such very happy results, I asked him, "At the time of your conversion, what was your chief inclination?" "The love of solitude," he replied. But here is precisely[21] the same inclination that I discovered afterwards in St. Teresa, who at the time of her second conversion said, "But what do you do above all during solitude? Read a lot, meditate without stop, make reflection upon reflection, prayer upon prayer?—Not at all. I often read, but very little; as for meditation, I didn't know how to do it, which greatly afflicted me; often I couldn't even pray in any way at all, which seemed unsupportable to me, for I was wanting to be meditating always, always praying.[22] Well then, I affirm, there the heart's secret desires [56] pray incessantly for you even during your longest dry periods; God sees these hidden desires even when you do not notice them and hears them even in the continual preparation of your heart, which God hears very well without words either vocal or silent.

"This heart, once deeply touched, only requires from time to time simple reflection on two or three words to put itself into pious motion and to continue in it. Recall the story of the publican. In your solitude do something like what he did in the back of the temple: 'Lord,' he cried out from time to time, 'have mercy on this sinner.'[23] But just

---

[21] Olphe-Galliard has "principalement" (principally) instead of the manuscript's "précisement" (precisely).

[22] She writes, "I read very little, for in picking up a book I become recollected in my contentment, and so the time for reading passes in prayer" (*Spiritual Testimonies,* no. 1, para. 7, in *Collected Works,* 1:312). Chap. 8 of her *Life* details her struggle with prayer.

[23] Quoting from memory: "Et publicanus a longe stans, nolebat nec oculos ad cælum levare: sed percutiebat pectus suum, dicens: Deus, propitius esto mihi peccatori" ("And the publican, standing afar off, would not so much as lift up his eyes towards heaven; but struck his breast, saying: O God, be merciful to me a sinner") (Luke 18:13).

like you, without repeating incessantly the same words,[24] he was trying to preserve the same sentiments and secret impressions as long as he could. This attitude visibly appears from the humble posture of his body so unpretentiously described in the Gospel, and in turn it clearly represents to us the humble posture of his soul, all confused interiorly, humiliated, and sighing before God. Thus he returns converted and [57] sanctified."

Q: What was the second thought about which you intended to speak?

A: The representative of all the sinners of the world, the Savior himself, who humbly prostrated himself in the garden before his Father, seems to have wanted to give us the model of this simple prayer, because all the evangelists agree in so expressly drawing to our attention that he is always repeating the same words: "Eundem sermonem dicens" ["Speaking the same words"],[25] and without doubt he did so after very long intervals, since on the one hand his words were so short and on the other hand his prayer lasted so long.

Q: What should the preceding example and your thoughts yield us?

A: We should endeavor to pray like the publican and like Jesus Christ himself, especially in reciting what he has taught us, since just one of his entreaties: "Fiat voluntas tua" ["Let thy will be done"][26] sufficed for such a

---

[24] Here we find expressed what today we call centering prayer, in which the prayer word is gently said and repeated when we become aware that we aren't saying it. The prayer word is not driving us with relentless repetition.

[25] "Et relictis illis, iterum abiit, et oravit tertio, eundem sermonem dicens" ("And leaving them, he went again and he prayed the third time, saying the selfsame word") (Matt. 26:44); and "Et iterum abiens oravit eumdem sermonem dicens" ("And going away again, he prayed, saying the same words") (Mark 14: 39). Here we see Caussade suggesting what we would call the use of a mantra.

[26] "Adveniat regnum tuum. Fiat voluntas tua, sicut in cælo, et

long prayer. This is what that pious widow of whom St. Teresa speaks[27] almost literally practiced. She sometimes spent whole hours [58] reciting a few Paters [Our Fathers]. And by the way, this is all that can ordinarily be done by most of the simple[28] but innocent and virtuous souls who are raised in the country or in hamlets.[29] Can we even require of them or teach them anything else? Also God often makes up [for whatever they lack] by impressions [so] secret that many of these good souls remain for whole hours in their churches without boredom, without disgust, and with a modest, respectful, and attentive demeanor that edifies and touches bystanders. Then ask them what they said to God. They will answer you, with tears in their eyes, that they don't know how to pray and never have been able to learn how. Good God! What are they doing there for such a long time and what secret charm holds them with such a great taste of piety and of so much peace and sweetness that they can hardly tear themselves away from the holy place? Yes, I dare to affirm, in the company of many holy country parish priests, that they are doing this heart-

---

in terra" ("Thy kingdom come. Thy will be done on earth as it is in heaven") (Matt. 6:10); see also Jesus' prayer at Gethsemani: "[D]icens: Pater, si vis, transfer calicem istum a me: verumtamen non mea voluntas, sed tua fiat" ("[S]aying: Father, if thou wilt, remove this chalice from me: but yet not my will, but thine be done") (Luke 22:42).

[27] She wrote in the first draft of the *Way of Perfection* that it was an elderly nun (chap. 30, par. 5, in *Collected Works,* vol. 2, chap. 30 [p. 471 n. 5]).

[28] Olphe-Galliard reads "saintes" (holy) in place of the manuscript's "simples."

[29] This notion of the spirituality of simple country souls goes under the title of "science du sauvage." See Michel de Certeau, "L'Illetré éclairé dans l'histoire de la lettre de Surin sur le Jeune Homme du Coche" (The enlightened illiterate in the history of the letter of Surin about the Young Man of the Stagecoach), 1630 ed. This letter is published in Surin's *Correspondance,* 140–44, and Caussade most likely read a different version, found in Surin, *Lettres Spirituelles,* 1721 ed., 1:1–15.

charged prayer, this prayer of faith, of the presence of God, this prayer of simplicity.

Many of our learned hardly [59] understand it and will never understand it as long as in following the heights and sublimity of their intelligences they evaluate it with those high and sublime ideas that they forge at will. Instead, they should look at it as the prayer of the small and humble, and to find it themselves by walking arm in arm with the humble in simplicity of heart according to the usual expression of the Scriptures.[30] Simplicity of heart so pregnant with the taste of God that, even in the Old Testament, the prophets never tired of repeating to the great kings of that time these short words: "If you walk before the Lord in simplicity of heart, if you look for him with simplicity of heart, you can expect all kinds of good things and graces."[31]

Q: But if, instead of what you have just said, we preach to these good souls to mistrust such a naive way of praying and this taste of piety that holds them so long in church on feast days, because it is mere imagination; [if we urge them] to mistrust this sweet rest in the presence of God because it is pure idleness; [if we urge them] to mistrust these attentive pauses and[32] the frequent pauses [occurring] during their vocal prayers as being very dangerous

---

[30] "Diligite iustitiam, qui iudicatis terram. Sentite de Domino in bonitate, et in simplicitate cordis quærite illum" ("Love justice, you that are the judges of the earth. Think of the Lord in goodness, and seek him in simplicity of heart") (Wisd. 1:1).

[31] "Innocens manibus et mundo corde, qui non accepit in vano animam suam, nec juravit in dolo proximo suo. Hic accipiet benedictionem a Domino, et misericordiam a Deo salutari suo" ("The innocent in hands, and clean of heart, who hath not taken his soul in vain, nor sworn deceitfully to his neighbor. He shall receive a blessing from the Lord, and mercy from God his Savior") (Ps. 23:4f.). Caussade may also have in mind "Quam bonus Israel Deus, his qui recto sunt corde!" ("How good is God to Israel, to them that are of a right heart!") (Ps. 72:1).

[32] The manuscript has "and," whereas Olphe-Galliard reads "so."

because they come very close to an error, to the [60] heresy that is called quietism—what will such preaching bring forth and yield?

A: You can judge well enough yourself. Fortunately, in the country they do not hear such learned preachers; for the most part we find there good parish priests who are simply convinced, as I am, that a good will is essential before God, and that in matters of good and evil it is the heart which accounts for all.[33]

Q: What other fruit should we draw from these examples and reflections?

A: 1. At the least [the purely heart-charged prayer of simple recollection] cuts away the superfluity of our meditations, readings, and vocal prayers to substitute assets, that is to say, attention of the heart, savor of the heart, peace and rest of the heart,[34] which many people hardly think of.[35]

2. Among many good Christians and people of virtue, [this prayer] abolishes a double illusion as nefarious as it is crude: illusion in the excessive earnestness of some, illusion in the pitiful discouragement of others, because they all think alike, convinced that they never meditate well, pray well, or read with fruit unless they are in perpetual agitation, piling up reflection upon reflection, [61] prayer upon prayer, reading upon reading. In this way they pass their whole life without ever wanting to learn from simple souls the great secret of knowing from time to time to restrain themselves a little in peace and in silence, attentive before

---

[33] For the word "heart" see *Dictionnaire de spiritualité*, s.v. "Cor et cordis affectus" (Heart and affection of the heart), vol. 2, pt. 2, cols. 2278–2307, and especially the section "Le coeur chez les spirituels du XVIIe siècle" (The heart among the spirituals of the seventeenth century), cols. 2300–2307.

[34] Olphe-Galliard omits the following words that are found in the manuscript: "savor of the heart, peace and rest of the heart."

[35] Olphe-Galliard has "dream of" instead of "think of."

God, not even when he seeks by some interior inclinations to draw them to this saintly and loving rest, which is the end and principal fruit of prayer, according to St. Bonaventure's opinion.[36] On the one hand, we only seek God to find him, to be united to him, and to rest in him who is the center of the heart and the unique object of its true rest, as St. Augustine says;[37] on the other hand, all of our holiness on earth consists in this holy union of heart, as in heaven all our happiness will consist in perfect union and eternal rest.

Alas! If with a little more distrust of ourselves, of our own skills, and of our customary undertakings, and if with a little more confidence in God[38] and abandonment to the Holy Spirit—whom the Church calls the finger of the right hand of the celestial Father,[39] because he engraves all that pleases him [62] in our hearts—if with this double awareness we were willing to try to practice, to proceed gently, and to make short attentive pauses during all our

---

[36] François le Roux writes: "Tout le fruit donc de l'oraison, son terme et son fin; c'est de s'unir à Dieu, et de devenir un seul esprit avec Lui; . . . toutes les forces de l'âme et ses puissances se rassemblent, et s'arrètant uniquement au seul bien véritable, souvrain et très simple, elle se transforme dans la ressemblance et la conformité très parfaite de Celui qui seul est permanent et éternel" (Thus all the fruit of prayer, its outcome, and its end are to be united to God and to become one mind with him; . . . all the forces of the soul and all its powers come together; and when it stops uniquely at the sole true good, sovereign and very simple, it is transformed into the likeness and very perfect conformity to him who alone is permanent and eternal) (*Traités spirituels tirés de St. Bonaventure,* 2:407f.); Bonaventure's *Itinerarium mentis in Deum* (Journey of the mind to God) argues that the end of the spiritual journey is peaceful rest and union with God.

[37] "[You stir man to take pleasure in praising you, because] you have made us for yourself, and our heart is restless until it rests in you" (*Confessions,* I, 1 (1) [p. 3 in Chadwick ed.]).

[38] Olphe-Galliard omits "in God."

[39] Hymn *Veni Creator* (Come Creator): "Digitus paternæ dexteræ" (Finger of the Father's right hand).

exercises of piety, confessors and preachers would not have so many reasons to berate us without end for the little fruit that we harvest from our prayers, spiritual readings, Masses, Communions, and especially from vocal prayer, which, not being animated by the heart, lacks this interior spirit and remains as if it was without effect and without soul.

Q: Since this double practice is so useful and, by the way,[40] so proper to introduce us little by little into this purely heart-charged prayer, I would like to know more in detail:

1. Why should prayer be made slowly and with pauses?
2. How can and ought we make these pauses?
3. What fruits do we inevitably collect?

A: This is what I shall try to answer in the following chapter.

---

[40] Olphe-Galliard drops the words "by the way."

Chapter 6

[ATTENTIVE PAUSES: WHAT, HOW, AND WHY?]

A: As for going slowly and gently word by word, either
        spoken or interior, all masters well acquainted [63]
with prayer teach the following about it:

1. Go slowly and gently to avoid, they say, every harmful effort and every struggle of the mind. Prayer, they add,
which causes a headache can hardly be good, because on
the whole prayer should be the work of a heart that speaks
with respectful freedom and filial confidence to him whom
Jesus Christ orders us to address as Father at the very start
of our prayer.[1]

2. What we usually reckon as fervor, far from being in
the heart or in the mind, is merely a flush of the blood or
imagination: purely natural acts[2] so apt to trouble the Holy
Spirit's actions that one of the major concerns of those who
are progressing consists in working to destroy this natural
activity,[3] which, if it opposes the gentle peace of the Spirit

---

[1] For the importance of the word "Father," see Teresa of
Avila, *Way of Perfection,* chap. 27.

[2] Antoine Guilloré has written thus: "Il y en a qui pensent
facilement que toute leur ferveur est un feu du Saint-Esprit" (There
are those who easily believe that all their fervor is a fire from the Holy
Spirit) ("Les illusions de la ferveur" [The illusions of fervor], *Oeuvres
spirituelles,* 757f.).

[3] The words: "so apt . . . natural activity" are missing from

of God, is a great imperfection, one which we ought to
tolerate only at the beginning.

Q: Shouldn't you back up the above paragraph with
       several examples?

A: Here are two taken from the Old Testament. The
       first is from the prophet Elisha,[4] who before starting
to pray realized that he needed to calm [64] his innermost
self, which was in truth holily agitated, but somewhat ex-
cessively so, after only a single spurt of his zeal for the
glory of God. From this I conclude with St. Teresa[5] that
every flush of zeal and devotion which disturbs the harmo-
nious dispositions of the interior and troubles its peace is in
no way characteristic of divine inspiration, but rather a
mixture of self-love that slides in everywhere—and that
mixes in all and spoils all, says St. Francis de Sales.[6] The
second is in chapter 19 of the third Book of Kings,[7] where
I strikingly see when and how God made [himself] heard
by the prophet Elisha on the mountain where he was ordered to go to hear him. It isn't at all when the prophet
heard an intense wind capable of uprooting mountains; no,
no, says Scripture,[8] it isn't during these intensities that God

---

Olphe-Galliard's edition.

[4] "Nunc autem adducite mihi psaltem. Cumque caneret psal-
tes, facta est super eum manus Domini, et ait . . ." ("Now bring me
hither a minstrel. And when the minstrel played, the hand of the Lord
came upon him, and he said . . .") (4 Kings 3:15 [in the current
Bible, 2 Kings]); Elisha is calmed by the singing of psalms.

[5] *Life,* chap. 13, para. 10.

[6] *Traité de l'amour de Dieu*, VIII, xii (Pléiade ed., 749f.); in
Oeuvres, vol. 5 (vol. 2 of *Traité*): 100f.; the same idea is found in his
letter of November 22, 1602, to the "Religieuses du Monastère des
Filles-Dieu" (The Nuns of the Monastery of the Daughters of God)
(*Oeuvres,* 12:145).

[7] 3 Kings in the Vulgate, which I am citing, but 1 Kings in
the current editions.

[8] "Et ait ei: Egredere, et sta in monte coram Domino: et ecce

speaks; it isn't when he felt the earth tremble under his feet; no, no, it isn't at all in these tremblings that God speaks; it isn't even when he saw a great fire lit before his eyes; no, no, it isn't at all in the middle of these waving flames that God speaks; so therefore when? It is precisely, adds the Scriptures, only when he had felt the agreeable touch of a gentle and very moderate breeze.[9] Why then? [65] Every ardor, by hampering interior peace, smothers there the peaceful Spirit of God or prevents feeling there the sweet impressions, just as we would not perceive the sweet stirring of a slight balmy breeze only rippling the surface of the water of a tranquil pond if at that time we threw in a stone.

Q: Why is it necessary to make these small and frequent pauses about which we are speaking?[10]

Dominus transit, et spiritus grandis et fortis subvertens montes, et conterens petras ante Dominum: non in spiritu Dominus, et post spiritum commotio: non in commotione Dominus" ("And he said to him: Go forth, and stand upon the mount before the Lord: and behold the Lord passeth, and a great and strong wind before the Lord overthrowing the mountains, and breaking the rocks in pieces: the Lord is not in the wind, and after the wind an earthquake: the Lord is not in the earthquake") (3 Kings 19:11).

[9] "Et post commotionem ignis: non in igne Dominus, et post ignem sibilus auræ tenuis. Quod cum audisset Elias, operuit vultum suum pallio, et egressus stetit in ostio speluncæ, et ecce vox ad eum dicens: Quid hic agis, Elia? Et ille respondit . . ." ("And after the earthquake a fire: the Lord is not in the fire, and after the fire a whistling of a gentle air. And when Elias heard it, he covered his face with his mantle, and coming forth stood in the entering in of the cave, and behold a voice unto him, saying: What dost thou here, Elias? And he answered . . ." (3 Kings 19:12f.).

[10] Caussade probably derived the idea of attentive pauses from Baltasar Álvarez, who said that he stopped "les discours par intervalles pour la présence de Dieu" (the conversation at intervals for the sake of the presence of God) (La Puente, *La Vie du père Baltasar Alvares,* in *Instructions spirituelles,* dialogue 5, question 2, bk. 2 [p. 139]). Caussade equates attentive pauses with what Álvarez said about stopping

A: I have just hinted at it: it is to listen to God after
         having spoken to him in different ways in the depths
of the heart.

[1.] Sometimes he speaks with those kinds of interior words that we hear in the depths of the soul, says St.
Teresa,[11] as if someone pronounced them out loud in our
ears; but here there isn't any question of such kinds of
words, since we are speaking only of something that arrives
during our commonplace recollection.

2. God speaks in intuitions and inspirations; it is therefore necessary to stop to receive them.

3. He speaks while acting, for in God, to speak and to
do what he wants are the same.[12] Therefore, it is necessary
to stop from time to time to make space for the impressions that God wants to imprint on our hearts [66] and
wills, which in an incomprehensible way he moves, turns,
and fashions as he wishes, as long as no obstacle at all is
found, much more easily than the most skillful craftsman
would know how to mold a piece of soft wax as he
wishes.[13]

4. God speaks in giving what we ask for, as the rich
answer the poor by giving alms. Therefore, imitate those
poor persons who, far from only crying and wailing without interruption, stop from time to time, hold out and
open their hands to receive alms. Likewise, let us stop now
and then, suspend our interior cries, give time for our
desires and for our confidence to expand well, and open
our hearts into which God, acting just as softly as he does

---

discourse.

[11] *Life,* chap. 25, par. 1, in *Collected Works,* 1:161f.

[12] "Quoniam ipse dixit, et facta sunt" ("For he spoke and they
were made[: he commanded and they were created]") (Ps. 32:9).

[13] See Francis de Sales, *Traité de l'amour de Dieu,* IX, iv, last
para.

secretly, will by his divine infusion pour the graces fervently hoped for and patiently awaited.[14]

Q: Are these pauses done, as some think, by a suspension of our interior acts?[15]

A: Those who view them this way imagine something absolutely impossible, for, [67] as the Scholastic philosophers and theologians say, our acts, specifically in this case the interior operations of our soul, are states of being one way at one time and another at another time. In other words, if you wish, just as our acts with respect to the soul are like shape with respect to the body, so our soul

---

[14] Surin writes: "Quoique rarement il arrive que les âmes parvenues à cet état, n'[?] aient par habitude quelque arrêt à la présence de Dieu, qui pour petit qu'il soit, leur doit suffire, sans recourir à leurs anciennes méthodes" (Although it rarely happens that souls arrive at this state, they have habitually a few pauses in the presence of God, which, as small as they might be, should suffice for them without recourse to their old methods) (*Catéchisme spirituel*, pt. 1, chap. 3 [p. 15 of Paris 1693 edition]). He also writes: "La seconde chose qu'elles doivent observer, c'est de tenir leur actvité suspendue sans interrompre par leur propre action humaine et base celle de Dieu si ce n'est qu'elles se sentent poussées de Dieu à cela, ou qu'elles connaisent que Dieu le permette, en quoi néanmoins elles ne se donnent point de peine mais procèdent avec grande liberté" (The second thing they should practice is to hold their activity suspended without interrupting that of God by their proper and lowly human action, unless they feel themselves pushed by God to do so or they know that God is permitting them to do so, in which case, however, they should in no way pain themselves but proceed with great freedom) (*Guide spirituel*, IV, I, para. 4 [p. 168]).

[15] The expression "interior acts . . ." comes from bk. 5 of Bossuet's *Instructions sur les états d'oraison*, entitled: "Des actes directs et refléchis, apperceus et non apperceus, etc." (On direct and deliberate acts, perceived and unperceived, etc.), 128f. In a footnote to chap. 31, sec. 34, of *Des grâces d'oraison*, Augustin-François Poulin explains that when we are distracted we do direct acts that differ from "réfléchis" (deliberate or conscious) ones. For instance, while brushing my teeth (a direct act), I'm hardly aware of what I'm doing and am thinking of something else (a distraction from the direct act of brushing my teeth).

can no more be without any activity than our body can be[16] without any shape; but just as a body can well have at one time one shape and at another time another shape—what was a square becoming round, thus losing one shape to receive another—likewise can our soul at one time be in a state with certain acts, at another time with certain other acts, dropping certain thoughts, certain feelings, in order to take up others, even contrary ones. Having established that interior pauses cannot be mere suspension of our acts, I will now explain how interior pauses can be done.

1. As we have already hinted, these attentive pauses are made precisely by a unique suspension of the acts, which we call usual, formal, explicit, and deliberate, in order to better[17] apply ourselves to the interior and to what goes on there. This kind of suspension happens when, thinking that[18] we are about to hear a beautiful voice or an agreeable symphony, we each during this expectation suspend our [68] thoughts, deliberations, and interior motions in order to be more attentive to what we are hoping to hear. Indeed, suspension and expectation would be in themselves evil if the awaited thing were [also evil]. Therefore, acts occur during this attentive suspension or, to speak more exactly, during the suspension itself. The awaiting itself is truly an act belonging to the kind that the bishop of Meaux calls direct, deliberate, and in a sense unperceived; that is to say, perceived not by explicit deliberation but only by awareness itself, which we find imperceptibly in the soul as we do in hundreds of purely natural cases.[19]

---

[16] Olphe-Galliard cuts out the comparison by dropping the words "without any activity than our body can be."

[17] Olphe-Galliard has "ainsi" (so) in the place of "better."

[18] The words "when, thinking that" are missing in Olphe-Galliard.

[19] See "Diverses causes par où il arrive qu'on ne connoist point les actes" (Different causes where it happens that we do not

2. Even the supernatural and divine suspension of which St. Teresa speaks,[20] which avoids the word "rapture," which astonishes us—even this suspension in rapture doesn't happen without acts, for God at that time suspends the powers of the soul and its usual operations only in order to lift the soul up and to make it perform acts even of a superior order, fully supernatural and divine. Concerning this, it is most fitting to underscore the misunderstanding and contempt of some writers [69] who mix all at the same time, mixing both the fully divine suspension, of which St. Teresa speaks, with what we are speaking of, and the most ordinary recollection with the extraordinary.[21] In order to combat simple recollection, these writers have taken it upon themselves to argue that accordingly we want to carry ordinary souls to a kind of prayer and[22] suspension so rare that St. Teresa[23] herself confesses to have never experienced it for longer than half an hour. After this, they add, the souls of fairly common virtue will claim to be able to remain in the same state for entire hours on end, although in simple recollection there is nothing of that sort. However, these books do not fail to leave strong impressions and to engender strange presuppositions against the truth.[24]

---

comprehend the acts), in *Instruction,* V, xvii (pp. 148f.).

[20] "When the Lord suspends the intellect . . . without reflection it understands more in the space of a Creed than we can understand with all our earthly diligence in many years" (*Life,* chap. 12, para. 5); see also *Interior Castle,* VI, chap. 4, para. 5, and chap. 10, para. 2.

[21] Nicole puts infused contemplation and acquired contemplation into the same category and consequently mixes them (*Réfutation quiétistes,* bk. 2, chap. 1 [pp. 150–54]).

[22] Olphe-Galliard omits "and."

[23] *Life,* chap. 18, para. 12.

[24] Caussade is referring to the literature of antimystical devotion whose exemplar is Pierre Nicole. See Henri Bremond, "Pierre Nicole ou l'anti-mystique," in *Histoire de sentiment religieux,* vol. 4, chap. 11 (pp. 471–588, esp. starting with p. 573).

Q: But from such a misunderstanding of the word "sus-
      pension," why and how could others have achieved
such contempt?

A: It is of small importance and maybe fairly difficult to
      guess why. For, on the one hand, it isn't at all by
ignorance, since these are clever writers and, rightfully, [70]
greatly esteemed. On the other hand, it cannot be by bad
faith, since their works are as filled with piety as with
understanding. Might it be for the reason that St. Bonaventure suggests?[25] Mystical theology[26] is completely different from dogmatic theology[27] which starts from theory,
whereas the former starts from experience or, as others add,
at the very least is supplied by extensive direction over souls
who have experience.[28] Now keeping in mind all that we
have just said, we easily understand whence arises and what
is the error of those who are scandalized when we advise
people about this recollection, urging that they should at
times hold themselves before God, either like a well-

---

[25] St. Bonaventure explains that we come to contemplation by
prayer and a holy life, which are conditions we have to meet to reach
wisdom (*The Soul's Journey into God,* chap. 1, para. 8 [p. 63]). Here
we see clearly that Caussade is not really a disciple of Bossuet, who
writes: "Je dis que l'experience qui peut bien regler certaines choses,
est subordonnée dans son tout à la science théologique qui consulte la
tradition et qui possède les principes. C'est icy une verité constante et
inébranlable qu'on ne peut nier sans erreur" (I hold that experience
which can well settle some things is as a whole subordinate to theological science, which takes stock of tradition and which possesses the
principles. Here is a constant and unshakable truth that cannot be
denied without error) (Introduction to his *Instructions,* pp. [15]–[16]).

[26] The text reads, "this science." As Caussade is writing about
deep prayer, I translated "this science" as "mystical theology."

[27] The text reads, "the others." As Caussade is contrasting the
study of deep prayer with regular theology or philosophy, I translated
"the others" as "dogmatic theology."

[28] In his *Traité de l'amour de Dieu,* Francis de Sales draws on
his own experiences and those of the Sisters of the Visitation who
shared with him their spiritual experiences (Fr. André Ravier's introduction to the *Traité,* in *Oeuvres,* Pléiade ed., 325).

stretched canvas in front of one who, with a brush in his hand, is going to paint on it,[29] or like a stone in the hands of one who turns it over and over to hew it and to fashion it as he wishes.[30] For then these [writers] imagine people in [71] total inactivity (as if that were possible, contrary to what we just have argued), instead of imagining them, as it really happens, in total abandonment, as would be the case for both this canvas and this stone if like us they were capable of awareness.

Indeed, for example, a man who wants to be cured of a sickness abandons himself like a dead body to all the actions of medicine and surgery, in spite of all his repugnances. Such is abandonment as we understand and recommend by these comparisons: a firm and sustained abandonment insofar as we can maintain it. Abandonment is one of the most heroic acts of perfect renunciation and death to oneself of which all writings speak, especially the *Imitation of Jesus Christ*.[31] I beg that those who, following their prejudices and false ideas, make [attentive pauses] a subject of scandal, would make several attempts at them during pauses in their prayers. Then they will discover by their own proper experience what it costs [72] nature, the mind, and the human heart. I am not begging them to remain a long time totally abandoned to God in the interior, but only to make a sincere attempt and to persist for one or two minutes, so utterly difficult is this supposed idleness and inaction that they have imagined.[32]

------

[29] See St. John of the Cross, *Living Flame of Love*, stanza III, para. 42 (pp. 625f.), for the image of a painting.

[30] Francis de Sales, *Traité de l'amour de Dieu*, VI, xi, para. 4 (Pléiade ed., 642).

[31] "On the Royal Road of the Holy Cross," bk. 2, chap. 12 (pp. 72–77 of Knox/Oakley translation).

[32] Interestingly, Guilloré doesn't seem to understand how difficult it is to rest in silence and argues that except for the few called by God to "oraison de simple repos" (prayer of simple rest), we should be "dans un soin perpetuel, de se remplir de saintes pensées,

Q: But in any event why should it be necessary to ex-
haust yourself with cogitation about a matter where,
so it seems, only affection would be necessary, as almost all
writers have held?

A: Happy is the time when nothing more is asked and
nothing more is necessary; but at other times, other
precautions [are necessary]. In effect, what purpose does it
serve that already there are many affection-filled books
concerning this matter if certain people of wit and even of
virtue continue to discredit them and to knock them down
in looking at them as if filled with fantasies or[33] dangerous
illusions? If instead these kinds of people (according to
whose opinion we guide ourselves)[34] could be convinced
once and for all of the contrary, they would find that they
themselves [73] put themselves into their pure fancies and
into a kind of illusion so prejudicial to the salvation and
perfection of souls.

---

pour n'être pas dans une oisiviété, ou dangereuse, ou criminelle" (with
unending attention filling ourselves with holy thoughts in order not to
be in either dangerous or sinful idleness) (*Oeuvres spirituelles,* chap. 2
[p. 36]). He also tells us that our duty is "de discourir, la raison
[nous] ayant été donnée, pour cet effet, et il n'apartient, qu'à Dieu, de
suspendre l'usage de cette même raison, par des occupations plus
élèvées. Elle est donc bien téméraire de faire cette espèce d'attentat, en
éteignant tout le discours, à qui Dieu seul a droit de faire commandement de s'arrêter" (to discourse because reason was given to us for
this, and it belongs only to God to suspend the use of this same
reason by superior activities. Thus it is quite rash to do this kind of
awaiting by extinguishing all discourse, which God alone has the right
to order to stop) (ibid., chap. 2 [p. 780]). Hence, Caussade differs
significantly from his predecessor Guilloré and opens the way to
gradual discovery of inner silence through active attention.

[33] Olphe-Galliard has "and" instead of "or."

[34] The parentheses don't appear in Olphe-Galliard.

Then books[35] that teach so well and with such facility how to meditate, honor, and pray to God, with all of the heart in pure spirit and in pure truth, far from being discredited, would be praised and applauded. They would read and recommend them, at the very least to people of piety, each of whom would profit from them in his or her own way according to inclination, attraction, and individual needs. Maybe then after they walk in simplicity of heart like our Fathers and enter into all our Fathers' sentiments, we would no longer see in their libraries so many pious books stacked with care, now covered with[36] dust, not so much because they dislike the style of writing, a little old-fashioned (to which they accommodate themselves for other works),[37] but because today they want, so they say, a less elevated and less sublime piety but [one that is], in fact, softer and more accommodating than that of some books, which leave nothing to human nature: not one desire, not one feeling, not one thought, holding that everything goes to God and is purely for God, even forbidding satisfaction in his gifts, graces, and the most spiritual [74] and the most holy joys he gives.[38]

---

[35] Caussade may be referring to Mme Guyon and others, such as Guilloré or Boudon, the new mystics whom Bossuet so roundly attacked. Bk. 1, dialogue 3, of Caussade's *Instructions spirituelles* presents Mme Guyon's work in such a way that the reader sees what is of value in her writings and understands that she has merely badly expressed herself. Caussade is adroitly defending her.

[36] Olphe-Galliard has simply "covered with dust," but the manuscript adds the word "rongé" [left untranslated in this edition— ED.].

[37] The parentheses don't appear in Olphe-Galliard.

[38] Olphe-Galliard remarks that Caussade is alluding to the spirituality called "God alone," which we find in the book *Dieu seul* by Henri-Marie Boudon; but the view expressed by Caussade can be found in Francis de Sales and Jane de Chantal. This ideal is well expressed in two quotations from Boudon (*L'homme intérieur or la vie du vénérable père Jean-Chrysostome* [Paris, 1684], 67f. and 134f.) given by Bremond in *Histoire de sentiment religieux,* 6:237 and 239.

Q: This suspension during pauses seems to me to be easy to understand and to practice, but I especially desire to learn how long it is necessary to do these pauses and what advantages can unfailingly be drawn from them.

A: 1. These pauses should be more or less long depending on each one's capacities, since beginners, who don't yet have the habit or facility to know how to hold themselves peacefully and silently attentive before God, have to make them fairly short; but as they advance, the pauses become, as naturally could be expected, easier and longer, either by virtue of acquired dispositions or of a small beginning of an ensuing attraction.

2. These pauses should last as long as we feel a good sentiment in our hearts, whether excited by a pious reflection or an affective act or any small interior attraction. When these interior movements appear, we gently try to stimulate them with the same affections or with other similar ones that likewise always lead to new attentive pauses; we continue in the same fashion until the end of prayer.

3. As it necessarily follows from the above,[39] we [75] should place ourselves in silence and remain there as if eavesdropping every time and as long as we feel either a desire to love and to unite ourselves with God or a sweet rest in his presence, a simple taste for piety or simply a great interior calm, a certain peace that we aren't in the habit of experiencing. The risen Jesus Christ always gave his disciples this peace when he approached them: "Pax vobis" ["Peace be with you"]. This profound calm of our passions shows, so says blessed John of the Cross, that God in his way [puts] both[40] peace and love at the bottom of our hearts.[41]

---

[39] Olphe-Galliard drops "from the above."

[40] Olphe-Galliard omits "both."

[41] See John of the Cross, *Living Flame of Love,* esp. stanza III, verse 3, paras. 18–69 (pp. 617–37).

Q: But what if after various attempts at attentive pauses,
      I don't feel anything like that at all?

A: Then it is necessary to do what God reveals in the
      Scriptures: bear up as we wait for the Lord.[42] We
must say to ourselves, as King David did in similar cases,
"With expectation I have waited for the Lord."[43] We must
do what is done with respect to temporal favors in the
courts of princes, where, no matter how little we hope, we
do not at all grow weary of waiting. We must do what
Jesus Christ taught us in the parable of the man who at
midnight comes to wake up his friend and ask him for
three loaves of bread.[44] First he is refused and [76] waits in
vain, but finally his noisy dunning and his redoubled efforts
obtain for him what he seemed to have asked for in vain
and waited for over a long interval. Finally, at this point we
should imitate what most of the poor do. Tired and weary
of having often waited at the door of the rich, they still do
not fail to return there again with the hope of a favorable
moment; finally, owing to the force of new lamentations
and repeated expectations, they come to obtain what was
refused to others who were less courageous in practicing
patience while waiting.

Q: But what if during the pauses I am exposed to all
      sorts of distractions and even to bad thoughts?

A: Since the most abominable distractions and thoughts
      are involuntary, as I suppose, they don't harm you
any more during these pauses than[45] during the remainder

---

[42] "Neque irrideant me inimici mei: etenim universi, qui
sustinent te, non confundentur" ("Neither let my enemies laugh at
me: for none of them that wait on thee shall be confounded") (Ps.
24:3).

[43] "Expectans, exspectavi Dominum, et intendit mihi" ("With
expectation I have waited for the Lord, and he was attentive to me")
(Ps. 39:2).

[44] Luke 11:5–8.

[45] By omitting "during these pauses than," Olphe-Galliard
loses the comparison.

of your prayer or during any of your other prayers. On the
contrary, patiently suffering them constitutes a great subject
of merit, for then, so say our masters, we are doing the
prayer of patience.[46]

Q: But still, if after a considerable time I have done my
     prayers with these attentive pauses without ever ex-
periencing at all what you have spoken of, then haven't I
wasted a lot of [77] time, especially the most precious time,
that devoted to prayer?

A: No, no, it is anything but lost time; it may be your
     best time spent in prayer. Why?

1. Just as fully as God sees the heinous intention of a
scoundrel who waits hour after hour to catch his prey,
doesn't he likewise see the good intention of your attentive
pauses to hear him better in silence and be better disposed
to receive his illuminations, impressions, and operations at
the very moment he wants? Therefore, it takes just as much
to be worthy as to be unworthy.

2. Doesn't God continue to see all the diverse acts
practiced, although unsigned, during these attentive and
silent pauses?

   a. He sees acts of keen faith, for I wouldn't have
been careful to remain thus in attentive silence if I didn't
firmly believe that God is everywhere, that he is looking at
me, that he penetrates right to the actual preparation of my
heart, and that he is strong and good enough to answer
with the graces that he knows that I most need.

   b. He sees acts of desire and hope that form the
essence [78] of prayer, for we wait only insofar as we desire
and hope.

---

[46] St. Francis de Sales and the Carmel teach this. Caussade
writes Sr. Anne-Marguerite Boudet de la Bellière, telling her that
prayer of inner silence consumes our bad inclinations (*Lettres,* 2:108–13).

c. He sees acts of a great mistrust of oneself and entire confidence in God, in that I stop my usual operations only because I count much more on those of God.

d. He sees acts of the greatest humility, when we want to remain in the presence of God, according to the expression of the prophet-king,[47] like a beast of burden to whom silence is more appropriate than words before the supreme Majesty of God.

e. He sees acts of resignation and perfect abandonment, because I am ready for all, willing to see my request denied or granted, to see myself rejected or heard as it pleases my God, before whom I remain firm in spite of all the inner distractions and dryness that occur during these now very painful pauses and very boring awaitings.

Q: But what if during these attentive pauses I don't any longer think about all the above acts?

A: Never mind, you are in reality practicing them and that's enough: your eager awaiting embraces all of them. When a sinner commits a crime, usually he is exactly concerned only with satisfying his passion, but not at all with his ingratitude, nor [79] with the abuse of grace, nor with contempt for God's words, promises, and threats, nor even with[48] the blood of Jesus Christ, nor with the so many breaches of duty for which books and preachers upbraid him endlessly. Why? Because, as theologians tell us, all these evils are contained in his free act of doing wrong. Consequently, he is presumed to will them all efficaciously and actually. In virtue of this principle, you are willing all the good acts of which I was speaking, because they are all enclosed in your voluntary, silent, attentive, eager, humble, and always resigned pauses.

---

[47] "Ut iumentum factus sum apud te, et ego semper tecum" ("I am become as a beast before thee: and I am always with thee") (Ps. 72:23).

[48] Olphe-Galliard has "for" instead of "with."

Q: Is there any further advantage in these attentive
      pauses?

A: Here, in my opinion, we find the most[49] outstanding
      advantage: by such an easy and, in a way, so natural
a means, all who regularly practice interior prayer or extended meditative reading find themselves quite ready to
enter into fully heart-charged prayer—but, in truth, more
or less so according to the good dispositions of which we
shall soon speak. But do they always find themselves ready
to enter without fear, presumption, and the necessity of
engaging in [80] long and difficult discussions? Am I really
called to this so simple interior prayer? do I have all the
tell-tale signs of which different authors have spoken?

Q: But how and why do those who pray find themselves
      entering into this holy recollection without risk and
without danger?

A: There's no danger if during these attentive pauses,
      without meddling within himself and without leav-
ing the path of either mental, vocal, discursive, or affective
prayer on which God and their directors have placed them,
they do precisely only what the poor do at the door of the
rich, where they wait for those alms that the rich are willing to give them. [The same is true] if, according to the
expression of St. Augustine, after having groaned, knocked
at, and struck the door of the heavenly Father, I often wait
without being discouraged in peace and in attentive silence
for what would please the goodness of God or his pure
generosity to grant me.[50] Whence there follow [four] great
indicators:

---

[49] Olphe-Galliard drops the superlative "most."

[50] Caussade may be referring to Augustine's letter to Proba
(paras. 16f.) in which the saint explains to her that when God doesn't
seem to answer our prayers, he is preparing us by increasing our desire
for him, our only true end, who can really satisfy us. He also may
have in mind a similar point that he makes in his *Enarrationes* on
Psalm 102. See Hugh Pope, *The Teaching of St. Augustine on Prayer,*
and Thomas A. Hand, *St. Augustine on Prayer,* chap. 5, pp. 86–91.

1. Some good souls who, without knowing it or without daring to flatter themselves about it, have already received great attraction to this prayer of simple recollection and enter into it, so to say, in full flight [81] at the least attentive pause.

2. Many other virtuous people who haven't yet felt such an attraction will receive it not merely in recognition of all those acts practiced during their painful pauses, but also for being themselves already in a state ready to feel this interior attraction, fully ready and disposed to give themselves up to it during the new pauses in which they will engage.

3. Still more for the same reasons God will accord a little of this state of recollection to people of goodwill but who are still very imperfect, so that, as St. Francis de Sales[51] says, they have, thanks to this powerful aid, more vigor and ease to quickly correct themselves of their faults and imperfections.

4. Sometimes even, as we have already hinted, the greatest sinners, vividly stung by their faults and by the desire to convert themselves, will find that by dint of humble, eager, and resigned attentiveness, their meditations, readings, prayers, and so on will soon be mixed with recollection, sometimes active, sometimes in part acquired and in part infused, [82] so that thus they may be able to come more effectively and more promptly to the full conversion for which they were already working with all their power. But nothing at all of this will happen or, at the minimum, will be felt or perceived in these or in others if they always surrender, on the one hand, to the anxiety of not being able to act according to their own taste and, on the other hand, to the frenetic or too active continuation of their ordinary activities, without realizing that they should give place to those of the Holy Spirit, as they have done so often and learned so well to do by means of their pauses, [which are]

---

[51] *Traité de l'amour de Dieu,* bk. 10, chap. 4, esp. para. 2 (*Oeuvres,* vol. 5 [vol. 2 of *Traité*]: 176–80 [Pléiade ed., 819–23]).

silent, attentive, desirous, and fully resigned to the good pleasure of God.

Q: But for a purely passive and infused recollection, can there be merit?

A: There is insofar as the soul voluntarily cleaves to and freely follows this infused attraction, just as we merit retribution when we voluntarily cleave to evil impressions that we receive in spite of ourselves from the devil, the flesh, or the world. In one and in the other case, this state cannot properly be called passive, but instead passively active or actively passive, because even if we feel ourselves pushed and swept along, we always freely follow the impulse that pushes and sweeps us along.

Q: But if, by sheer force of practicing what you have said [83] and by means of experiencing from God what you describe, my prayer were bit by bit to change into pure recollection and sweet rest of the heart in God, how should I be preparing myself? What preparation is there for such a prayer?

A: Since we don't know for how long God wants us to remain in peace and fully recollected in his presence, we still need to prepare and begin as we usually do.

Q: But what if, with time and the sheer effort of so spending all or almost all of the time of my[52] prayer in this holy and sweet recollection, it were to become rather habitual in a recollection of God and a holy impression that would last all day?

A: In this case I don't see the need nor[53] even the means to prepare yourself better, for what better preparation is there than what the Holy Spirit himself has already accomplished in you by this continual presence of God? Moreover, when a soul has arrived there, we can say

---

[52] Olphe-Galliard has "our" instead of "my."

[53] Olphe-Galliard has "and" instead of "nor."

that the time of its prayer only continues or, if you prefer, renews prayer.

Q: But in this case what happens to the good resolutions that we are accustomed to make during meditation?

A: 1. We have already said that there is a time for everything.[54]

2. Formerly you made a great number of resolutions, maybe without much success, but now you carry them out. Why? Because during this prayer your heart, which has given itself up to and totally abandoned itself to the stimuli of the Holy Spirit, is moved, formed,[55] and fashioned as he wishes [84] and, on account of this, finds itself much better disposed and much more ready to avoid evil and do good when the opportunity arises than it would have been on account of all our usual resolutions. You will experience this proportionally as you acquire this infused or[56] mixed recollection.

Q: How does this courageous and virtuous disposition of the heart work in us?

A: 1. That it does is confirmed by the masters and a variety of experiences, although how it is achieved may be as incomprehensible as it is for many other supernatural matters where we cannot understand how they are produced, so limited is our mind. For example, who understands how sanctifying grace in a single moment wipes away from our souls all the stains of the most enormous sins and in an instant sanctifies the greatest sinners?

2. Doesn't our soul make itself virtuous proportionally as it practices virtuous acts? But what we can achieve only after a very long time with ordinary grace, the Holy Spirit achieves in us and with us in a very short time with the grace of holy recollection.

---

[54] See the last response of chap. 1.

[55] Olphe-Galliard drops "formed."

[56] Olphe-Galliard has "and" instead of "or."

3. In this prayer—have we not said so since the beginning?[57]—our heart does with respect to God what the miser does in thinking about his treasure and the worldly lover fully occupied by his object; that is to say, our heart conceives a liking for, turns to, yields to, pours out to, [85] unites with, and rests in God, who is its[58] center. There it is—have we not already said it?[59]—the pure language of the heart. God, for his part, speaks to it and answers it likewise by yielding and bending over as if in a living tabernacle, even taking delight there, as he himself says.[60] But as God is fully good, fully virtuous, fully holy, isn't it wonderful that in proportion to the different degrees of love and of union, which go to infinity, we find all in him who is the All? Hence, sometimes, those doing this prayer will often practice some virtues for the first time with as much facility as those who by dint of hard work practice them habitually. Moreover, as our masters say, sometimes in this prayer our imperfections are consumed as straw is in fire, yet without our becoming[61] exempt from every sin that is characteristic of our nature and necessary for humility.[62]

Q: We only enter therefore into this prayer with the help of attentive pauses, as you[63] have said, in proportion to the good dispositions each one of us has; but in what do they consist?

---

[57] See response 1 of chap. 2.

[58] Olphe-Galliard has "our" instead of "its."

[59] See the last response of chap. 1.

[60] "Ludens in orbe terrarum; et deliciæ meæ esse cum filiis hominum" ("Playing in the world: and my delights were to be with the children of men") (Prov. 8:31).

[61] Olphe-Galliard has "being able to become" instead of "becoming."

[62] This process of purification of our imperfections Caussade develops in his *Sacrament of the Present Moment,* 46–48.

[63] Olphe-Galliard has "we" instead of "you."

A: To facilitate memory and understanding, I summa-
          rize them in four expressions: purity of conscience,
of heart, of mind, and of action, which will constitute the
subject of the following chapter.[64] [86]

---

[64] Actually the next two chapters. In a letter to Marie-Anne-
Thérèse de Rosen, Caussade writes: J'ai seulement ajouté, avec le Père
Surin et les auteurs qui en parlent, qu'on peut indirectement et de loin
se disposer á recevoir ce grand don du ciel, en ôtant les obstacles par
une grande puretè: (1) de conscience, (2) de coeur, (3) d'esprit,
(4) d'intention" (I only add with Father Surin and the authors who
write of it that we can indirectly and from a distance dispose ourselves
to receive this great gift of heaven by removing the obstacles through
a great purity: [1] of conscience, [2] of heart, [3] of mind, [4] of
intention) (*Lettres,* 1:229f.) Here in Caussade's treatise intention
becomes action. These four points are not listed as such in Surin's
*Dialogues spirituels, Catéchisme spirituel, Secrets de la vie spirituelle, Lettres
spirituelles,* and *Fondements.*

Chapter 7

[PURITY OF CONSCIENCE]

Q: What is purity of conscience? Why and how should we acquire it?

A: [1.] It consists in a firm disposition of the heart never to want to consent to the least offense against God through deliberate purpose. This habitual disposition can subsist very well alongside many other contrary ones that, however, are forthwith given up.

2. This disposition is needed to succeed well at attentive pauses in prayer. Why?

[a.] When it is simply a question of acquiring active recollection by means of ordinary grace, won't grace be more effective insofar as we are more faithful to want to avoid even the least sin that could soil the conscience?

b.[1] If it is a case of infused recollection, how dare[2] we expect this special grace from God as long as we have for him so little love and so little filial fear that we fear offending him merely from self-love, that is to say, being concerned whether the offense will lead to our downfall, and not at all whether it will merely displease him without putting at risk our salvation?

---

[1] Olphe-Galliard has "1" instead of "2" [in this edition, however, printed as *b*.—ED.].

[2] Olphe-Galliard has "can" instead of "dare."

c.[3] We can acquire bit by bit this purity of conscience by following the recommendations of spiritual writings and directors, but especially by paying great attention to all our [87] interior agitations, so that the continuous perception of our own weaknesses leads us to have recourse to God at every occasion of a fall and to repent and humiliate ourselves after the least failings.[4]

Q: How must we repent and humble ourselves?

A: [1.] This repentance must be neither worrisome nor turbulent but moderate and peaceful; for, as St. Francis de Sales says, "Mustn't we even at the bitter end from the pain of our sins find peace there?"[5]

2. This interior humiliation must likewise be exempt from bustle, sorrow, resentment against oneself; for not only do agitations unsettle the soul and solve nothing, they are likewise new faults often more dangerous[6] than the

---

[3] Olphe-Galliard has "2" instead of "3" [in this edition, *c*—ED.].

[4] Here we see the influence of St. Ignatius of Loyola's rules 9–13 for the discernment of spirits (*Spiritual Exercises,* nos. 322–24).

[5] "Rien que le péché ne nous doit desplaire et fascher, et au bout du desplaisir du péché, encor faut il que la joye et consolation sainte soit attachée" (Nothing but sin should displease and anger us, and at the end of the displeasure of sin we must still discover that joy and holy consolation are attached) (letter of March 8 or 9, 1621, to Mme de la Chapelle, in *Oeuvres,* 20:31f.). See also *Introduction à la vie dévout,* III, ix, where Francis de Sales advises "la douceur envers nous-mêmes" (gentleness with ourselves), and his third conference, "De la confiance et abandonnement" (On confidence and abandonment) (*Entretien spirituel,* in *Oeuvres,* 6:19–30 [Pléiade ed., pp. 1020–30]). In *Oeuvres* it is called the second *entretien* and carries as its full title "Auquel on demande si l'on peut aller à Dieu avec une grande confiance, mesme ayant le sentiment de nostre misère et comment et du parfait abandonnement de soy mesme" (About which we ask whether we can approach God with great confidence, even when we have a sensation of our wretchedness and how to do so, and about the perfect abandonment of ourselves).

[6] Instead of "likewise new faults often more dangerous," Olphe-Galliard reads "themselves new faults more dangerous."

initial ones. Why? Because they arise from vexed self-love
and pride scandalized at seeing ourselves still so imperfect.
Therefore, St. Francis de Sales continues, drop all that
sorrowful, anxious, and resentful humility that consequently
is full of pride; learn to accept yourself just as you must
accept your neighbor; with the same charity, practice kindness towards yourself just as you do towards others, by
correcting yourself without anger, bitterness, and spite. This
brings you back to God with the same confidence as if
nothing has happened to you. This is the great secret [88]
for quickly acquiring great purity of conscience and, in the
meanwhile, perfect knowledge of yourself and deep humility of heart founded on frequently experiencing our pitiable
weakness. In this way, all things turn to the advantage of
people of goodwill.[7]

Q: Isn't it rash and presumptuous to expect such
    prompt forgiveness of our daily and frequent faults?

A: Here is what *The Spiritual Combat*, a book greatly
    esteemed, especially by St. Francis de Sales, says: I
assume that you have fallen not many times, but one hundred times in one day, not inadvertently but with full
knowledge, not into small faults but into very grievous
ones. After you have asked forgiveness for them and have
been humiliated by them for the last time, just as for the
first time, without wasting any time, return to God and to
yourself and take up your occupations and habitual exercises, with the same confidence as if you hadn't at all
failed.[8] Model yourself on the example of a wise traveler

---

[7] Here Caussade is summarizing Francis de Sales's chapter "La
douceur envers nous-mêmes" (Gentleness with ourselves) of *Introduction à la vie dévout*; see also the April 15–18, 1605, letter to Mme
Bourgeois in *Oeuvres,* 13:27–33, and the January 20, 1609, letter to
Mme de la Fléchère in 14:120.

[8] Caussade is paraphrasing chap. 26 of Lorenzo Scupoli's
Spiritual Combat. See Francis de Sales's letter of July 20, 1607, to
Jeanne de Chantal (*Oeuvres,* 13:304) and letter 104 in *Correspondance:
Les lettres d'amitié spirituelle,* 239), in which he writes: "Ma chère fille

who is as courageous in spirit as he is weak in body.[9] If he

[Mme de Chantal], lisez le 28e [26e?] chapitre du *Combat spirituel,* qui est mon cher livre que je porte en ma poche il y a dix-huit ans, et je ne le relis jamais sans profit. Tenez ferme à ce que je vous ai dit" (My dear daughter, read chapter 28 [26?] of the *Spiritual Combat,* which is my precious book that I have been carrying in my pocket for eighteen years and have never reread without profit. Hold on solidly to what I told you). Jean-Pierre Camus in *L'Esprit de saint François de Sales* (vol. 1, pt. 3, sec. 12 [pp. 164f.]) writes: "Le *Combat spirituel* [le livre St. François conseillait le plus]: c'estoit son cher livre, son favori. Il m'a dit plusieurs fois qu'il l'avoit porté plus de dix-huit ans dans sa pochette, en lisant tous les jours quelque chapitre, ou au moins quelque page. . . . [Il] conseilloit la lecture de ce livre . . . à tous ses devots. Je luy demandois un jour que estoit son directeur. Il tira de sa pochette le livre du *Combat spirituel,* et me dit: 'Le voila; c'est celuy que avec Dieu m'enseigne dès ma jeunesse, c'est mon maistre aux choses de l'esprit et de la vie interieure.' . . . Il estimoit beaucoup le *Combat* pour le regard de la vie active et de la pratique" (The *Spiritual Combat* [the book that St. Francis recommended the most]: it is his precious book, his favorite one. He told me several times that he had carried it for over eighteen years in his pocket and that every day he read a chapter or at least several pages. . . . He recommended to all his pious followers that they read this book. I asked him one day who his spiritual director was. He drew from his pocket the book *Spiritual Combat* and said to me: "Here it is; it is this book that has been teaching me since my youth; it is my master for things of the spirit and of the interior life." . . . He valued greatly the *Combat* to guide him in the practicalities of his active life) (ibid., pt. 14, sec. 16 [pp. 125–28]). The abridgement of Camus by Pierre Collot (2nd ed., Paris, 1731) reads: "Le *Combat spirituel* étoit son cher livre, son livre favori. Il m'a dit plusieurs fois qu'il l'avoit porté plus de dix-huit ans dans sa poche, y lisant tous les jours quelque chapitre, ou au moins quelque page. Il conseilloit ce livre à tous ceux qui s'addressoient à lui. . . . Plus je le lis, plus j'y remarque, comme en sa semence, toute la doctrine spirituelle de notre Bienheureux" (The *Spiritual Combat* was his precious book, his favorite one. He told me several times that he had carried it in his pocket for over eighteen years and that every day he read a chapter or at least several pages. He recommended this book to all who sought his advice. . . . The more I read it, the more I discover, as in its seed, the full spiritual doctrine of our Blessed [Francis]) (pt. 3, chap. 7 [p. 104]).

[9] Instead of the imperative "imitez" (imitate) Olphe-Galliard

happens to fall, he gets up right away and continues his journey without wasting time uselessly lamenting; if, several paces later, he again falls, [89] he thinks only of getting up again and always courageously continuing his journey in spite of his many repeated falls; finally he completes his journey, although later than others.[10]

Q: Can you justify such conduct for the path of salvation and perfection?

A: Because we are always duty-bound to return necessarily to God, is it possible for us to do so too quickly? Furthermore, such eagerness reveals a good will in spite of its great weakness and a proper confidence in God, because only in him can we expect goodness such that it always covers the multitude and enormity of our sins. To behave otherwise is wicked distrust of God's mercifulness. We would have a hard heart little responsive to the mischief of having displeased him or the evil shame of a conceited soul. Such a soul so often cannot bring itself to acknowledge its infidelities and ingratitudes, or such love of freedom that, instead of looking at these frequent reversals as encouragements to do better, we avoid binding ourselves and refuse to commit ourselves to anything. What does this lead to? We become further separated from God and weaker and weaker; we fall more often, more seriously, and make our renewal more difficult.[90]

Ah, if some spiritual people understood this maxim well, we wouldn't at times see them after a relapse so conceitedly distressed and demolished that they even abandon their exercises of piety and dare not, so they say, present themselves before God after such infidelities. Moreover, they flatter themselves for this as if such feelings came from

---

has the present participle "imitant."

[10] Fénelon advises us to continue walking without looking back in "Discours sur la dissipation et la tristesse" (Discourse on dispersion and dejection), no. 6 of "Lettres et opuscules spirituels," in *Oeuvres* (Pléiade ed.), 575.

real affliction and true humility.[11] The truly spiritual have
very different feelings and act very differently. Strongly
imbued with their nothingness, with both[12] their misery
and their weakness, they are neither discouraged nor devastated nor even surprised by their relapses. From them they
learn to know themselves better, to humble themselves
always more and more profoundly, to mistrust themselves,
and even to despair of themselves fully, in order to place
their confidence exclusively in God alone and to wait for no
more than his goodness.

Q: What you have just said seems to lead to rejoicing in
       our faults rather than being afflicted by them.

A: Distinguish well the faults always worthy of our
       regret from those having fortunate consequences, as
does the Church when in speaking of the fall of the first
man it exclaims, "O fortunate fault"—fortunate not in itself
but "for having merited such a redeemer."[13] Likewise, to
view in a better light our poorly understood pain and [91]
humility after our relapses, let us right away screw up our
courage and hope by keeping in mind that God is strong
and merciful enough to give us even in the middle of our
relapses the precious treasure of true humility. With its
total mistrust in ourselves and perfect confidence in God,
which are like the two poles of the spiritual life, humility
forms the foundation and guardian of all the virtues.

Also, when a soul has progressed to this point, God
lavishes his gifts and favors upon it. Why? He no longer
risks that we will purloin any of his glory by appropriating

---

[11] St. Teresa of Avila tells us about this temptation and warns
us against it in her *Life,* chap. 7. paras. 1 and 11.

[12] Olphe-Galliard omits "both."

[13] "O felix culpa, quæ talem ac tantum meruit habere
Redemptorem!" (Oh fortunate fault, which merited to have so great
and such a Redeemer!) (Præcomium paschale ["Exsultet"] from the
vigil of Easter, in *Missale romanum,* 32nd ed., 230f.).

anything to ourselves.[14] Therefore, we understand from our own experience that beautiful maxim of a great servant of God that a well-known affliction is better than an angelic virtue which we appropriate to ourselves by vain complacency.[15] For this reason God sometimes leaves in very elevated souls some faults well below their elevated path with the purpose of having them exercise at the same time both humility and charity towards others.[16]

Q: How can it be that souls well nurtured and cherished by God can have such faults and not have them harm their perfection?

A: 1. These blemishes are not found in them[17] as in the imperfect who foster or tolerate their cherished faults, [92] but rather these faults are hated, detested, and unremittingly fought off. Because the attachments of the heart uniquely define its orientation, these cherished souls do not displease God as the imperfect do. By God's permis-

---

[14] See what Francis de Sales writes about generosity in "Entretien spirituel sur le sujet de la Générosité" (Spiritual conference on the topic of Generosity) (Conference 19, in Pléiade ed., p. 1271–80, and Conference 6, in *Oeuvres,* 6:74–85).

[15] Without doubt Fénelon is the great servant of God who is quoted here by Caussade. Madeleine Huillet d'Istria writes: "Caussade est nettement le disciple de saint François de Sales et de Fénelon. Sur les points où Fénelon fut condamné . . . Caussade adopte en général la position salésienne. Sur les points où Fénelon ne fut pas condamné, et où il se montra simplement en opposition avec Bossuet, sans que l'Eglise ait tranché en faveur de l'un ou de l'autre, Caussade est du côté de Fénelon" (Caussade is manifestly the disciple of St. Francis de Sales and of Fénelon. On the points for which Fénelon was condemned . . . Caussade generally adopts the position of de Sales. On the points for which Fénelon was not condemned, in which he was simply in opposition to Bossuet, and on which the Church had not taken a stand in favor of the one or the other, Caussade stood on the side of Fénelon) (*Le Père de Caussade et la querelle du pur amour,* chap. 2 [p. 72]).

[16] See Caussade, "The Mystery of God's Grace, This Diet of Dust and Ashes," in *Sacrament of the Present Moment,* chap. 7 (pp. 46–48).

[17] Olphe-Galliard erroneously reads "themselves."

sion there remains only weakness, the pure[18] misery of our nature, so apt to keep these souls, in spite of their elevation, always interiorly humble and often even exteriorly so.[19]

2. In them, these involuntary faults receive admirable compensation as the soul acquires heroic virtues, but always accompanied with the most profound humility that develops under the aegis of these same faults which they themselves never succeed in correcting. This admirable divine guidance should alone[20] render us more reserved in our judgments about people whose interior is unknown to us and often disguised under appearances so deceptive that it ought to be enough for us to have seen or heard cited only one example to persuade us to suspend at the very least the wickedness of rash judgments and, even more, of our ill-advised conversations.

---

[18] Olphe-Galliard reads "poor" instead of "pure."

[19] For this very Fénelonian teaching see letter 9 in Le Brun's article "Textes inédits du Père de Caussade III," *Revue d'ascétique* 46 (1970): 326–35, especially p. 329, or the version given by Olphe-Galliard in Caussade's *Lettres spirituelles,* 2:71–79, especially p. 75, and Francis de Sales, "Que l'humilité nous fait aimer notre propre abjection" (Let humility lead us to love our own abasement), in *Introduction à la vie dévout,* pt. 3, chap. 6 (Pléiade ed., 145–48; Image Book ed., 135–38).

[20] The manuscript here reads, "Cette conduite admirable de Dieu qui seule devrait . . ." (This admirable divine guidance which should alone . . .). Because this reading omits the main verb of the sentence, I drop the word "which."

Chapter 8

[Purity of Heart, Mind, and Action]

Q: What is purity of heart? Why and how should we
       acquire it?[1]

A: The heart is free from every attachment: not only
from evil ones [93] but even from those that we call innocent, because in truth these never can be fully innocent,
since the heart, which is only made for God,[2] leaves room
for creatures. But how will a heart thus divided—and usually most unequally—succeed at these pauses needed to
enter fully into this prayer? Let us recall what we have
written. This prayer is a sweet rest of the mind and heart in
God, as we have said.[3] But how can a heart that is accustomed to letting its thoughts and affections rest on the
objects to which it is attached really rest in God unless it

---

[1] Lallemant calls his third principle purity of heart (*Doctrine
spirituelle*, 136–67); Caussade seems to tend towards Ignatian indifference, one objective of which is to prepare the way for contemplation.

[2] Recall St. Augustine's "Because you have made us for yourself, and our heart is restless until it rests in you" (*Confessions*, I, i [1]
[p. 3 in Chadwick ed.]). Surin writes: "Le coeur recueilli est celui qui
s'arrête dans l'intérieur avec Dieu et ne se laisse pas emporter et dissi-
per au dehors par l'attache aux objets de cette vie" (The recollected
heart rests within itself with God and does not let itself be carried out
and dissipated outside by attaching itself to the objects of this life)
(*Dialogues spirituels*, 1:65).

[3] See chap. 2, response 1, no. 1.

has killed its initial attachments, in order to[4] carry itself to God and rest there as it did formerly on its deeply cherished attachment? Purity of heart is taste for God.[5] But how can a heart that dotes on sensible goods and the pleasures of the senses, such as honor, esteem, reputation, idleness, and commerce with the worldly, taste God unless it purifies itself of its terrestrial, carnal, human predilections? Purity of heart is a gaze fixed on God.[6] But how can this gaze of pure faith be sustained through the thick clouds of ideas and sensible images, when even one attachment fills the mind and the imagination?

Purity of heart is recollection in God.[7] But how can we gather our powers, thoughts, desires, and emotions into God if it only takes one foreign object to hold them as if tied and chained or to call them back to itself by the same [94] charms by which it knew how to capture our heart in the first place? Finally, purity of heart is an interior silence of respect, admiration, and love.[8] But how can we enter or remain in this deep interior silence in the middle of the noises and clamors of thousands of pressing desires, so many anxious hopes and afflicting fears, with a heart that sighs without end, almost in spite of itself, for any object but God?

Q: Isn't this prayer restricted to the perfect, because attentive pauses require such purity and detachment? And doesn't it follow that these pauses are useless for the prayer of those who are not perfect?

A: Doesn't this detachment which creates a pure heart[9]

---

[4] The manuscript has "par" (by); but as this doesn't make sense, I follow Olphe-Galliard's reading of "pour" (in order to).

[5] See chap. 2, response 1, no. 5.

[6] See chap. 2, response 1, no. 2.

[7] See chap. 2, response 1, no. 3.

[8] See chap. 2, response 1, no. 4.

[9] "Detachment and purity go hand in hand, for purity is but detachment of the heart" (Evelyn Underhill, *Mysticism: A Study in the*

have different degrees, as does prayer of the heart?[10] Great facility for entering into this prayer and doing it well corresponds to great detachment of heart; to lesser detachment, lesser facility. Let's explain this principle. Those who, by dint of purifying their hearts of the least attachment, have come to love only God or all things for God enter into this prayer full of love like fish into water; or if you want, we can offer a comparison still more developed and based on the views of Saint Paul,[11] who holds that every [95] ardent

---

Nature and Development of Man's Spiritual Consciousness, 205).

[10] Jane de Chantal writes in *Vive Jésus réponses,* "Or il y a divers dégrez en cette manière d'oraison, comme en toutes les autres" (But there are different degrees in this way of praying as there are in all the others) ("Réponse sur l'article vingt quatrième, Des retraits" [Response to article 24, On retreats], 510); and she continues, "Celles qui sont conduites par cette voye, sont obligées à une grande pureté de coeur" (Those who are lead along this path need great purity of heart) (ibid., 511).

[11] "Quorum finis interitus; quorum deus venter est; et gloria in confusione ipsorum, qui terrena sapiunt" ("Whose end is destruction; whose god is their belly; and whose glory is in their shame; who mind earthly things" (Phil. 3:19); and "Fornicatio autem, et omnis immunditia, aut avaritia, nec nominetur in vobis, sicut decet sanctos: aut turpitudo, aut stultiloquium, aut scurrilitas, quæ ad rem non pertinet: sed magis gratiarum actio. Hoc enim scitote intelligentes: quod omnis fornicator, aut immundus, aut avarus, quod est idolorum servitus, non habet hæreditatem in regno Christi et Dei" (But fornication, and all uncleanness, or covetousness, let it not so much as be named among you, as becometh saints: Or obscenity, or foolish talking, or scurrility, which is to no purpose; but rather giving of thanks. For know you this and understand, that no fornicator, or unclean, or covetous person [which is a serving of idols], hath inheritance in the kingdom of Christ and of God") (Eph. 5:3–5); and "Tenebris obscuratum habentes intellectum, alienati a vita Dei per ignorantiam, quæ est in illis, propter cæcitatem cordis ipsorum, qui desperantes, semetipsos tradiderunt impudicitiæ, in operationem immunditiæ omnis in avaritiam" ("Having their understanding darkened; being alienated from the life of God through the ignorance that is in them, because of the blindness of their hearts; who despairing, have given themselves up to lasciviousness, unto the working of all

love for a creature is idolatry of the heart.

Look at a worldly lover who is interiorly preoccupied with the beauty that he idolizes. Won't he find in this interior pursuit sweet rest for his heart, enjoyment as delightful as it is sinful? This unfortunate recollection, which lets him only think of his idol, seems to absorb all the faculties of his soul and reveals quite a continuity in the inner gaze fixedly attached to his idol. Doesn't he fall into a deep interior silence that suspends any other sentiment in order to give place only to an outburst of love? During the course of prayer, this is more or less the holy and blessed state of those who are truly detached and fully occupied with their divine object.[12] Such is a rough image of these most holy and most meritorious dispositions in which any can have shares proportional to their degree of purity and love.

But here is something rather surprising, at least to me. When it is merely a question of a heart possessed by profane love, we easily understand all its evil dispositions and even the vocabulary especially designed to express them. But what happens when there is question of a heart given over to the impressions of divine love? [96] Then all the holy dispositions become incomprehensible; all these expressions become too mystical even for some pious persons. Consequently, do they really believe that this love, which is stronger than death and hell, has lost all of its strength and past rule over hearts; or that there are no longer those who can feel these movements; or that these movements, even though they are less sensible and less palpable than those of worldly love, are less real and less true?[13]

---

uncleanness, unto covetousness") (Eph. 4:18f.).

[12] See St. Francis de Sales, *Traité de l'amour de Dieu*, bk. 6, chap. 8 (Pléiade ed., 632–35; *Oeuvres*, vol. 6 [vol. 1 of *Traité*]: 330–333) for the idea of resting quietly with one's beloved.

[13] Caussade is thinking quite likely about the Jansenists, especially the writings of Nicole; he may also be expressing his feelings about the way he was viewed by some. See his *Lettres spirituelles,*

Let them listen to the great bishop of Meaux [Bossuet]. During these purely spiritual processes, so he says, our soul seems to lose consciousness, to forget itself, yet it never functions better.[14] Let them listen to the masters of the art: one will tell them that in these kinds of processes the most tangible grace is, so to speak, only the residue;[15]

1:49f.

[14] Caussade attributes the following words to Bossuet: "During these purely spiritual operations, although our soul seems to vanish and escape from itself, it exercises more than ever its true and natural operations" (*Instructions spirituelles,* 185 in Thorold ed.). But Bossuet actually wrote: "Mais c'est proprement dans la contemplation que recueillie en elle-même elle [l'âme] commence à se demêler comme expérimentalement d'avec le corps, dont elle se sent apesantie, et à séparer ses occupations intellectuelles, qui sont ses véritables actions, d'avec celles des sens et de la partie imaginative. . . . L'âme donc dans cette ignorance, naturellement dominée par l'habitude de sentir et de croire en quelque façon que rien n'est réel que ce qui se sent, ce qui se touche, ce qui se manie, en se réduisant peu à peu à la pure intellection, s'échape à elle-même, et ne croit plus opérer pendant qu'elle commence à exercer ses plus véritables et plus naturelles opérations" (But it is properly in contemplation that once recollected into itself, the soul begins to extricate itself as if experimentally from the body by which it feels weighed down and to separate its intellectual operations, which are its veritable actions, from those of the senses and of the imaginative part. . . . Therefore in this state of ignorance, the soul naturally dominated by the habit of feeling and believing in some way that nothing is real except what is felt, touched, or handled, in confining itself bit by bit to pure intellection, escapes from itself and no longer believes that it is working while it is beginning to practice its most true and most natural operations) (Bossuet, *Instruction* V, xix [pp 150f.]).

[15] In bk. 2, dialogue 2 of *Instructions spirituelles* (p. 185 in Thorold translation), Caussade attributes to Louis Lallemant the metaphor: "[The] most perceptible . . . is merely, so to speak, the secondary distillation" ("le marc," which I translate as "the residue of grace"). Rigoleu uses the same metaphor: "Ce que l'on ressent de la grâce n'en est que le marc et la lie" (What we feel of grace is only the residue and dregs) *(La vie du père Rigoleu,* letter 6 [p. 383], in *Lettres spirituelles).*

another will teach them that the more these processes are deep-seated, delicate, and almost imperceptible, the more they are perfect, since they are the more spiritual and the more detached from the senses.[16]

Q: If the degree of facility to enter into this prayer and to do it well is in general proportional to the degree of purity of the heart, what hope is there for those who have hardly any facility? [97]

A: At the very minimum they must have the least, the lowest degree, which is the sincere desire to acquire it, to work on it, and to use varied means, even[17] this prayer in particular, which is one of the most efficacious means. God would delight in this goodwill of those who at present don't know how to do better. Then if, in reward for this goodwill, God lets himself be felt and tasted from time to time in a soul, even if only for a few instances during this holy recollection, ah, how this soul will soon make great progress in this detachment. Why?[18] Our hearts are so made for God that, when once we savor him, everything else seems insipid. This impression of the taste of

---

[16] Jane de Chantal wrote, "Cette manière est très-bonne, disoit notre bienhereux Père [François de Sales], parce qu'elle est plus épurée des objets sensibles" (This way is very good, said our blessed Father [Francis de Sales], because it is the most purged of sensible objects) ("Réponse sur l'article vingt quatrième, Des retraits," in *Vive Jésus réponses* [1665 ed.], 508) (Response to article 24, On retreats). And de Maupas du Tour writes about Jane de Chantal, "Et cet amour separant en apparence, faisoit une secrette union d'autant plus parfaite et amoureuse, qu'elle estoit separée des sens" (And this love, which seems to separate, achieves a secret union all the more perfect and loving as it is separated from the senses) ("De son amour patissant et operant pour l'oraison [On her burning and working love for prayer] (*Vie,* pt. 3, chap. 4 [p. 403]).

[17] Olphe-Galliard reads "elle-même" (itself) instead of "même" (even).

[18] The Olphe-Galliard edition drops the following words from the manuscript: "In this detachment. Why?"

God in a heart is a secret charm that makes it turn incessantly towards God, almost as the needle of a compass turns without ceasing to the rising sun.[19]

God, says St. Augustine, brings about in the order of grace this second wonder by pouring into the soul this celestial delight, which surpasses every earthly consolation and gives us the strength to triumph![20] Now the onset of purity and unattachment in a heart produces in its turn [98] a new taste, a new attraction, and a new facility for recollection. Such rapidity in the progress of both occurs— that is to say, in the progress of purity of heart facilitating recollection and in that of recollection increasing unattachment—that directors themselves are surprised at it, especially in the case of people hitherto so weak that they didn't

---

[19] The metaphor of the sun, which dates back to Plato's *Republic* (507d–509d), is applied to God by St. Augustine in the *Soliloquies,* bk. 1 (see Fulbert Cayré, *Initiation à la philosophie de saint Augustin,* 107–10); the simile of the magnet is found in Francis de Sales, *Traité de l'amour de Dieu,* bk. 6, chap. 7, para. 2 (Pléiade ed., 629). Pierre de Bérulle calls Jesus a new light in the world ("Grandeur de Jésus"; Disc. 11, "Seconde naissance de Jésus") [The greatness of Jesus; Disc. 11, The second birth of Jesus], in *Oeuvres complètes,* 4:359–61).

[20] In dialogue 2, response 8, in bk. 2 of *Instructions spirituelles* (p. 186 in the Thorold translation), Caussade writes similarly about the taste of God in the heart and quotes the following words, translated below, from St. Augustine: "Dando menti cælestem delectationem qua omnis terrena delectatio superetur" ("Sermo XLII: De capitulo evangelii ubi dicit, Remittite et remittetur vobis, date et dabitur vobis" [On the gospel chapter where it is said: Forgive and you shall be forgiven. Give and it shall be given to you] [Luke 6: 37f.], p. 506, lns. 76–78, in *Corpus Christianorum,* vol. 41). Augustine writes: "He shall free you from yourself. How does he free you from yourself? By forgiving sins, by giving merit, by giving you the strength to fight against your concupiscence, by inspiring virtue, by giving [dando] your mind the celestial delight by which every terrestrial delight is surpassed [superetur]" (lns. 74–78). For a discussion of delectation in St. Augustine, see Fulbert Cayré, *Les Sources de l'amour divin,* 211–18. See also *Imitation of Christ,* bk. 3, chap. 34.

have the courage to overcome anything or the fortitude to detach themselves from the least trifle.

Q: What is purity of mind? Why and how should we acquire it?[21]

A: 1. It consists in conquering a certain aimlessness of the mind that naturally drifts about considering anything that pleases it, even when nothing wrong is involved; and at the very least it consists in having acquired enough sway over the mind in order to stop and temper its natural activity to run unceasingly after all the vain images of sensible objects, just as children run after butterflies.

2. Why is purity of mind absolutely necessary? If the mind in this way accustoms itself to dissipating itself vainly by continual running about, how will it enter into itself, especially during times of interior prayer, which, more than any other kind, requires a tranquil mind, [99] since it is the prayer of recollection itself?

3. How can a mind that is always flitting and wandering about all those agreeable or entertaining objects turn its inner gaze to fix it either on God or on the incomprehensible objects of faith? Furthermore, even when it can do so for several instants, won't the many different ideas and flattering images, which come continually and in swarms to display themselves in its imagination, be with regard to the mind like a cloud of dust lifted up by a whirlwind around a traveler, who will no longer know where he is going or where he is or even see himself? Therefore, it is necessary to resist continually the natural aimlessness of the mind and

---

[21] The manuscript has at the start of this question the number 3. At the end of chap. 6, Caussade said that in the next chapter he would deal with purity of conscience, heart, mind, and action. But in the manuscript purity of conscience is the topic of chapter 7, and purity of heart, mind, and action that of chap. 8. However, purity of mind is the third topic and the topic raised by the current question is the third kind of purity.

to curb continually its natural activity by never permitting it to look willingly at itself and to stray with vain or[22] useless thoughts and, even worse, to hold onto them, to feed on them, and to live on them. Therefore, it is necessary to look at all these merely useless or frivolous thoughts in the same way as good people look at truly evil ones in order to behave likewise as soon as we are aware of them.[23] [100]

Q: So, it seems to me, isn't this purity as explained the most difficult of all?

A: It certainly is, but grace makes easy what appears impossible to man. Once we have tasted God and God's peace within us, this enticing taste calls us without cease with a gentleness that easily leads us to forget everything else; and this same enticement gives us an aversion to creatures: we think no more of them except reluctantly. Then, what freedom of mind we have in being attentive only to God and celestial matters.[24] But to arrive at this bit by bit, here is what it behooves you to do:

1. By recourse to recollection itself, we must work at weakening and destroying our unfortunate predilections. Just as for all most compelling thoughts, the most difficult

----

[22] Olphe-Galliard reads "and" instead of "or."

[23] See Surin, "Du coeur recueilly" (On the recollected heart) (vol. 1, bk. 2, chap. 1 [pp. 65–72]); "Du vice interieur de la multiplicité" (On the interior vice of multiplicity) (vol. 2, bk. 5, chap. 7 [pp. 238–42]); and "De l'emportement de l'âme hors d'elle-même" (On the displacement of the soul outside of itself) (vol. 2, bk. 5, chap. 8 [pp. 46–250]); all of the above citations are from *Dialogues spirituels*.

[24] This passage calls to mind Ps. 4:2, which reads in the Douay-Rheims version, "When I called upon him, the God of my justice heard me: when I was in distress, thou hast enlarged me. Have mercy on me: and hear my prayer"; about these lines St. Augustine writes, "[God] in this way shows what it is to cheer a heart; i.e., to have already in the heart an infusion of God with whom it converses interiorly" (*Enarratio Ps. 4,* p. 14, lns. 17–19); see also his *Confessions,* especially bk. 13, chap. 26, para 40, and the *Dictionnaire de Spiritualité,* s.v. "la contemplation augustinienne," vol. 2, pt. 2, cols. 1912–21.

to divert come solely from our predilections; but in proportion to their weakening, we feel less hesitancy in withdrawing the mind and thought from what we have already started to leave in heart and affection.

2. Since it is principally by the pleasure of the heart and vain delights that the mind fixes its interior attention on the objects from which these agreeable feelings come to it, as soon as we feel natural pleasure, we must no longer pause to taste these feelings, to savor them, [as we would do] if they were [101] heinous pleasure; and at the occasion of the least joy from either good news or happy success or an advantageous event, we must right away withdraw from it,[25] wean the heart from it, and sidetrack it by giving the heart its true object, which is God, in order to accustom ourselves to take pleasure, to rejoice only in God. For the same reason we must do the same thing with regard to other strong feelings arising in the soul, such as hope, fear, sadness, affliction, and the like, for fear that our spirit will absorb all these thoughts.[26]

3. As for other less stimulating thoughts, which are really only useless or frivolous, we must either drop them like a stone into water[27] or without hesitation[28] let them rush by like garbage floating in the middle of a torrent that sweeps it away; but if inadvertently we let ourselves be led astray, right away we must gently and without effort call back our mind from its least detour, either by simply remembering God, by elevating the heart to God, or by

---

[25] Olphe-Galliard reads "se" (ourselves) instead of "en" (from it).

[26] See Surin, "Du coeur recueilly" (On the recollected heart), vol. 1, bk. 2, chap. 1 (pp. 65–72), in *Dialogues spirituels*.

[27] Fénelon writes, "Il faut laisser tomber toutes ces choses comme une pierre au fond de l'eau" (Let all these things fall like a stone into the bottom of water) ("Sur le renoncement à soi-même" [On self-denial], *Lettres et opuscules spirituels, no. 13,* in *Oeuvres spirituelles,* vol. 1 [in Pléiade ed., p. 620.])

[28] Olphe-Galliard, misplacing the "or," reads "without hesitation or."

recalling pious thoughts prepared in advance and well cal-
culated to turn our minds back [to God] when necessary.

Q: Doesn't the innocent freedom of pondering its own
          thoughts, cherishing its ideas, nourishing itself with
its own reflections give the mind its most treasured delights? Consequently, isn't abandoning all of these the se-
verest subjugation of the mind, and perhaps [102] the most
crucifying interior abnegation and interior death?

A: Exactly for this reason we must be on watch all the
          more against the surprises of self-love, which so jeal-
ously gives free rein to its thoughts, which constitute the
food and life of the mind, whose activity cannot be con-
fined within the proper limits of the purely necessary.
Hence, we find so many paths leading to detrimental, excessive preoccupations, such as

   1. Under the pretext that we must think about what we
ought to do and say, how futilely and unnecessarily we
ruminate and reflect, even though the time we waste in
deliberation and introspection over the least things would
often have been long enough to accomplish them?

   2. Under the pretext of scrutiny and introspection after
some speeches, conversations, or the affairs that we have
already dealt with, no matter what were the circumstances,
time, or place, we will not fail to examine, exactly recall,
words spoken or frivolously blurted out, and thus immediately open the gates to a crowd of very futile reflections.
Usually these only serve to incite vain joys, melancholies,
fears, or even vainer hopes; but in turn all these only increase without end the dispersion of the mind and over-
throw interior peace by carrying anxiety and trouble right
into the depths of the soul.[29] [103]

   3. Under the pretext of thinking of however many
necessary things, or of what we think are necessary but for

------

[29] See Surin, "Du coeur libre" (On freedom of the heart), in
Dialogues spirituels, vol. 1, bk. 2, chap. 3 (pp. 57–61).

which we aren't able to know whether they will happen all at once, or even, perhaps, whether one alone will happen—how, during the time when we are reflecting, we let rise up in the soul a state of confusion, a chaos of thoughts and reflections[30] that agitate, worry, upset the whole interior and so overwhelm the mind that it no longer knows how to call itself back to God or to itself or to that with which it should begin.[31]

4. Under the pretext of spiritual progress, how often and vainly do we reflect and plan worthless projects upon which self-love ruminates[32] all the more uselessly, because this wastes the present time and is fruitless for the future, a future that will not turn out as we expect, for we shall find ourselves[33] in other circumstances.[34]

5. Finally, under the pretext of foreseeing what can happen, in order not to tempt Providence, as it is said, how long do we spend in turning over thought upon thought, reflection upon reflection, and plan upon plan? We wear ourselves out with anxious forethoughts, with distressing solicitudes, with fully futile precautions, since when the time comes, things have changed or we ourselves have changed our minds and feelings. We take up new measures often contrary to those very ones that we previously had

---

[30] The following were omitted by Olphe-Galliard: "during the time . . . we let rise up in the soul a state of confusion, a chaos of thoughts and of reflections."

[31] See Caussade, *Sacrament of the Present Moment,* 15–19, 62–83).

[32] Olphe-Galliard reads "s'assurer" (establishes itself), whereas the manuscript has "s'aviser" (ruminates).

[33] Olphe-Galliard has "even often" instead of "ourselves."

[34] See Francis de Sales, "Quatrième entretien: De la désappropriation" (Fourth conference: On renunciation) (Pléiade ed., pp. 1031–38); called "Huitiesme entretien: De la désappropriation et despouillement de toutes choses" (Eighth conference: On renunciation and relinquishment of every thing) (*Oeuvres,* 6:120–30). See also "De l'inquiétude" (On anxiety) (*Introduction à la vie dévote,* in *Oeuvres,* vol. 3, pt. 4, chap. 11 [pp. 310–13; in Pléiade ed., pp. 271–74]).

and so needlessly [104] imagined and so vainly determined.

But the great remedy for all these harmful and endless miseries of the human mind would be to tell yourself according to the occasions: Such and such a thing has happened; what good is it for me to continue busying myself with it? For what is left over to undertake, do, or say, God will provide. "To each day suffices its tribulation";[35] don't tomorrow and the following days bring with them their own graces? Let us think only of profiting from the present moment as God gives it to us, and leave the past to his mercy, the future to his providence. Cast upon his paternal bosom all our worries and all our solicitudes, because he takes care of us, says St. Peter.[36] Do what Jesus Christ recommended to St. Teresa,[37] to St. Catherine of Siena, and to many others, when he said, "My daughter think of me and I will think of you."[38] Let us practice what still today so many good souls do who, in similar encounters, with a simple renewing of abandonment and confidence in God, know in an instant where[39] to remedy everything: "Lord, I

[35] "Nolite ergo solliciti esse in crastinum. Crastinus enim dies sollicitus erit sibi ipsi: sufficit diei malitia sua" ("Be not therefore solicitous for tomorrow; for the morrow will be solicitous for itself. Sufficient for the day is the evil thereof") (Matt. 6:34). Closer to the Latin, the manuscript reads "son mal" (its tribulation), whereas Olphe-Galliard gives "sa peine" (its suffering).

[36] "Omnem sollicitudinem vestram proiicientes in eum, quoniam ipsi cura est de vobis" (Casting all your care upon him, for he hath care of you) (1 Pet. 5:7).

[37] *Interior Castle,* VII, 2, para. 1.

[38] "Ma fille, pense en moy, & je ferai le semblable de toy" (My daughter, think of me and I will do the same for you), in Raimondo da Capua (in French: Raymond de Capoue), *Vie de sainte Catherine* (1615 ed.), chap. 18, p. 97. Francis de Sales (*Traité,* bk. 9, chap. 15 [Pléiade ed., p. 802]) writes, "Pense en moi, lui [le Christ] dit-il [Catherine of Siena], et je penserai pour toi" (Think like me, Christ said to Catherine of Siena and I will think for you). Caussade seems to be citing from memory.

[39] Olphe-Galliard has "how" instead of "where."

hope that at the time and place you will give me the grace, thought, impulse, and facility to undertake or execute such or such things which so[40] inopportunely come to present themselves to my mind. I abandon them all to you with their outcomes, with the intention of only paying attention to you and of waiting for all to happen at the pace of your wise and sweet providence."[41] It is in virtue of [105] this double sacrifice and of this continual preparation of mind and heart that this loving providence, always attentive to their needs and to their style of acting, disposes in the favor [of these good souls] and arranges right down to the least details apparently accidental opportunities and the most favorable encounters. Moreover, by frequent experiences of these happy arrangements, their confidence and abandonment continually increase. Happy, therefore, are those who, to be more recollected in God and more fit for this prayer, know how to constantly banish every useless pursuit from their minds, in order to retain only what is absolutely necessary both with regard to the present time, which is so fleeting—and that is little enough at this point—but especially with regard to the future, which has yet to unfold and may perhaps never unfold for us.

---

[40] Olphe-Galliard has "often" instead of "so."

[41] The prayer starting with "Lord" ends here. It clearly embodies Caussade's theme of abandonment and reflects the theme developed by Fénelon in "Sur le détachement de soi-même" (On indifference to self), in *Lettres et opuscules spirituels,* no. 14, *Oeuvres spirituelles,* vol. 1 (Pléiade ed., pp. 623–28). A slightly modified version reads: "O Lord, while I do not wish to neglect anything of what thou ordainest for me, for the good of my soul or my body, I hope that in due time and place thou wilt grant me the thought, the movement and the facility to undertake and carry out such and such things which come so often and at such inappropriate times to present themselves to my spirit; I give them all up to thee with their various outcomes, with the intention of occupying myself more freely with thee, of waiting patiently and with complete resignation for everything to happen at the will of thy wise Providence (*Instructions spirituelles,* bk. 2, dialogue 3 [pp. 192f. in the Thorold translation]).

Q: What is purity of action? Why and how should we
         acquire it?[42]

A: 1. It consists, not in the substance of our actions,
         but in the purity of the motives that propel us to act.
This purity boils down to acting precisely only for the love
of God or according to God's plan and perspectives.

   2. If we lack this, our conduct will never be anything
but purely natural, generally infected by the corruption of
nature, and consequently completely filled with sins or
coarse imperfections. Now[43] [106] the readiness to practice
a prayer that unites us to God more intimately than any
other necessarily supposes in the soul a degree of purity in
every facet proportional to its degree of union with the
God of total purity.

   3. This purity of action is primarily acquired by three
means:

   a. Purity of conscience in heart and mind leads to it.
Why? Insofar as we make it a point to avoid all that might
displease God, attach ourselves only to God, and occupy
ourselves only with God, don't we inevitably find ourselves
fully disposed to act only for God or according to God's
perspectives?

---

[42] The manuscript has at the start of this question the numeral
4. At the end of chap. 6, Caussade said that in the next chapter he
would deal with purity of conscience, heart, mind, and action. But in
the manuscript purity of conscience is the topic of chap. 7 and purity
of heart, mind, and action that of chap. 8. However, purity of action
is the fourth topic and the topic raised by the current question is the
fourth kind of purity.

[43] The manuscript reads, "or sans cela" (now lacking this), but
Olphe-Galliard has "or sont-ce là" (now these are those). Neither
reading seems correct: the manuscript's version contradicts the
thought being developed, while Olphe-Galliard has two main verbs
one after the other. In the interpretation that I adopt, the "lacking
this" comes from repeating the "lacking this" that appears right after
the numeral 2, so I drop it.

b.[44] Purity of action is acquired by continual vigilance in the beginning of our actions and especially as they unfold. I say in the beginning, because if these actions are so agreeable and in conformity with the inclinations of nature, right away they are carried forward by their own motion through the sole attraction of pleasure or interest. But to prevent the will from being immediately drawn by the force of natural motions that flatter and captivate it, how much mastery and how much vigilance should we not have over ourselves?

c.[45] I said, especially in the unfolding of our actions. Although at first we may have had the strength to renounce every flattering enticement [107] of the senses or of self-love in order to follow in everything only the views of the faith with pure intention, if then we forget to keep careful watch over ourselves, the real satisfaction either with the good that we are experiencing or with the advantages that we discover as we enjoy what we are doing inevitably exerts greater and greater pull. Thus the heart weakens bit by bit, and our natural inclinations, although mortified by early sacrifices, wake up and regain their ascendancy.

But soon self-love, cunningly and almost[46] unnoticed by us, slides in its self-seeking views and substitutes them for the good motives with which our actions were taken up and begun. Wherefore there occurs—who knows on how many occasions?—what St. Paul said, that after having started with the mind, we finish with the body;[47] that is to say, with base, worldly, ambitious, sensual, or self-serving views that cause us to lose or to corrupt all the purity and merit

---

[44] Olphe-Galliard omits the letter *b*.

[45] Olphe-Galliard omits the letter *c*.

[46] Olphe-Galliard gives "prepare" instead of "prèsque" (almost), which appears in the manuscript.

[47] "Sic stulti estis, ut cum spiritu cœperitis, nunc carne consummemini?" ("Are you so foolish that, whereas you began in the spirit, you would now be made perfect by the flesh?") (Gal. 3:3).

of an infinite number of undertakings and actions of piety, charity, zeal, justice, and love for order and the public good, reaching right into the most holy ministries and sacred functions.[48] [108]

Q: How do we acquire the perfection of this purity?

A: We acquire it by trying on every occasion to act not only according to the divine ordering of things but even more so with with the sole intention of pleasing God. The excellence of this pure motive, which is stripped of every advantage, even the spiritual, enhances our least actions so much before God that even only one such pleases him more and is of greater merit than a hundred others, even the greatest, although praiseworthy and holy but done with inferior motivation.

That is why someone who accomplishes little in a state of life that affords little opportunity for accomplishments, at least such as appear great in the eyes of the world, or one who must labor under restrictive circumstances can nonetheless become more holy and lay up greater stores for eternity than can others who, in far superior states of life, in quite different circumstances and professions, might accomplish many things, even important things, but would not act out of love, or out of pure love. This is the case because it is the degree of our love and its purity that confer value on everything. The truth of this

---

[48] Caussade summarizes what Rigoleu writes: "La garde du coeur . . . n'est autre chose que l'attention qu'on apporte aux mouvements de son coeur et à tout ce que se passe dans l'homme intérieur, pour régler sa conduite par l'esprit de Dieu et l'ajuster à son devoir et aux obligations de son état" (Watching over the heart . . . is nothing other than the attention we bring to the movements of our heart and to all that goes on in the interior man, in order to regulate our conduct by the spirit of God and to adapt our conduct to our duty and to the obligations of our state) ("Traitez de spiritualité," treatise 3, sec. 1, in *La vie,* 216).

statement can humiliate some while consoling and encouraging others.[49]

Q: What kind of impurity of action should be most [109] feared, especially for spiritually minded people?

A: Vanity, whether outward or inward. In most of our actions, outward vanity directs its attention and biases to what will be said[50] and thought by such or such a person whose esteem and approval are most cherished and most precious, because we make into an idol a certain reputation that, if we don't renounce it once for all, will become, as St. Teresa says,[51] like a worm that attacks the roots of a plant, imperceptibly gnaws at them, destroys them, and causes the plant's fruit and leaves to fall. On the contrary, once we know how to trample underfoot all[52] that others consider esteem, praise, and approval and be satisfied with pleasing only God, then we will find ourselves in one of the most valuable stages of the spiritual life, one that places us in a state ready to delight in God not only during prayer but also in every occasion and in every place.

Inward vanity appears to me even more ominous, not just because it also is evil, but because it is much more covert. First of all, it consists in puffed-up self-esteem, which causes us to prefer ourselves to others, to measure ourselves, and incessantly to compare ourselves with them. It gives birth to contempt and scorn, then envy and jealousy. Second, it is a swollen self-confidence that [110]

---

[49] Here we find Fénelon's doctrine of disinterested love; see Fénelon's "Sur le pur amour" (On pure love), *Lettres et opuscules spirituels,* no. 23, in *Oeuvres spirituelles,* vol. 1 (in Pléiade ed., 656–71); also see d'Istria, "La notion de l'amour pure chez Bossuet et Fénelon" (The notion of pure love in Bossuet and in Fénelon), chap. 1, in *Le Père de Caussade,* 21–70.

[50] Olphe-Galliard adds "et ce qu'en feront" (and what will be done), which does not appear in the manuscript.

[51] *Life,* 31: paras, 12–21, esp. 21.

[52] Olphe-Galliard omits "all."

unnoticeably leads us to rely much more on our own enlightenment, resolutions, and forces than on the grace of
God. We count much more on a foundation of virtue or[53]
acquired merit than on the pure mercy of God, although
often we assert the contrary and are truly persuaded of it.
Third, it is an almost continuous rekindling of secret[54] self-
satisfaction through which, without reflection, we attribute
to ourselves all the good we accomplish and all we do for
God, for salvation, and for perfection. But,[55] as all our
masters say, is there anything more against the spirit of
God and of this holy prayer than these smoke screens of
vanity which give birth to such a profound hidden pride
that we begin to recognize it only insofar as we begin to be
cured of it?

Q: Why haven't you said anything about exterior morti-
        fication, which by common assent so greatly helps
prayer?

A: Because no one overlooks its usefulness. All spiritual
        books recommend it, all preachers preach it; but in a
brief work, we must stick to the essentials. But[56] I do know
that the author of the *Spiritual Combat*[57] and all our other
masters[58] teach that exterior mortification is only a means
for acquiring interior mortification, which truly constitutes
real holiness and real perfection. But how could the persis-

---

[53] Olphe-Galliard has "and" instead of "or."

[54] Olphe-Galliard has "certaine" instead of "secrete," which
appears in the manuscript.

[55] Olphe-Galliard has "and" instead of "but."

[56] Olphe-Galliard has "and" instead of "but."

[57] Lorenzo Scupoli, "Preliminary Words on Perfection," chap.
1, pp. 1–7.

[58] See for instance Guilloré, who writes, "Il ne faut pas avoir
tant d'application aux austeritez du corps, afin que l'esprit vacque à
l'intérieur avec plus de liberté" (We must not pursue corporeal auster-
ity so radically that the spirit wanders about in the interior with
greater freedom) ("Des illusions des austérités" [Illusions of austerity],
in *Oeuvres spirituelles,* chap. 6 [pp. 649–50]).

tent attempt to acquire these four kinds of purity not finally achieve complete interior abnegation? This abnegation will leave nothing to be sacrificed [111] in our conscience, heart, or mind, not even the least desire or most trifling thought; it operates by interior principles rendering the senses and all our nature powerless to be vainly[59] self-satisfied with anything at all.

Moreover, isn't it interior mortification that carries us outward, animates us, and purifies us of all the stains of so many instances of vain contentedness, hidden pride, and secret overconfidence? Without it, all we esteem so much in exterior mortification has slight value, because we can too often meet in the uncircumcised[60] heart all the liveliness of unrestrained desires and the violence of unmortified passions. This formerly[61] led St. Francis de Sales to say about a man as distinguished by his merits as by his profession, "I would never have thought that with such exterior mortification he would have so little in his interior."[62]

Even more so, doesn't interior mortification have two additional advantages? First, we can pursue it as far as we want without having to fear exceeding or over-stepping the limits of discretion. Second, because it strives without respite to extinguish all the passions in the heart, the enemy no longer finds a handhold for his temptations, not even for the least figment of one,[63] because they can only come

---

[59] Olphe-Galliard gives "vraiment" (truly) instead of "vainement" (vainly), which appears in the manuscript.

[60] "Uncircumcised" is missing in the Olphe-Galliard's edition.

[61] Olphe-Galliard omits "formerly."

[62] I have been unable to find out who this person is and where Francis de Sales writes the lines that Caussade quotes. But this paraphrases "Des exercices de la mortification extérieure" (On exercises of exterior mortification), pt. 3, chap. 23 of *Introduction à la vie dévote*, Pléiade ed., pp. 194–99, especially the last long paragraph on pp. 198f. [*Oeuvres*, 3:216–22]).

[63] The manuscript reads, "à aucune sorte d'illusion" (the least

from self-love residing in itself or in one of its offspring, unhappy fruit of [112] the accursed stock of Adam.[64]

Q: Why not at least speak of peace of soul, since most authors lay it down as the foundation of the prayer of simple rest in God and of all the interior life?

A: I admit that they are correct and that we will never build anything solid except on the unshakable foundation of this peace. First, without doubt the spirit of God lives and functions only in peace.[65] Second, a soul lacking this peace is like a body lacking health; just as disease, in weakening bodily forces, renders them[66] unable to take care of the needs of the body, so likewise all that troubles the

---

figment of), whereas Olphe-Galliard has "à une sorte d'illusion" (a kind of).

[64] The danger of self-love being a major block to spiritual progress constitutes an important theme of spiritual direction; for instance, see Jane de Chantal's warning against self-love, "Quatorzième traité: De la mortification, du mal de l'amour-propre and dommages causés par l'amour-propre" (Fourteenth treatise: On mortification, on the evil of self-love, and on the harm caused by self-love), in Denys Mézard, *Doctrine spirituelle de . . . Chantal,* chaps. 3–4 (pp. 323–26); or see what Fénelon writes at the beginning of "Sur le renoncement à soi-même" (On self-renunciation) (*Oeuvres spirituelles,* no. 13, in *Lettres et opuscules spirituels,* Pléiade ed. pp. 613–15); or see Rigoleu, who reminds us that "l'amour propre se glisse mesme dans les choses les plus saintes" (self-love slides into even the most holy things) ("Avis pour les âmes qui entrent dans les voyes extraordinaires de la grace" [Advice for souls who are entering into the extraordinary paths of grace], chap. 3, no. 9, of "Traité no. 10: Instructions pour les trois états de la vie spirituelle" [Instructions for the three states of the spiritual life], *La vie,* p. 342). The *Dictionnaire de spiritualité* treats of self-love in vol. 1, cols. 339ff.

[65] "Et factus est in pace locus eius, et habitatio eius in Sion" ("And his place is in peace: and his abode in Sion") (Ps. 75:3).

[66] Olphe-Galliard reads "la maladie . . . est dans l'impuissance" (the disease . . . is in the inability), whereas the manuscript has "la maladie . . . mest dans l'impuissance" (the disease . . . renders . . . unable). Reading "met" for "mest," I translate it "renders."

health of the soul renders it feeble, listless, totally sick, and almost unable to function spiritually. This explains why St. Francis de Sales so often repeated in his works that other than sin nothing is more pernicious for the soul than agitation, grief, worry, and gloom, which are the soul's true diseases.[67] Once more I acknowledge all of this, but by not speaking of it directly, perhaps I am accomplishing more by teaching the practice of the four kinds of purity.[68] These are the infallible means of coming to such a solid, profound, infallible, and well-established peace that henceforth the soul can no longer be troubled by the following:

- harassing remorse that comes only from impurity of conscience or[69] inattention to its promptings [113]

- the cruel tyranny of our attachments, which have no other source than the impurity of a heart that lets itself be captivated by the lures of material goods

- the violence of the passions, which initially arise in the impurity of a mind delivered up to the wandering of its thoughts

- the pressing desire of pleasing men or the vain fear of displeasing them; these come only from a lack of purity in the motives of our actions

Q: Might[70] you have some recommendations for those who, by means of their attentive pauses, have for a

---

[67] "De la tristesse" (On despondency), in *Introduction à la vie dévote,* pt. 4, chap. 12 (Pléiade ed., 274–76, or *Oeuvres,* 3:313–16); and "L'Inquiétude, mère de la mauvaise tristesse, est le plus grand mal qui puisse arriver à l'âme, excepté le peché" (Anxiety, mother of pernicious despondency, is the greatest evil that can happen to the soul except sin) (Opuscules X, Séries 6, in *Oeuvres,* 26:226).

[68] Purity of conscience, of heart, of mind, and of action.

[69] Olphe-Galliard has "and" instead of "or."

[70] The manuscript reads, "n'auriez vous" (might you), not "n'aviez vous" (have you), as Olphe-Galliard gives.

little while begun to really enter into the simplicity of this prayer, and for those who are well advanced, and even for those who by their fidelity have made great progress in it?

A: I have, so it seems to me, fairly important advice, but perhaps it will appear so only to those who are interested, or perhaps to each according to his path in life, as we shall see in the following chapter.

Chapter 9

SOME IMPORTANT RECOMMENDATIONS FOR THOSE WHO, THANKS TO ATTENTIVE PAUSES, HAVE BEGUN TO ENTER INTO THIS PRAYER

Q: What do you believe are the most important recommendations?

A: We should pay great attention to knowing how to profit from every favorable occasion for this prayer, just as [114] in the courts of kings we know very well how to take advantage of the least occasion or of a favorable audience with the prince. Even during the course of the day, sometimes after a holy thought or a fitting movement of the heart toward God, sometimes after some great sacrifice or even a little victory, at other times after Communion, during Mass, during pious reading, and in many other occasions, those of whom we are speaking happen all of a sudden to feel a certain recollection of the mind, a sudden delight in God, or some other stirring and sensible affections. Here arrives the Holy Spirit, here comes the favorable moment, no longer to speak[1] to God, but rather to listen to God himself in deep silence in the depths of the

_____

[1] Olphe-Galliard has just "not to speak" instead of "no longer to speak."

heart, fearing to disturb there his divine action merely by the exercise of our ordinary actions. Therefore, we must suspend them, as has been said, and be content with remaining there listening as long as we can with an inner attention whose motive and all the actions that flow from it God sees well.[2] Two main advantages follow from this:

1. God, who is moved by[3] good dispositions and especially by a soul abandoning itself to his good pleasure, brings about in it according to his wishes what he alone knows is the most suitable for him.

2. We thus establish bit by bit the happy [115] habit of knowing how to hold ourselves in rest and in attentive silence before God, which is much more difficult than we think.

Q: Where can this difficulty come from, for at the outset it seems that nothing is easier than this silent rest?

A: First of all, this difficulty comes from hidden presumption and vain confidence, both so profoundly rooted in every heart that unless in practice we take care, we become as if effectively persuaded that nothing can be achieved unless we are fully involved, and that unless we do it ourselves, all will be lost if we let all be done by God.[4] Listen to the way Jesus Christ explains this to St. Catherine of Sienna. Once she said to him: "But, my Lord and my God, let me ask you why is it that at the time of the Apostles you communicated yourself so abundantly and that now we see nothing like it?" "My daughter," replied Jesus

---

[2] This theme of attentiveness to God is a classical one going under various names such as "spiritual discernment" (St. Ignatius of Loyola), "spiritual ruminating" (St. Francis de Sales), "docility to the directions of the Holy Spirit" (Louis Lallemant), and "watch over the heart" (Jean Rigoleu); the *Dictionnaire de spiritualité*, in vol. 1, cols. 1063–66, develops "Attention: role dans la spriritualité; oraison" (Attentiveness: role in the spirituality; prayer).

[3] Olphe-Galliard adds "these."

[4] The words "unless we do it ourselves" found in the manuscript are not in Olphe-Galliard's version.

Christ, "in the past, men were extremely unpretentious and extremely wary of themselves, expecting all from me; but now they are so filled with themselves, so occupied with what they are doing, with what they are telling me and repeating endlessly as if I would forget, that they hardly give me the time to carry out what I want to do, because they want to say and do everything in their own way, as if my grace should accommodate itself to them rather than they to my grace."[5]

Furthermore, this difficulty arises because it [116] costs a good deal to renounce oneself and one's own ideas, reflections, functions, and customary undertakings in this way, in order to hold oneself to the simplicity of these direct acts of the heart, which are, we have said, a kind of death for the natural activity of the mind. Perhaps it is even the most mortifying and most humiliating abnegation of oneself.[6] As a matter of fact, this ought to be most difficult, since Mme de Chantal thought it necessary to be explicitly commanded in order to succeed at it: "My father," she wrote[7] to her holy director, "order me to hold myself in simple rest; I hope that my mind will respect your orders."[8]

---

[5] I don't know where Caussade got his quotation, but it isn't in her *Dialogue* or in the French edition of Raimondo da Capua, *La Vie miraculeuse de la seraphique et devote Ste. Catherine de Siene* (the copy of this work that is preserved at Les Fontaines at Chantilly came from Monastère de la Visitation Ste. Marie de Reims); nor is it in Conleth Kearns's English translation, *The Life of Catherine of Siena*. Caussade cites similar words of Catherine of Siena in letters 50 and 51, *Lettres spirituelles*, 1:178, 180–82.

[6] See chap. 8, response 6.

[7] Olphe-Galliard has "said" instead of "wrote."

[8] Jeanne de Chantal writes, "C'est pourquoi je demande encore à mon très cher Seigneur l'aide de la sainte obéissance pour arrêter ce coureur, car il m'est avis qu'il craindra le commandement absolu" (This is why again I asked my very dear lord [Francis de Sales] the help of holy obedience to stop this vagabond, for my impression is that it fears the peremptory command) (Maupas du Tour, *La vie de . . . Jeanne Françoise Frémyot*, pt. 2, chap. 7 [p. 195], and also in

Didn't St. Francis de Sales experience the same difficulty? For some fairly long time he felt great attraction to this simplicity of prayer; often he himself responded to it. "My mind," he said, "why do you always want to busy yourself like Martha rather than holding yourself in rest like Madeline?" Finally, one day during his prayers, piously stirred up against this activity of the mind, he cried out from a holy transport, because he found such difficulty in doing what it pleases certain spiritual persons to call pure idleness, "My God, you yourself stop this vagabond."⁹

Q: If these¹⁰ favorable moments for this attentive silence arrive during vocal prayer or spiritual reading, should we abandon them both?

A: [1.] According to St. Thomas,¹¹ vocal prayer is not

Jeanne de Chantal, *Vie et oeuvres,* 2:41).

⁹ Jean Nyon attributes to Francis de Sales the following words: "O Dieu! Arrêtez ce miserable coureur, ô qui me fera cette grace, sinon vous, ô mon Jésus, par les prières de votre très digne Mère" (O God! Stop this miserable vagabond, O who would give me this grace unless you, O my Jesus, by except prayers of your most worthy Mother) (*Les Reliques,* 115).

¹⁰ Olphe-Galliard has "the" instead of "these.

¹¹ Olphe-Galliard adds "if" here. In *Summa Contra Gentiles,* bk. 3, chap. 96, para. 4, Aquinas explains that contemplation, devout affection, and humble but firm intention draw us near to God and render our prayer capable of being heard by God. In *Summa Theologica,* IIa,–IIae, q. 83, art. 12, he writes: "Hence then alone [in private prayer] should we use words and suchlike signs when they help to excite the mind internally. But if they distract or in any way impede the mind, we should abstain from them; and this happens chiefly to those whose mind is sufficiently prepared for devotion without having recourse to those signs. Wherefore the Psalmist (Ps, 26:8) said: 'My heart has said to You: My face has sought You,' and we read of Anna (1 Kings 1:13) that she spoke in her heart." Hence prayer is primarily in the mind and secondarily in words. In q. 180, art. 3, *ad* 1, he writes: "Meditation would seem to be the process of reasoning from certain principles that lead to the contemplation of some truth. . . . But contemplation regards the simple act of gazing on the truth." In q. 182, art. 1, he writes: "The contemplative life is simply more

necessary. We should leave it behind to turn to [117] interior recollection whenever the occasion presents itself, because we would be leaving behind the most imperfect prayer for the most perfect. So, following the same principle, I would add, when vocal prayer is a duty, such as reciting the divine office, if we are reciting it in private and are sure to have time to finish it, we would be wise to stop reciting it to take advantage of such fortunate moments; and afterwards, taking it up at the same place, to continue with it, but this time with greater affection and greater devotion. However, the most perfect way would be to recite it in a spirit of recollection in the presence of God.

2. Similarly, interrupted reading could only be more profitable. Doubtlessly it is beneficial to listen to the writers who tell us about God, but isn't it even better to listen to God himself speaking in the depths of our hearts in the way that we have explained? Concerning this, we should never forget the beautiful maxim of a great servant of God that, except for the case of needed instruction, we must pay attention to the words that we read only insofar as it is necessary for the heart to taste them; and only by this peaceful tasting do we enter much better into the truths of the faith and its mysteries than by all the cogitations of the mind; in a word, the words we read are only the pulp, but the taste of God that we derive from them is like the sap by which our soul is fed and nourished.[12] [118] St. Francis de

---

excellent than the active. . . . Sixth, because the contemplative life consists in leisure and rest, according to Ps, 45:11, 'Be still and see that I am God,' " and in art. 2, "The contemplative life pertains directly and immediately to the love of God; for Augustine says (*De Civ. Dei*, xix, 19) that 'the love of' the Divine 'truth seeks a holy leisure,' namely, of the contemplative life." Augustine actually writes: "And therefore holy leisure is longed for by the love of truth" (*City of God* [New York: Random House; Modern Library, 1950], 698).

[12] In a letter to Bourcier de Monthureux, Caussade attributes the advice and the metaphor of sap and pulp to Fénelon (*Lettres spirituelles*, 2:56). Olphe-Galliard was unable to find this metaphor in Fénelon. However, a similar metaphor serving to describe the impor-

Sales also sets as much store in this simple spiritual tasting when he speaks of certain saints whose lives are more to be admired than to be imitated; and after having presented to himself this objection, "What fruit can we draw from these readings?" right away he answered, "A great taste for piety."[13]

Q: Are there other recommendations?

A: There is a second, but it is extensive; it pertains to the way in which we should conduct ourselves concerning the sensible tastings and consolations of holy recollection. Since beginners need, as St. Paul explains,[14] to be enticed by sweetness and nourished, like children, with the milk of spiritual consolations, God very often gives us those which are so delicious and abundant that we need much detachment, restraint, wisdom, and moderation.

   1. We should not go to prayer with self-seeking views, but only to carry out the will of God and to learn to con-

---

tance for the spiritual life of examining the acts of the heart is developed by Boussuet, who writes: "C'est une écorce, il est vray; mais à travers cette écorce la bonne seve se coule: c'est la nége sur le bled, qui en le couvrant engraisse la terre, et fournit au grain de la nourriture: on en vient peu à peu aux actes du coeur que nous avons expliqués autant que Dieu l'a permis à notre foiblesse" (It is the pulp, this is true; but the good sap flows through this pulp: it is the snow on the fields, which by covering them enriches the earth and nourishes the seeds: we come bit by bit to the acts of the heart that we have explained as well as God has conceded to us in our weakness" (*Instructions*, V, xxiii [p. 155]). Jean Rigoleu writes, "Ce que l'on ressent de la grâce n'en est que le marc et la lie. Quant à la grâce, on ne la ressent point parce qu'elle n'est pas sensible" (What we feel from grace are merely the residues and the dregs; as for grace, we cannot feel it at all because it is not tangible" (Letter 6 to Soeur Catherine de St. Bernard, *Vie*, 383).

[13] See *Introduction à la vie dévote*, pt. 2, chap. 17, para. 3 (Pléiade ed., 109; *Oeuvres*, 3:108), where he actually writes, "However they don't fail to give us a great general taste of the holy love of God."

[14] 1 Cor. 3:1f.; Heb. 5:11–14.

form always to it more and more, because perfection consists in this perspective.

2. We should not let ourselves become elated by succumbing without restraint, as would a starved and thirsty[15] individual presented with a meal and a pleasing drink. God asks for moderation in all. Here we ought not to halt too often at sensible tastings, which are not the means always directly leading to him who gives them to us only to draw us on. They have value only insofar as they are aids for the weak and a powerful help for detaching ourselves from creatures. In a word, we must in good times act somewhat like a reasonable person at a feast: he barely thinks [119] of food, of the maintenance of his life, of his health, of his strength, and scarcely keeps an eye out to indulge in them and to be engrossed with them.[16]

3. So we should carefully protect ourselves from the longing to do many acts, because when naturally talkative joy begins redoubling interior activity, we easily stifle the soft breath of the Holy Spirit. By clumsily wanting to pronounce inner words of thanksgiving and of love, we soon find ourselves falling out of recollection and feel its sweet peace troubled and its fervor extinguished. Why? As St. Teresa says,[17] we have acted indiscreetly, like a person with only a spark of fire, who instead of adding very little fuel and blowing on it softly, decides to throw on huge logs, which immediately snuff it out. One or two interior words spaced further and further apart suffice well, adds the saint, to sustain this faint divine fire that begins to burn in the interior.

---

15 Olphe-Galliard omits "thirsty."

16 St. John of the Cross discusses spiritual gluttony (*The Dark Night*, I, 6); Guilloré warns us to be on our guard against being deceived by sensible tastings ("Les illusions des douceurs intérieures, des soupirs, et des larmes" [the illusions of inner delights, of sighs, and of tears], in *Oeuvres spirituelles*, 792–97).

17 *Life*, xv, paras. 6 and 7.

4. The curiosity to examine at that time what is going on inside us must be put aside. We confusedly feel what is happening, just as when we are above a mine, we feel from slight tremors that there are workers who are toiling in the bowels of the earth, but we must not want to penetrate further. God reserves the secret to himself. We can well put our trust[18] in him; what results will tell us more.

5. So [we should] avoid as much as we can every kind of rumination about ourselves and our recollection, because this would be turning these[19] interior awarenesses away from God [120] and consequently distracting ourselves. Also, when speaking of this recollection, St. Francis de Sales was accustomed to say that the most certain way of keeping it was not to look at it,[20] and apropos of this cited the words of the bridegroom to the bride in the Song of Songs: "Your eyes . . . have made me flee away."[21]

6. Don't be eager to have or keep this sweet recollection.

a. As to having it, God usually does what a wise mother does for the education of a child whose whims she thwarts without respite to teach him to have no other than her wishes: she makes him come and go as she wishes, in a short time do and undo the same thing, drop what he has taken up and then take up again what he has just dropped. Likewise, to render a soul perfectly supple and docile to

---

[18] Olphe-Galliard reads "confidence" instead of "trust."

[19] The manuscript has "ses" which, as often happens in the manuscript, surely is phonetic spelling for "ces" (these), whereas Olphe-Galliard has "nos" (our).

[20] Francis de Sales writes, "et la juste règle de le bien affectioner, c'est de ne point l'affecter" (and the correct rule for cherishing it well is not to simulate it) (*Traité de l'amour de Dieu,* bk. 6, chap. 10 [Pléiade ed., p. 638], *Oeuvres,* 4:337); the Song of Songs is not quoted in de Sales but in St. John of the Cross, *Ascent of Mount Carmel,* II, chap. 29, 7 (p. 205).

[21] "[Sponsus:] Averte oculos tuos a me, quia ipsi me avolare fecerunt" (Turn away thy eyes from me, for they have made me flee away) (Song 6:4).

every one of his interior movements, God takes pleasure in thwarting its urges, most holy but ever so slightly mixed with self-love. Hundreds of times in a very short time he will make[22] it feel the approaches of this divine recollection, which vanishes right away: here he's coming, appearing and disappearing almost in the same instant; I'm here, I'm not here. Often such is our prayer, but I dare say it is one of the most fruitful, because God makes us practice here in very subtle ways the most blind submission to his will and [121] the most heroic renouncement of ours.

b.[23] Nor should we be avid to keep it, for this would be wanting to appropriate to ourselves God's gift and make ourselves its owners, just like naturally bad or badly brought-up children, from whose hands we have to snatch what once we had put there.[24]

c.[25] Furthermore, we shouldn't slide into grasping at safeguards, which St. Teresa characterizes as superstitions when she speaks of people so jealous of their gift of recollection that they do not dare to cough or to move, almost not to breathe, as if by these necessary actions, adds St. Francis de Sales, God would want to take away from us the favor which He has just given us.[26]

---

[22] Olphe-Galliard has the present tense instead of the future.

[23] Olphe-Galliard omits the number 2 [in this edition *b*—ED.].

[24] Caussade writes, "Ce qui s'appelle s'approprier les dons de Dieu" (It is called appropriating the gifts of God) (*Lettres,* 1:172). Fénelon writes: "Quand on pense aux grâces de Dieu, c'est toujours pour soi, et c'est l'amour du moi qui fait presque toujours une certaine sensiblité qu'on a pour les grâces" (When we think of God's graces, it is always for the self, and it is love of the ego which inevitably leads to a certain feeling for graces) (*Lettres et opuscules spirituels,* in *Oeuvres spirituelles,* Pléiade ed., 604).

[25] Olphe-Galliard misnumbers this as "8."

[26] *Traité de l'amour de Dieu,* bk. 6, chap. 10 (Pléiade ed., p. 638), in *Oeuvres,* 4:337; St. Teresa, *Way of Perfection,* vol. 2, chap. 31, no. 6 (pp. 155f.), and *Life,* vol. 1, chap. 15, no. 1 (p. 102).

d.[27] Furthermore, we must know to relinquish it and even deprive ourselves of it for some time, not only from obedience and duty but more so from charity and zeal, and even at the least intrusion often arranged by Providence with the intention of testing the docility of a soul that God wants to strip of all its proper initiatives in order to clothe it with his own.

Q: Won't these people have distractions and do you have any advice to give them about this?

A: It is true that they have them but [they are] very special kinds.

1. Distractions arise that don't turn them at all from their prayer, because these are only inconsistent thoughts that do no more than pass by, appear and disappear just like flashes of lightning. We should in no way trouble ourselves over them, since the sweet repose of the soul, which is stronger, prevails over its[28] frivolous distractions, just as the pleasure of hearing [122] a beautiful concert or a beautiful voice prevails over the few noises arising around me[29] that would not prevent me, if I want, from hearing or savoring the sweet harmony.

2. Sometimes distractions favor our recollection, in two ways:

a. Because the fear alone of losing what we already feel we possess redoubles the attention of the mind and heart.

b. Because God uses them to make us understand better whence comes this sweet recollection. Also, as it often happens to us, after we with effort acquire a recollection that we painfully try to preserve, our mind escapes by accident and stops outside in useless considerations; but, in the same instant that we become aware of this, there occurs

---

[27] Olphe-Galliard misnumbers this as "9."

[28] Olphe-Galliard has "the" instead of "its."

[29] Olphe-Galliard has "soi" (the self) instead of "moi" (me).

in the soul some interior motion or sudden retiring of the spirit within itself; we feel all of a sudden that we are returning into ourselves. Without knowing why or how, we find ourselves in a wholly other recollection—sweet, peaceful, profound, durable, even effortless. By these frequent experiences, God makes souls really feel that he is communicating in the depths of the heart, and that this kind of recollection is not at all the fruit of man's labor and activities, but the pure effect of the all-powerful goodness of him who gives, using naturally opposite ways.

c. At other times there are distractions, which to a considerable extent, divide the faculties [123] of the soul. In order the better to recognize their features and differences, it is now very important to untangle them. These distractions are filled with foolish things and are very often found only in the imagination; but meanwhile, the mind finds itself occupied with a general notion of God, and the heart, with a feeling of love corresponding to this confused notion.[30] On the one hand, this is a very painful situation, which St. Teresa in the beginning suffered for a long time without being able to find, so she says, other remedies besides patience. Concerning these, in accord with her character, she very agreeably adds the Spanish proverb, "Let the millclapper make as much noise as it wishes, provided that the mill makes flour."[31] Her disorderly imagination was

---

[30] Thus for Caussade there are three faculties of the soul: imagination, mind, and heart. In a few lines he makes the will synonymous with the heart. But in a similar passage of the *Instructions spirituelles* (p. 299; pp. 227f. in the English edition), he drops the word "will." Sensible distractions are primarily found in the imagination. For St. Teresa, the names are intellect, memory, and will (*Way of Perfection,* vol. 2, chap. 31, no. 3 [p. 154]); only the will is stilled and captured by God; the intellect, the imagination, and the mind seem to be the same faculty that is distracted (see vol. 2. chap. 31 [p. 471 n. 6, in the Rodriguez and Kavanaugh ed.]).

[31] *Interior Castle,* vol. 2, IV: 1, no. 13 (pp. 321f.); also no. 8–12 (pp. 319–21). See also Surin, *Catéchisme spirituel,* 2:375.

the annoying clapping of the mill,[32] and her heart,[33] her will, was the mill working so usefully at what makes spiritual food. At other times the mind itself went astray, following the imagination; and with such turbulence that the saint adds more: "My mind was running like a madman from room to room;[34] but we must be careful not to run after it," she adds furthermore, for by acting under the pretext of stopping these follies, these extravagances, and thus driving back to ourselves the imagination and the mind, we run the risk [124] of losing a holy repose and the heart's inclination. Therefore, we have only to hold ourselves firmly in the simple repose of the heart, which by the sweetness of its enticements little by little calls back this errant mind, this vagabond imagination—"a bit," says St. Francis de Sales, "like calling back bees into their hive by the sweetness of an agreeable sound or by the charm of a good aroma."[35]

Here's what many good souls still experience today, who in similar circumstances feel very firmly, they say, as if there were two different things [faculties] within them, which meet and unite in the heart in order to participate,

---

[32] Olphe-Galliard reads "le tracas incommode du moulin" (the inconvenient worry of the mill), but the manuscript shows "le tracat [surely *traquet,* millclapper] incommode du moulin" (the annoying clapping of the mill).

[33] The words "and her heart" found in the manuscript do not appear in Olphe-Galliard's edition.

[34] For the image of a madman, but not exactly as employed by Caussade, see *Way of Perfection,* vol. 2, 31, no. 8 (p. 156), and *Life,* vol. 1, 17, no. 7 (p. 115); and vol. 1 30, no. 16 (p. 201). Fénelon refers to Teresa of Avila for the same metaphor (*Lettres et opuscules spirituels,* in *Oeuvres spirituelles,* Pléiade ed., 574). For a discussion of mistranslations of St. Teresa's use of the metaphor of a madman, see Robert Ricard, "La Folle du logis" (*Vie et langage,* no. 100 [July 1960], 387–389); his "La Loca de la casa" (*Mélanges de la casa de Velasquez* 3 [1967]: 487–91) may be of interest.

[35] *Traité de l'amour de Dieu* (bk. 6, chap. 7 [Pléiade ed., 629] or *Oeuvres,* 4:327).

so it seems, in the same happiness. After this they no longer feel anything separated in the interior but all well-unit-
ed as in a single point; and during this total calm of the
faculties, it seems as though they have nothing else to desire.

Q: But how can it happen that the faculties of our soul
      come in this way to part company and then to meet
again[36] like that?

A: 1. This question, I would say, seems to demean
      those who always need unrefined comparisons to
understand and maybe to believe what their piety alone
should render indubitable to them concerning the witness
of the saints, whose deeds, even apart from the sanctity of
those who perform them, are more than enough to [125]
demonstrate that they have even greater insight than we do.[37]

   2. Doesn't what you have a hard time believing or
understanding here take place in everyday life? How many
times do we feel in our hearts a sweet feeling, whereas the
imagination and the mind only mull over sad and painful
thoughts? But the secret enticement of the heart little by
little also calls back the other two faculties, wins them over,
takes possession of them by its winning attractiveness.
From then on, no more sad and[38] painful thoughts, no
more divisions nor[39] interior contradictions—all is in agree-
ment, united, in peace, and by the same occasion in a more
or less evil[40] tranquility according to the object of this sweet
feeling.

---

[36] The manuscript reads "et puis à se revoir" (and then to
meet again), whereas Olphe-Galliard has "puis à se réunir" (then to
assemble again).

[37] Olphe-Galliard omits "their."

[38] Olphe-Galliard has "or" instead of "and."

[39] Olphe-Galliard has "or" instead of "nor."

[40] Olphe-Galliard has "continuelle" instead of "criminelles"
(evil), which the manuscript shows.

Chapter 10

RECOMMENDATIONS APPROPRI-
ATE FOR THOSE ADVANCED IN
THIS PRAYER

Q: What is the first recommendation?

A: It deals with aridity in recollection by which God
       begins to wean them from the consolations given to
beginners. We call this recollection dry or arid because it
[126] really is such, and in it we find the most prevalent
recollection of advanced souls.[1] Why? Because,[2] now that
they are no longer in spiritual childhood, as St. Paul says,[3]
God begins to give them food that is in truth less delicious,
less savory than at the beginning, but now more solid,
more nourishing; but a soul accustomed to feelings or
consolations has a great deal of trouble accommodating
itself to this new food. However, it is necessary to harden

---

[1] Fénelon writes, "Que la voie de la foi nue et de la pure
charité est meilleure et plus sûre que celle des lumières et des goûts"
(That the path of naked faith and pure charity is better and more
certain than that of enlightenment and of feeling) (*Lettres et opuscules
spirituels,* no. 25, in *Oeuvres spirituelles,* Pléiade ed., 673–76 and 1447);
and "Sur la prière" (On prayer) (ibid., no. 12, Pléiade ed., 609–13
and 1433–34). Both of these documents were published in the 1718
and 1738 editions of *Oeuvres spirituelles,* but "Sur la prière" was also
published in the 1713 and 1715 editions of *Sentiments de piété.*

[2] Olphe-Galliard omits "because."

[3] 1 Cor. 13:11.

oneself against [this new nourishment], because this is[4] the will of God and his usual conduct based both on the interests of his glory, which requires that we serve him with noble disinterestedness, and on our own advantage, because it is in this way that we advance in the practice of pure love, which constitutes the totality of perfection.[5]

1. We must not be pained, worried, or grieved like children who cry when they are reduced to eating dry bread. At the very least, we ought to humble ourselves by just feeling this weakness and honestly recognizing this underlying affliction of self-love that attaches itself to everything, that corrupts all, even the very holiest things, and that at the same time[6] forces the wise goodness of God not to take away his favors from us forever, but really to defer them for a time according to how much self-love there is to purify.[7]

---

[4] The manuscript reads "se raidir contre parce que cela est" (. . . this is), but Olphe-Galliard shows "se raidir contre cela parce que c'est" (. . . it is).

[5] The path of pure love is what Fénelon calls "la voie marquée par le bienheureux Jean de la Croix, qui veut qu'on croie dans le non-voir et qu'on aime sans chercher à sentir" (the path marked out by Blessed John of the Cross, who wants us to believe in the unseen and love without seeking feelings) (*Lettres et opuscules spirituels,* in *Oeuvres spirituelles,* Pléiade ed., 675).

[6] Olphe-Galliard drops "that corrupts all, even the very holy things, and that at the same time."

[7] Fénelon writes: "N'est-ce pas là ce qui fait mourir le vieil homme, plutôt que les belles réflexions où l'on s'occupe encore de soi par amour-propre, et plutôt que plusieurs oeuvres extérieures par lesquelles on se rendrait témoignage à soi-même de son avancement" (Doesn't this cause the old man to die rather than the beautiful considerations that we use to continue focusing on the self out of self-centeredness, and rather than many exterior deeds that we use to validate our own progress?) (no. 12, Pléiade ed., 611). See also John of the Cross, "The Harm Caused by Reflection upon This Supernatural Knowledge" (*Ascent of Mount Carmel,* in *Collected Works,* bk. 3, chap. 8 [pp. 225f.).

2. Hence, we must be fully on our guard against the temptations and tricks of the enemy who, to divert souls from such a dry and arid prayer, takes advantage of these circumstances to tempt them in thousands of different ways. [127]

Q: What is the first and the most dangerous temptation?

A: It is the inordinate fear of having lost recollection, based on the excuse that we no longer feel the same consolation or the same attraction.[8]

Q: But for matters of salvation, shouldn't we always fear?

A: Yes, without doubt, we should, and in this case not to have the least fear is generally a sign of self-deception. But this fear must be what we call chaste and pure, that is to say, without agitation, without worry, peaceful and reasonable, because, though it lacks the certitude that we shall never have for anything, the soul knows it can reassure itself with suitable reasons.[9]

Q: Then what are the well-founded reasons against these excessive fears, doubts, or perplexities?

A: Aside from the feelings and the consolations, we still have the solid foundation of recollection.

1. The mind, in spite of the dryness of its prayer, is not at all occupied with any sensible thing but with an invisible

---

[8] Fénelon writes: "On ne prie jamais si purement que quand on est tenté de croire qu'on ne prie plus: alors, on craint de prier mal; mais on ne deverait craindre que de se laisser aller à la désolation de la nature lâche" (We never pray as purely as we do when we are tempted to believe that we no longer are praying: then we fear that we are praying badly, but we should fear nothing except that we are letting ourselves fall into the despondency of our cowardly nature" (no. 12, Pléiade ed., 612).

[9] Lallemant warns us that the demon is revealed when our inner peace is troubled. He, however, considers the fear of God the most important of the gifts of the Holy Spirit (*Doctrine spirituelle*, 242).

and incomprehensible something that exists; in actuality this is God and can only be God.

2. The heart rests quietly in a dry peace and in a simple desire of love and union.

3. All the time spent in such an arid prayer doesn't seem long; usually we feel no boredom or distaste; or if sometimes we perceive this, we bear up under it courageously for God's sake and soon it ceases.

4. Nevertheless, we leave this prayer with a recollected mind or with one that desires to be so. [128]

5. Taking pleasure in nothing, we inevitably find ourselves with greater distaste for creatures.

6. We feel that dread of sin grows with the firm resolve to belong to God, which becomes always more profound.[10]

Q: Should we be thinking these thoughts during this prayer, in order to reassure ourselves about our fears and doubts?

A: We must beware of them, for they would be so many more distractions. We must think of them ahead of time, so that merely keeping them in mind or merely remembering them prevents every fear or voluntary doubt to enter and disturb the fragile rest of this prayer and carry off all the fruit. When necessary we can only say this: I thought carefully about this beforehand. I have adopted my point of view on good grounds, on wise advice, and[11] after many edifying experiences. Consequently, in this case I am not tempting God; therefore, here I can abandon myself to him as in all other cases and await all with confidence.[12]

---

[10] Caussade is summarizing Fénelon, "De la nécessité de connaître et d'aimer Dieu" (On the necessity of knowing and loving God) (*Lettres et opuscules spirituels,* in *Oeuvres spirituelles,* Pléiade ed., 697–717).

[11] Olphe-Galliard omits "and."

[12] Fénelon writes, "Ne soyez donc jamais inquiéte de ce que cette présence sensible de Dieu vous aura échappé; mais surtout garder-vous bien de vouloir une présence de Dieu raisonnée et sou-

Finally, if the temptation of fears and[13] doubts becomes more pressing, these words alone suffice: It is no longer the time to examine; we can do it afterwards, as is done at the end of meditation.[14]

Q: But when subsequent recollection becomes very arid and very painful to sustain,[15] isn't it therefore infused recollection?

A: Well! What does it matter whether it is either acquired or infused? Isn't it certain that one or the other is truly prayer? Therefore, I can righteously be bent [129] on persevering in spite of everything that wants to turn me away from God's presence, which, at the very least, I possess in desire and which constitutes the spirit and essence of every prayer.[16]

Q: But if distractions come and add to our drynesses, what should we do, since no sensible consolation or attraction is present to call the distracted faculties back to us?

---

tenue par beaucop de réflections" (Never be anxious if this sensible presence of God escapes you, but above all keep yourself from wanting the presence of God through thought sustained by many considerations" (*Lettres et opuscules spirituels,* no. 6, in *Oeuvres spirituelles,* Pléiade ed., 575); and "On cherche souvent dans ces réflexions le repos de l'amour-propre" (We often seek in these considerations the repose of self-love) (no. 12, Pléiade ed., 612).

[13] Olphe-Galliard omits "and."

[14] See St. Francis de Sales, "Quelques avis très utiles sur le sujet de la méditation" (Useful advice about meditation), in *Introduction à la vie dévote,* pt. 2, chap. 8 (pp. 89–91, esp. 91); *Oeuvres,* 3:84; in Ryan's English edition, 86f.; Note, however, that Ryan translates "Au sortir de cette oraison cordiale" by "After finishing this mental prayer" rather than "finishing this heart-charged prayer.")

[15] Olphe-Galliard had "entretenir" instead of "soutenir."

[16] Fénelon writes, "Le désir du recueillement est une espèce de recueillement qui suffit" (The desire of recollection is a kind of recollection that suffices) (*Lettres et opuscules spirituels,* in *Oeuvres spirituelles,* no. 15, Pléiade ed., 628).

A: Everyone agrees that involuntary distractions neither
       should nor can prevent any kind of prayer and even
less this one. Why?

1. Because when we have arrived here, we find ourselves detached enough from everything that at least we do
not have those enticing and unwelcome distractions which
fix the mind on a tantalizing object or which entice it re-
lentlessly in spite of itself.

2. Because a soul already accustomed to interior recollection clearly perceives the least distraction sooner than
would someone else and stops the distraction more easily at
its beginning.

3. Because, once we have caught on to simple interior
attentiveness, as soon as we perceive the mind wandering,
all we have to do inside ourselves is what is done exteriorly
by those who, when in the presence of a highly esteemed
person, find themselves turning their eyes hither and yon;
they simply begin to turn them modestly and without any
effort to the person to whom they owe respect; [130]
likewise we have only to turn our inner attention, which
has wandered elsewhere, to God.[17]

Q: But this turning [to God] is not as easy or as percep-
       tible as turning the eyes of the body.

A: I agree, especially for those who don't understand
       what this simple activity of the soul is. But those of
whom we are speaking have experienced this a million
times and practice it as often as they wish. Furthermore,
even when sometimes they doubt that they are doing it,
they at least know that they have the will to do so, which
suffices for them and calms them down.[18]

---

[17] See Fénelon, "De la présence de Dieu" (On the presence of
God) (*Lettres et opuscules spirituels,* in *Oeuvres spirituelles,* no. 15, Pléiade ed., 628–30).

[18] See Fénelon, "Sur la prière" (On prayer), *Lettres et opuscules
spirituels,* in *Oeuvres spirituelles,* no. 12, Pléiade ed., 609–11.

Q: But suppose that during these dry states, distractions become continual, violent, and overwhelming.

A: To push this objection even further in order to console and fortify[19] the most timid, I would like to imagine all of these distractions mixed with lunacies, extravagances, and the most terrible temptations, as we are told about in the lives of some saints, and as happened for a full year to the famous founder of the Capuchins of Barcelona,[20] who, as a matter of fact, was only engaged in the simple prayer of which we are speaking. Don't we have the certitude that it is only the will which is absolutely within our control? Therefore, only the will engenders the full merit or demerit through its free consent; since this is my cross and a kind of martyrdom, I am likewise certain that I [131] consented to nothing. Here we find the best of all disavowals; the heart without saying anything disavows unceasingly. How? By the continual pain that it suffers, without which I might well be doing what are commonly called acts of disavowal, but which will merely be vain interior words that often deceive many people.[21]

Q: What you are saying evidently shows that in all of this there is no offense at all[22] against God; but then where is the merit and harvest which I expect from my prayer?

---

[19] Olphe-Galliard has "reassure" instead of "fortify."

[20] Father Arcangel de Alarcon (born in Tordesillas, died in Barcelona, 1598) founded the first Capuchin monastery in Spain in 1578, the Conventus S. Eulaliæ, V. et M., at Sarrio in Barcelona.

[21] Fénelon writes, "Ainsi on est secrètement en paix par cette volonté que se conserve au fond de l'âme pour souffrir la guerre" (Thus we are secretly in peace, possessing a will that protects itself in the depths of the soul to endure the battle) (*Lettres et opuscules spirituels,* in *Oeuvres spirituelles,* no. 12, Pléiade ed., 612f.). See Caussade, *Lettres spirituelles,* 2:175.

[22] Olphe-Galliard has "aucune" (no one) instead of "nulle" (not at all).

A: 1. Since I am supporting[23] these interior pains with God's will in view, I am truly doing this prayer of patience and sacrifice that the saints value so much.

2. After having served God at his expense as is said—that is to say, well paid on the spot by his favors and consolations—at present I serve him, so to speak, at my own expense. But, as our masters tell us,[24] the most perfect prayer is not the one that we receive from God, but the one that we give him by the sacrifices that we make of our dearest desires.

3. Then don't I really have the greatly desired solace of being able to make sure of my own heart before God and of its good dispositions, since I am unable to have the slightest fear or doubt that I am approaching him solely attracted by his kindness and wanting to follow him only upon Mount Tabor?[25] [132]

Q: But what if I have grounds to fear that I myself caused[26] these drynesses, distractions, temptations, and similar experiences?

A: Even if you were assured that you had done so, you only have to detest your fault and to support patiently the punishment, just as one should who by his disordered state has fallen into great illnesses or infirmities.

Q: But if I were to think that this is only a test from God, this thought alone would encourage me by alleviating the pain.

A: That is the way secret pride speaks, since the word "test" pleases and flatters it, whereas the word "pun-

---

[23] Olphe-Galliard has "suppose" instead of "suporte."

[24] For instance, see Surin, "De la mort mystique" (On mystical death), in *Dialogues spirituels,* vol. 1, bk. 3, chap. 4 (pp. 166–74).

[25] Mount Tabor signifies the sensible consolations of God's presence.

[26] The manuscript reads "avoir donné sujet moi-même" (I myself caused), whereas Olphe-Galliard has "avoir donné moi-même" (I attribute to myself).

ishment" shocks and humbles it. But isn't it as equitable and meritorious to bear up under the blows of God's justice as it is to bear the blows and trials of his mercy? By the way, how do you understand it? Is there any pure[27] punishment in the distressing woes of life? Aren't justice and mercy mixed hand in hand with them, as the Scriptures say?[28] Therefore, nothing unfortunate occurs that is not a combination of justice and mercy or punishment and trial all mixed together—punishment because we merit still more for our least faults, and trial because the goodness of God turns and directs all for our advantage.[29] Even more so, says a Father of the Church: the goodness of the celestial Father for us [is such] that even his anger and blows spring from his mercy.[30]

Q: Although I understand that we can merit [133] much by such apparently badly done prayers, [I do] not [understand] that [thereby] we can advance on the path of perfection; without doubt it is precisely this that disheartens, discourages, and worries a good many people who have an ardent desire to advance always.

---

[27] The manuscript reads "pure punition" (pure punishment), whereas Olphe-Galliard has "pires punitions" (worse punishments).

[28] "Misericordia et veritas obviaverunt sibi; justitia et pax osculatæ sunt" ("Mercy and truth have met each other: justice and peace have kissed") (Ps. 84:11.)

[29] "Scimus autem quoniam diligentibus Deum omnia cooperantur in bonum, iis qui secundum propositum vocati sunt sancti" ("And we know that to them that love God, all things work together unto good, to such as, according to his purpose, are called to be saints") (Rom. 8:28).

[30] See Fénelon, *Lettres et opuscules spirituels,* in *Oeuvres spirituelles,* Pléiade ed. 32:707f., 714f. In Caussade we find the following Latin text: "Tanta est summi patris pietas ut etiam ira ejus ex misericordia sit" (Such is the tenderness of the supreme Father that even his anger rises from mercy) (*Instructions spirituelles,* 308). These or similar words were not found in a computer search of the Corpus Christianorum and Patrologiæ cursus latinæ.

A: [1.] Such desire is most praiseworthy, but if no trace
        of pride or self-love enters into it,[31] then it will al-
ways be most obedient to the will of God and consequently
untroubled, without anxiety or discouragement, because in
desiring my perfection I only want it to the exact degree
and at the time set by the will of God, by the means and
the manner pleasing to God.[32] Otherwise we would want to
progress in order to gratify ourselves with our own accomplishments rather than to please God. To want the virtues,
even to be enriched by them, in order to see ourselves
adorned and well embellished to our liking rather than to
be agreeable in the eyes of God—in brief, this constitutes
wanting perfection less for the love of God than for the
love of self.[33] My God! How many attempts to achieve an
exact and delicate self-love escape the notice of those who
ought to be striving to cure us of them! How many false
ideas, biases, and deceptions concerning progress are found
in the circle of our spiritually minded, just as[34] there are
concerning devotion in that of conventionally devout people![35]

---

[31] In "Sur le renoncement à soi-même" (On self-denial) (*Lettres et opuscules spirituels,* in *Oeuvres spirituelles,* no. 13, Pléiade ed. 613–
23), Fénelon describes the insidiousness of self-love and pride even in
seeking to love purely.

[32] Olphe-Galliard has "him (God)" instead of "God."

[33] See Fénelon's letter to the Marquis de Blainville (*Lettres et
opuscules spirituels,* in *Oeuvres spirituelles,* no. 35, Pléiade ed., 724–27).
See also letter no. 36, in which he writes: "Ne craignez rien dans le
chemin où vous marchez. Dieu vous menera comme par la main,
pourvu que vous ne doutiez pas et que vous soyez plus rempli de son
amour que de crainte par rapport à vous" (Be not afraid along the
path you are following. God will lead you as if by his hand provided
that you do not doubt and that you are more filled with his love than
with fear for yourself) (ibid., no. 36, 728).

[34] Olphe-Galliard writes "soit comme" (say as) instead of "tout
comme" (just as).

[35] See Fénelon, "Sur le renoncement à soi-même" (On self-
denial) (*Lettres et opuscules spirituels,* in *Oeuvres spirituelles,* no. 13,
Pléiade ed., 616 and 620).

2. Just exactly what is true progress in a soul? I confess that I know no other than always to progress by continually practicing acts of the heart, following the inner way of most perfect submission to all the [134] wishes of God. Whoever loves me, says Jesus Christ, will do the will of my Father; because I love him, I always do what pleases him and am always pleased in what he does.[36] Jesus adds in many places in the Gospel, Here is my food, my life, and what is chiefly said about me.[37]

---

[36] Caussade is paraphrasing John 14:15, 21–24, and 8:29: "Si diligitis me, mandata mea servate" (If you love me, keep my commandments). "Qui habet mandata mea, et servat ea: ille est qui diligit me. Qui autem diligit me, diligetur a Patre meo: et ego diligam eum, et manifestabo ei meipsum. Dicit ei Juda, non ille Iscariotes: Domine, quid factum est, quia manifestaturus es nobis teipsum, et non mundo? Respondit Jesus, et dixit ei: Si quis diligit me, sermonem meum servabit, et Pater meus diliget eum, et ad eum veniemus, et mansionem apud eum faciemus: Qui non diligit me, sermones meos non servat. Et sermonem quem audistis, non est meus: sed ejus, qui misit me, Patris" ("He that hath my commandments, and keepeth them; he it is that loveth me. And he that loveth me, shall be loved of my Father: and I will love him, and will manifest myself to him. Judas saith to him, not the Iscariot: Lord, how is it, that thou wilt manifest thyself to us, and not to the world? Jesus answered, and said to him: If any one love me, he will keep my word, and my Father will love him, and we will come to him, and will make our abode with him. He that loveth me not, keepeth not my words. And the word which you have heard, is not mine; but the Father's who sent me.")

"Et qui me misit, mecum est, et non reliquit me solum: quia ego, quæ placita sunt ei, facio semper" ("And he that sent me, is with me, and he hath not left me alone: for I do always the things that please him").

[37] Caussade has in mind John 4:34 and 5:30: "Dicit eis Jesus: Meus cibus est, ut faciam voluntatem ejus, qui misit me, ut perficiam opus ejus" ("Jesus saith to them: My meat is to do the will of him that sent me, that I may perfect his work"). "Non possum ego a meipso facere quidquam. Sicut audio, judico: et judicium meum justum est: quia non quæro voluntatem meam, sed voluntatem ejus, qui misit me" ("I cannot of myself do anything. As I hear, so I judge: and my judgment is just; because I seek not my own will, but the will

Read spiritual books, consult the Old and the New Testament, the Fathers, the theologians; they all will unanimously tell you that the true love of God, which is the true perfection of the soul, consists precisely in wanting in everything only what God wants. But isn't it a matter of faith that, except for sin, all that occurs comes from the will of God, even[38] the fall of a single hair from our head[39] or of a single leaf from a tree in the forest.[40] Therefore,[41] the most afflicting things that I suffer in my prayers and all the times that I suffer these because God wills them—all these are quite as many acts and form a long chain of acts through which I progress more and more in submitting my will perfectly to that of God and from which I proceed by thousands of new and[42] different degrees to achieve at last the uniformity[43] of will that Jesus Christ asks for us when he says to his Father, "Just as you and I are only one, bring it about that they be only one in us."[44] This obviously can

---

of him that sent me").

[38] Olphe-Galliard writes "qu'à" (as) instead of "jusqu'à" (even).

[39] Caussade is drawing on Matt. 10:30f. and Luke 12:7 and 21:18: "Vestri autem capilli capitis omnes numerati sunt. Nolite ergo timere: multis passeribus meliores estis vos" ("But the very hairs of your head are all numbered. Fear not therefore: better are you than many sparrows"). "Sed et capilli capitis vestri omnes numerati sunt. Nolite ergo timere: multis passeribus pluris estis vos" ("Yea, the very hairs of your head are all numbered. Fear not therefore: you are of more value than many sparrows"). "Et capillus de capite vestro non peribit" ("But a hair of your head shall not perish").

[40] Fénelon says God knows the number of hairs on our heads and the leaves on trees ("Discours sur la croix" [Discourse on the Cross], *Lettres et opuscules spirituels,* in *Oeuvres spirituelles,* no. 21, Pléiade ed. 652). See also Catherine of Siena, *The Dialogue,* chap. 60 (p. 114).

[41] Olphe-Galliard has "dans" (in) instead of "donc" (therefore).

[42] Olphe-Galliard omits "and."

[43] Olphe-Galliard writes "conformity" instead.

[44] Citing John 17:21 from memory: "Ut omnes unum sint, sicut tu Pater in me, et ego in te, ut et ipsi in nobis unum sint" ("That they all may be one, as thou, Father, in me, and I in thee; that they

only be accomplished when, by dint of wanting only what God wants, how he wants it, and because he wants it,[45] our will [135] finds itself as if lost and transformed into the will of God right up to the point of forming one will with him. How does this happen? Because from then on,[46] properly speaking, no longer do I have my own will, but just that of God who guides me, conducts me, and directs me in all and everywhere.

Here's what they call the deiformity, for which Jesus Christ lead us to ask in these words: "Thy will be done on earth as it is in heaven."[47] Here there is not only conformity or uniformity of the will with his, but true deiformity[48] still more perfect than that of St. Paul, who said, "It

---

also may be one in us").

[45] Olphe-Galliard omits "and because he wants it."

[46] "Because from then on" translates the manuscript's "Parce que délors," and not Olphe-Galliard's "Parce qu'alors."

[47] "Fiat voluntas tua, sicut in cælo, et in terra" ("Thy will be done on earth as it is in heaven") (Matt. 6:10).

[48] For the expression "deiformity" at the end of the seventeenth century, see *Dictionnaire de spiritualité,* vol. 3, cols. 428f. and 1452–56. Surin describes deiformity: "[L'âme] se trouve entièrement en Dieu, ne voyant plus rien qu'en Dieu même" (The soul finds itself fully in God and sees nothing anymore except in God himself) (bk. 5, chap. 2, of *Fondements* [ed. F. Cavallera, 1930], 253). The idea of deification is found in Pseudo-Dionysius, who writes: "This can only happen with the divinization of the saved. And divinization consists of being as much as possible like and in union with God" (*The Ecclesiastical Hierarchy,* chap. 1, sec. 3, 376a [p. 198]). Mme Guyon calls perfect union with God deiformity (*Torrents,* pt. 2, chap. 3, secs. 1–2 [pp. 260f.]); and in the last chapter of her *Moyen court* (chap. 24 [pp. 70–78]), she argues that her prayer from the heart prepares the soul for perfect union, a point of view that Caussade seems to follow. Francis de Sales implies deiformity at the end of bk. 6, chap. 11, of his *Traité* (Pléiade ed., 643). Caussade seems influenced by Isabelle Bellinzaga's *Breve compendio,* but there is no evidence that he read her. Perhaps he was aware of Francis de Sales's reservations about the *Breve compendio (Abrégé de la perfection);* see de Sales's letter to Mme Brulart, ca. November 2, 1607 (*Oeuvres,* 13:334f.).

is no longer I who live but it is Jesus Christ who lives, who speaks, who sees and rules in me."[49] St. Teresa, who learned it well just from the school of the Holy Spirit, who abides in the depths of the heart, said to her daughters, "Of all the unions of which I have told you, the most precious, the most desirable in my view, is the union of the will."[50]

Q: This being the case, although it may never happen to us in prayer, we should firmly align ourselves[51] with the will of God, which wants all that is not sin. Then we may persevere in peace[52] and likewise emerge.

A: Not only can we but we should,

1. because sorrow, agitation, worry, during or after prayer, cause all its fruits to be lost;

2. because one of the principal fruits of prayer is to [136] pacify the heart;

3.[53] Because we merit in proportion to afflicting dryness, annoying distractions, humiliating and crucifying temptations;

4. because we progress insofar as we learn how to submit ourselves wholeheartedly to God's wishes in every

---

[49] Citing Gal. 2:20 from memory: "Vivo autem, iam non ego, vivit vero in me Christus" ("And I live, now not I; but Christ liveth in me").

[50] Teresa of Avila writes: "This true union . . . to make your will one with God's. This is the union that I desire and would want for all of you, and not some absorptions, however delightful they may be, that have been given the name 'union' " (*Foundations,* vol. 3, chap. 5, para. 13 [p. 122]). See also "Fifth Dwelling," *Interior Castle,* vol. 2, chap. 3, para. 3 (p. 349). Francis de Sales also speaks in the same sense in his *Traité de l'amour de Dieu,* bk. 6, chap. 11 (Pléiade ed., p. 643; *Oeuvres,* vol. 4 (vol. 1 of *Traité*): 342f.).

[51] Olphe-Galliard adds "only."

[52] Olphe-Galliard omits "in peace."

[53] Olphe-Galliard omits "Because one of the principal fruits of prayer is to pacify the heart; 3."

kind of cross, but especially in the interior ones that wound the heart in its most delicate places;[54]

5. because what we are suffering is much more conducive to our progress than whatever we do, for it is a received maxim that we advance more in suffering than in doing.[55] Why? Because other than that it is naturally more painful to suffer than to act, we almost always act according to our own wishes and suffer according to the wishes of God.

Q: Then why is it that within themselves so many people, even the spiritually minded, get confused, worried, annoyed even in prayer and most often leave it fully disgusted, discouraged, so they say, and strongly tempted to abandon its practice?

A: 1. Some give themselves false ideas about it and also about devotion and perfection by placing all in the sensible, by thinking that they have devotion only insofar as they feel themselves aroused or stirred, and by believing that they pray only insofar as they produce sensible and palpable acts that they can count like the [137] beads of the rosary. Won't we ever learn to seek God by rectitude of the

---

[54] Fénelon writes of the "Nécessité de la purification de l'âme par rapport aux dons de Dieu, et spécialement aux amitiés" (Need for the purification of the soul as regards the gifts of God, and especially as regards friendship) (*Lettres et opuscules spirituels,* in *Oeuvres spirituelles,* no. 11, Pléiade ed., 606f.).

[55] Bossuet writes: "Il faut expliquer . . . que ce qu'on appelle pâtir et souffrir . . . qui est opposé au mouvement propre et à l'action qu'on se peut donner à soi-même. . . . Denis Areopagite disoit que c'estoit 'un homme qui non seulement operoit mais encore enduroit les choses divines'; c'est-à-dire, qui recevoit des impressions de Dieu, où il n'avoit point ou très-peu de part" (We must explain . . . what we mean by being afflicted and suffering . . . which are opposed to our own movements and our own activities. . . . Denis the Areopagite said that it was "a man who not only performed but also endured divine things"; that is to say, who received impressions from God in which he had no part or very little) (*Instruction sur les états d'oraison,* VII, ii [p. 233]).

heart, in simplicity of the heart, in pure faith, as St. Paul says?[56]

2. There are some who, though they pretend that they have only good intentions, are actually guided by other lights than spiritual goods and the graces of God. These still attend very much to themselves and want to do and feel all according to their whims at the time and in the way that they wish; and they hope for these as if God's wishes shouldn't be the rule and measure of our good desires and of our most holy expectations.[57]

Q: But also [what are] the means of leaving prayer content and in peace when, having in view nothing else than salvation and perfection, we haven't achieved anything of what we wanted or obtained anything of what we asked for?[58]

---

[56] 2 Cor. 5:7.

[57] Fénelon writes: "Ce n'est pas que l'homme simple et détaché de soi-même ne travaille à sa perfection; il y travaille d'autant plus qu'il s'oublie davantage et qu'il ne songe aux vertus que pour accomplir la volonté de Dieu" (It is not that a man, one uncomplicated and unattached from self, does not work for his perfection; he works at it all the more when he forgets himself and does not think of virtues except to do the will of God) ("De la vraie liberté" [On true freedom], *Lettres et opuscules spirituels,* in *Oeuvres spirituelles,* no. 28, Pléiade ed., pp. 688f.). Francis de Sales has this to say: "Que peut donc faire l'âme qui est en cet état [de sécheresse], Théotime? Elle ne sait plus comment se maintenir entre tant d'ennuis et n'a plus de force que pour laisser mourir sa volonté entre les mains de la volonté de Dieu" (What can a soul do when it is in this state of dryness, Theotime? It no longer knows how to hold its ground surrounded by so many difficulties and has no longer any strength except to let its will die in the hands of the will of God) (*Traité de l'amour de Dieu,* bk. 9., chap. 12, Pléiade ed., p 794; *Oeuvres,* vol. 5 [vol. 2 of *Traité*]: 148). The manuscript reads "esperances" (hopes), not "aspirations" (aspirations), as given by Olphe-Galliard.

[58] Teresa of Avila emphasizes the great importance of perseverance in prayer (*Life,* chap. 19, para. 4, in *Collected Works,* 1:123f.); Francis de Sales advocates "l'union de notre volonté au bon plaisir de Dieu par l'indifférence" (the union of our will to the good pleasure of

A: Oh! How transactions with God differ from those
       with men, in which, if after our keen efforts and our
earnest requests we can obtain nothing, we have grounds to
go away discontented because we go away empty-handed.
But in dealing with God, I can always part company con-
tented, because it depends on me never to part empty-
handed but always full. Well, with what? With him, and
like him, I accept even his refusals; like him I am pleased to
see myself humiliated and mortified in his presence by his
manifest rebuffs; [138] his divine satisfaction follows me
because it causes mine; and in everything and everywhere I
only want his good pleasure, to the extent that I consider
myself most satisfied even with my own dissatisfaction
when it gives him satisfaction.

       Such is the behavior that so many[59] clever attendants
adopt in the presence of the rulers[60] of the world. Well,
why shouldn't I expect it[61] with respect to a God? Far from
worrying and complaining like so many others, far from
considering myself poor and miserable, I want the complete
opposite: O my God, I want to consider myself richer than
those who have succeeded better according to their own
wishes. Why? It appears to me, my God, that I will be
enriched, clothed, adorned,[62] and well embellished only by
what is the most precious of your divine treasures, the most
agreeable in your eyes.[63] I am speaking about the continual,
most humble, most respectful, most disinterested, and most
loving submission of the heart to your adorable wishes[64] at

---

God by indifference) (*Traité*, bk. 9, chap. 4, Pléiade ed., 768–70).

[59] Olphe-Galliard writes, "tout habile courtisan" (every clever
attendant), but the manuscript has "tant d'habiles courtisans" (so
many clever attendants).

[60] Olphe-Galliard has "sovereign" in the singular.

[61] Olphe-Galliard writes "le tendrais-je" (I proffer it), whereas
the manuscript has "l'attendrais-je" (I expect it).

[62] Olphe-Galliard omits "adorned" (paré).

[63] Olphe-Galliard omits "the most agreeable in your eyes."

[64] The manuscript reads, "the continual, most humble, most

the expense of my own, in spite of all of mine that I have sacrificed and placed at the feet of your throne, like Jesus Christ, by Jesus Christ, with Jesus Christ, and in Jesus Christ, so using,[65] O my God, the same words which your holy spouse puts into my mouth every day in the sacred canon of the Mass: "Per ipsum et cum ipso," and so forth. [139]

Q: Might you still have some other recommendations to give to these advanced people?[66]

A: There remain two, but I reserve them for the next chapter.

---

respectful, the most disinterested, the most loving submission of the heart to your adorable wishes," but Olphe-Galliard has "the continual most loving submission to your divine wishes."

[65] Olphe-Galliard writes, "et en Jésus Christ, ô mon Dieu," whereas the manuscript has "et en Jésus Christ, me servant ainsi, ô mon Dieu"; thus he drops "me servant ainsi" (so using).

[66] This last question summarizes the principal theme of Caussade's *Sacrament of the Present Moment* and reflects the views of Fénelon and St. Francis de Sales.

Chapter 11

EMPTINESS OF MIND, THE IMPO-
TENCY THAT FOLLOWS, AND
THE EXTRAORDINARY REBEL-
LIONS OF THE PASSIONS

Q: What do you mean by emptiness of the mind?[1]

A: The expression "emptiness" almost explains itself:
it is a mind empty, as it seems to itself, of every
thought of either God or of the world. Whereas to purify a soul, to detach it, and to have it advance more and
more, God holds it in this state, it seems to itself that it
has fallen into a state of stupidity and folly,[2] since it

---

[1] This chapter was published by Jacques Le Brun in "Textes
inédits du Père de Caussade" (Unedited texts of Father de Caussade),
Revue d'ascétique et de mystique 46 (1970): 99–114. The theme of
emptiness can be found in St. John of the Cross, especially in the
expressions "the nakedness of the intellect and emptiness of the memory." See *Ascent of Mount Carmel,* bk. 2, chaps. 7ff., and bk. 3, chaps.
2–15; and *Dark Night,* bk. 1, chap. 9, and bk. 2, chap. 7.

[2] Caussade wrote Sr. Charlotte-Elisabeth Bourcier de Monthureux on Dec. 4, 1733, reassuring her about her spiritual difficulties
and in particular about "Cet état de vraie bêtise" (This state of true
folly) (*Lettres spirituelles,* 2:30). In a letter to Sr. Marie-Antoinette de
Mahuet (ibid., 71–79), he writes: "La seconde manière de ne penser
qu'à Dieu, c'est qu'à force de laisser tomber les pensées inutiles on
parvient à une sorte d'oubli général de toutes choses, en sorte que,
durant quelque temps, on passe les journées entiéres sans penser, ce

passes whole[3] days, so it seems to itself, without thinking of anything, no more than a stump or a trunk of a tree would, according to words of those [in this state].[4] From this there follows what we call the inability to attend to God or to any good thought.

If the soul wants to reflect, the mind, straying off somewhere, loses sight of itself or remains fully dazed; if the soul wants to pray, all the ordinary acts are lifted from it; if it wants to enter into itself, it doesn't know how to find the way in and discovers itself as if banished, exiled from its own heart, as *The Imitation of Jesus Christ* says.[5] Finally, if the soul wants to devote itself to pious reading, what St. Teresa reports [140] for a similar case takes place: "I was reading," she says, "up to two or three times the same passage in a book, without understanding any more

---

semble, à rien, comme si on était devenu stupide. Souvent même Dieu met cetaines âmes dans cet état qu'on appelle le vide de l'esprit" (The second way of thinking only of God is, after by dint of letting fall useless thoughts, we come to a kind of general forgetfulness of everything, so that for a while we pass full days without thinking, which seems like doing nothing as if we had become stupid. Often even God places some souls in this state, which we call emptiness of mind) (72). See *Sacrament of the Present Moment*, 7f.

[3] Olphe-Galliard has "ces jours" (these days) instead of "les jours" (days).

[4] Caussade writes thus: "On devenait comme stupide et hébété, ne pensant presque à rien . . . presque insensible à tout comme une bête, comme un tronc d'arbre" (We become as if stupid and witless, thinking of almost nothing . . . almost indifferent to everything like an animal, like a tree stump) ("Abrégé de quelques principes et pratiques pour l'oraison intérieure" [An abstract of several principles and practices for interior prayer]) (*Lettres spirituelles*, 2:240).

[5] Bk. 2, chap. 9 reads: "Magnum est et valde magnum tam humano quam divino posse carere solatio, et pro honore Dei libenter exsilium cordis velle sustinere et in nullo seipsum quærere, nec ad proprium meritum respicere" (What is difficult . . . is the ability to do without both, God's comfort and man's, the will to endure cheerfully having one's heart an outcast from happiness, to seek in nothing one's own profit and to have no regard for one's own merit) (66).

than if it were written in Greek or in Hebrew. What multiplies this inner cross, so mortifying and so annihilating, is to compare this state with the preceding ones. In it we seem to be as if suspended between the heavens and the earth, where we don't receive any consolations either from one or the other, or either from outside or inside."[6]

Q: Is it,[7] perhaps, a savage attack of melancholy or fully natural stupidity?[8]

A: Not at all, for

1. it happens that those following this path are frequently, and sometimes even more than frequently, possessed of a most lively disposition and, by the way, of an active intellect as well;

---

[6] See *Life,* 30, section 12 (with regard to reading) and 13 (with regard to being harshly treated by her confessors). Fénelon describes such a state as being in a "bourbier" (mud pit) (no. 6, Pléiade ed., 578).

[7] Olphe-Galliard omits "est-ce" (is it).

[8] Surin writes: "C'est de quoi se rient non seulement plusieurs personnes grossières, mais encore plusieurs savants qui, faute d'entendre les secrets de la conduite de Dieu sur les âmes, prennent les peines dont nous parlons pour les effets d'une pure mélancolie. Cependant c'est par là que Dieu conduit les âmes au plus sublime degré de la mort mystique, où l'on se trouve denué de tous les goûts spirituels, de toutes ces belles idées de vertue, de tous ces désirs ardents, qui n'étoient pas exempts d'interêt propre. Ensuite l'on en vient à un simple regard de Dieu, on ne veut que lui . . . on mène une vive toute divine" (Not only many coarse people, but also many of the learned make fun of this. Since they do not understand the secrets of God's guidance of souls, they consider the difficulties of which we are speaking the effects of pure melancholy. However, it is through these that God guides souls to the most sublime degree of mystical death, where they find themselves stripped of all spiritual consolations, of all those beautiful ideas of virtue, and of all those ardent desires, all which are not exempt from being self-regarding. Then they arrive at a simple gaze of God and want only him . . . they lead a fully divine life) ("De la mort mystique" [On mystical death], in *Dialogues spirituels,* vol. 1, bk. 3, chap. 4 [p. 172f.]).

2. in the necessary exchanges with neighbor, the same people during this sorrowful inner condition will, as a rule, not fail to appear to others wholly different from what they feel, in fact, speaking to the point, reasoning,[9] and even writing about divine matters with a facility and a flow at which they themselves are surprised, as thousands of others have experienced, among them the venerable Mother de Chantal.[10] Charged with leading a large community and with replying to all the daughters of her order while undergoing such a deplorable situation, which even for her lasted a very long time and attained a degree [141] of impotency so terrible that she was no longer able to do the least inner act of piety, she believed herself without faith, without hope, without charity, and without religion,[11] all of which

---

[9] The manuscript's "resonant" (ringing) doesn't make sense; surely "raisonnant" (reasoning) was meant.

[10] De Chaugy writes: "Elle [Jane Frances de Chantal] disait, en pleurant à grosses larmes, qu'elle se voyait sans foi, sans espérance et sans charité, pour celui qu'elle croyait, espérait et aimait si souverainement" (Jane Frances de Chantal, shedding heavy tears, said that she saw herself without faith, hope, and charity for him whom she believed in, hoped in, and loved so extremely) (*Oeuvres,* 1:510). See Thorold's edition of Caussade's *Instructions spirituelles,* where we read the following: "Here is her own confession, in a letter to a Superior of her Order: 'You give me good cause for confusion,' she says, 'in asking what is my way of prayer; alas! my daughter, it is usually nothing but distraction and some suffering; for how could a poor miserable soul like mine do otherwise, filled as it is with a thousand affairs? but I may tell you in confidence, and simply, that it is twenty years since God took from me all power of acting in prayer with understanding, consideration, or meditation, and that I only know how to suffer and to keep my spirit simply in God, cleaving to his works by simple surrender, but without performing any acts except when I am stimulated by his movement, waiting for what it pleases him in his goodness to grant' " (*On Prayer,* bk. 1, Dialogue 12, sec. 4 [p. 119]). Thorold gives bk. 5, Letter 37, as the source for what is written by Jane de Chantal; this surely was written in the margins of Caussade's original 1741 edition.

[11] Olphe-Galliard omits "sans religion" (without religion).

threw her into a state of suffering very difficult to imagine when we haven't undergone it.[12]

Q: Then what's[13] going on inside ourselves, for you said[14] that our soul can never be without activity any more than a body can be without shape?

A: Although as a consequence of diverse degrees of darkness, of inner impotencies, we can place in different classes the diverse people on this path and in this transitory state, I hold, however, without any distinction that they are all almost continually attentive to God each in his or her way, in truth, not by reflected and known acts, but by simple, direct, unperceived acts[15] that collectively produce both merit and martyrdom without being recognized.

Q: How do you know that something like this happens?

A: For this I don't need to consult books,[16] because these people, without wanting to do so, without thinking so, let me know it well enough:

1. As some people say, it is very distressing, very painful to spend the time of prayer, whole days, being unable either to recollect themselves, [142] pray, read, lift their hearts to God, or even to think of him or settle on anything good. Although they vainly desire it, excite them-

---

[12] See "De ses [Jane de Chantal] peines intérieur, et la mort des premières Mères de l'Institut" (On Jane Frances de Chantal's interior pains and the death of the first Mothers of the Institute), pt. 2, chap. 24 (319–38); and "De son amour souffrant" (On her suffering love), pt. 3, chap. 6 (pp. 417–27), in Maupas du Tour, *Vie . . . Chantal.*

[13] Olphe-Galliard has "dans quoi" (in what) instead of "de quoi" (what's).

[14] Chap. 6, response 4.

[15] See Bossuet, "Des actes directs et refléchis, appperceus et non apperceus, etc." (On direct and deliberate acts, perceived and unperceived, etc.), in *Instructions sur les états d'oraison,* bk. 5 (pp. 128–77).

[16] The text literally reads, "our writers," but it is clear that Caussade means consulting what the writers write.

selves, force themselves, all is useless and lost time; thereupon, they complain like poor people reduced to begging. The sinners, the tepid, and the worldly, don't they have similar difficulty; don't they make the same complaints? But these people simply press on with a most forceful desire to be able to occupy themselves with God during prayer and with the overwhelming difficulty of wanting to do so, and of even vainly trying to do so—and perhaps even too often with efforts that they should never exert. Here, therefore, are hearts completely filled with the best of intentions, filled with holy desires, but that are berated for being unable to engender them in order to have the consolation of having them and perhaps of admiring themselves, which God knows so well how to prevent. Let these people, therefore, humble themselves and remain in peace, happy with their own discontent, since it engenders God's contentment and his good pleasure.[17]

2. As some others say, in their darkness, their futilities, their stupidity,[18] what distresses them is not this state, so humbling, so crucifying, but the fear of no longer belonging to God, of having lost God, of being rejected, abandoned by God, perhaps even of having given occasion to it by some hidden [143] infidelity; distressing reflections unceasingly occupy them, crucify them. Whence can such feelings come except from an admirable foundation of filial fear or ardent love that devours, that consumes their souls by thousands of impotent yearnings?[19] Nevertheless, just as God "sees fruit in the sprout," as Msgr. de Meaux [Bossuet] says,[20] doesn't he see these yearnings, so hidden and

---

[17] Caussade discusses the advantages of this state in various letters; see *Lettres spirituelles,* 1:121f. and 2:111f.

[18] Olphe-Galliard has "simplicité" instead of "stupidité."

[19] See Caussade, *Lettres spirituelles,* 1:92f. and 2:64–67.

[20] Bossuet writes, "Dieu voit le fruit commencé dans le noeud et la prière dans l'intention de prier" (God sees fruit beginning in the seed and prayer in the intention to pray) (*Instructions sur les états d'oraison,* bk. 5, chap. 24 [p. 157]).

buried that they remain deep in the heart without being able to blossom except in the form of a few sighs that escape?

Let them, therefore, remain in peace, satisfied with conforming to the will of the celestial spouse.[21] Even though they don't see themselves either adorned or embellished as they wish, but rather completely deformed in their own eyes, such a state itself becomes more agreeable to God as they grow in dissatisfaction with themselves, says St. Augustine.[22]

3. Finally, as others say, their condition always gets worse; there is no longer any way of continuing; every means, every support is lacking. Formerly their feelings, even their resignation, served to reassure them, to calm them, but now there is nothing left that is good inside of them. They find themselves unfeeling, hardened like a stone, or discover in themselves a heart that, far from being subjugated, rebels against every act of subjugation that they try to [144] impose.

Such is the summit of their hardness, whence is born[23] a kind of despair that tears at the gut. Here, therefore, they are fully devastated at no longer feeling devastated[24] or[25] fully desperate at no longer achieving any resignation; but it is precisely on account of this that they should remain in peace before God with only this thought: Formerly my feelings, my feeble desires, in accord with my resignation, were rising up from[26] the bottom of my heart towards the throne of God; now there rises despair alone caused by the fear of having lost every remaining good

---

[21] Olphe-Galliard omits "with conforming to the will of the celestial spouse."

[22] I have been unable to discover where Caussade found this thought in the writings of St. Augustine.

[23] Olphe-Galliard drops "born" (nait).

[24] Olphe-Galliard writes "consolation" instead of "désolation."

[25] Olphe-Galliard has "and" instead of "or."

[26] Olphe-Galliard has "au" (in) instead of "du" (from).

sentiment. Doesn't it speak even more strongly? These are wails more profound, more impenetrable, less comforting for me, but aren't they also more keen, more touching for a God who hears them?[27]

Q: Aren't you pushing things too far here [at this point in the discussion]?

A: No, for there is nothing more established, and every reasonable mind will understand it quite well without having experienced it; moreover, these are only several small attributes of this desperate love or of this desperation of love, of which Msgr. de Meaux [Bossuet] speaks;[28] but perhaps while reading his *Instructions* you were so taken up with the errors and evils that he was condemning that you paid no attention to the good and truth in what he was saying. [145]

Q: Would you have a major principle to back up your ideas and feelings?

A: I find it in these very profound words of Jesus Christ: "There where your treasure is, there also will be your heart";[29] doubtlessly and especially in its feelings

---

[27] Guilloré describes in detail the frustration arising from being repeatedly subjected to strong temptations and urges steadfast courage ("Sur l'excès des tentations" [On too many temptations], in *Oeuvres spirituelles*, 516–21).

[28] In letter to Sr. Louise-Françoise de Rosen, Caussade wrote: "Ces efforts pour s'élancer vers Dieu, suivis de l'impuissance, sont dans quelques âmes si violents qu'ils produisent ce que Msgr de Bossuet appelle l'amour désespéré ou le désespoir d'amour, qui, dans le fond, est le plus violent de tous les amours. Voilà, dit ce grand évêque, comme la grâce imite quelquefois ce que fait faire à des insensés l'amour profane des créatures" (These efforts at straining towards God followed by incapacity are in some souls so violent that they produce what Bossuet calls desperate love or the despair of love, which fundamentally is the most violent of all loves. See, says this great bishop, how grace sometimes imitates what the profane love of creatures does to the foolish) (*Lettres spirituelles*, 1:318). Le Brun, the expert on Bossuet, could not find in Bossuet what Caussade refers to.

[29] The manuscript has "là est aussi et sera votre coeur" (where

and simple movements, which the common people don't consider acts because they aren't counted among reflected, sensible, and tangible ones, and which for this reason they call simple direct acts, as a rule unperceived. The beautiful reflection of St. Augustine develops it even better: everything, he says, is moved by its proper weight, the light upward, the heavy downward; my weight, he continues, is my love; by it I am carried everywhere I go. Then he adds that we live less in ourselves than in the object of love, because it is there that generally are found our desires and our affections, which are the life of the heart.[30]

-----

it is, there also will be your heart), whereas Olphe-Galliard has only "là est votre coeur" (there is your heart). The allusion is to Matt. 6:21 ("Ubi enim est thesaurus tuus, ibi est et cor tuum" ["For where thy treasure is, there is thy heart also"]) and Luke 12:34 ("Ubi enim thesaurus vester est, ibi et cor vestrum erit" ["For where your treasure is, there will your heart be also"]). In the second half of the expression, Caussade combines the present tense of Matthew with the future tense of Luke.

[30] *Confessions,* bk. 13, chap. 9 (10) (pp. 278f.) in the Chadwick ed.; Oxford, 1:187 and commentary in 3:354–59; for the theory of love in Augustine, see Gilson, *Introduction à l'étude de saint Augustin,* 170–84, and the note in French edition of the *Confessions* (*Bibliothèque augustinienne,* vol. 2, no. 14 [pp. 617–22]). In a parallel passage (*On Prayer,* bk. 2, dialogue 8 [p. 246 of the English translation of *Instructions spirituelles*]), Caussade wrote: "This is why St. Augustine said that 'the ardor of charity, which consists in an excellent will, is the cry of the heart'; that is, the fervor of the prayer of the heart ['Flagrantia caritatis clamor cordis']." Augustine writes: "Frigus caritatis, silentium cordis est; flagrantia caritatis, clamor cordis est. Si semper manet caritas, semper clamas; si semper clamas, semper desideras; si desideras, requiem recordaris. Et rugitus cordis tui ante quem sit, oportet ut intellegas" (Frigidity of charity is the silence of the heart; ardor of charity is the cry of the heart. If you always let charity endure, you are always crying out; if you are always crying out, you are always desiring; if you are desiring, you are calling rest to mind. And it is fitting that you understand in whose presence is the outcry of your heart) (Ps. 37:14, *Enarrationes in psalmos,* p. 392); for a discussion of the end of charity, see Gustave Combès, *La Charité d'après saint Augustin,* 101–30.

So it follows from this that as soon as a confessor has discovered the dominant tendency of a miser or a rake, he then confusedly catches sight of sin in the heart; I am not speaking of sins which are known and committed by reflected acts, but of another kind, hidden and unknown in an impenetrable abyss of sin, with which an impassioned heart stains itself endlessly by these simple and almost continual movements [146] of the passion of which it has become the slave.

Likewise, once a director has, on the basis of certain traits or words blurted out, recognized the acquired and dominant habitual disposition in one of the people of whom we are speaking, he easily understands that in spite of the faults inextricable from our fragility or human weakness, generally the whole inner life of this soul tends towards God. Why? Because where its treasure is, there also its heart is and will be, by the agency of these simple movements and affections, which are truly acts, although common people don't know this, and more so by all these diverse feelings, whether of love or of hate, of hope or of fear, of joy or of sadness, whether such people perceive them or they don't perceive them.[31] Again why? Because the weight of love often unrecognized, a secret charm that is in the soul, sustains the soul wherever the soul betakes itself—either in mind or heart, with or without reflection, says St. Augustine—living in this object more than in itself without knowing it does.[32] Also, as soon as the soul believes that it has found the treasure that it believed lost,

---

[31] In the manuscript at Nancy (no. 1092), we find the following Latin text distorted: "Ibi et cor meum erit" ("There also will be my heart"); see Jacques Le Brun in *Revue d'ascétique et de mystique* 46 (1970): 108.

[32] Augustine writes, "Quid est ergo amor nisi quædam vita duo aliqua copulans vel copulari appetens, amantem scilicet et quod amatur?" (Thus, what is love other than a certain life that unites two beings or seeks to unite them: him who loves and the object loved?) (*De Trinitate,* VIII, x, 14 [pp. 290f.]).

inside all is calm and serene; peace and joy gush right up to the surface.

Q: What you have just said appears to me most comforting and encouraging for those who [147] have truly given their hearts to God and who want to please only God; but I would decidedly like to know in a few words what we should be doing above all else during the time of these trials and similar conditions.

A: I have already explained this or hinted at the answer:

1. Avoid willful troubles and discouragements in order to hold ourselves in peace by means of trust and total abandonment to God;

2. Expect solace only from God alone; don't go begging among his creatures, not even among his ministers, except for pressing needs and[33] for necessary instruction.

Q: But what is to be done to arrive at these two levels of detachment?[34]

A: 1. Once and for all abandon yourself to God without aim, without limit, without any reservations, for it is an established maxim that it is only these reservations which block the flow of grace and the progress of a soul.

2. Convince yourself once and for all that any great affliction that occurs is wisely arranged by a Providence so loveable, so splendid; and that, if we were to understand the great good which it hopes to draw from these sufferings, we would consider this purgatory as one of the greatest favors of heaven; indeed after we have passed through it and have experienced its precious advantage, we can't give enough thanks.[35] [148]

---

[33] Olphe-Galliard puts "or" instead of "and."

[34] This reflects what Caussade teaches in "The Virtue and Practice of Surrendering Ourselves" and "Surrendering to God: The Wonders It Performs," in *The Sacrament of the Present Moment,* chaps. 3 and 4 [pp. 15–27].

[35] Fénelon writes, "Si quelque chose est capable de mettre un coeur au large et en liberté, c'est l'abandon" (If one thing is able to

Q: But if, in spite of myself, I find myself assailed by
     difficulties and involuntary despondencies?

A: Again, it is necessary to resign yourself to the will of
     God, patiently to let yourself be crucified, as we do
in the case of overwhelming sickness when every remedy is
useless.

Q: But what if I cannot make any perceptible acts of
     resignation, confidence, and abandonment?

A: You must tell yourself on these occasions: Now
     then! Didn't I want to do these acts? God, therefore,
has fathomed my desires; this suffices, for in all that precisely concerns the inner life, the will does all, and God sees
it in its depth, which is the most removed from my[36] senses.[37]

Q: But if during[38] these sad and distressing delibera-
     tions, I sometimes voluntarily admit some impa-
tience, distress, agitation, or despondency?

A: After you are humbled by these and have repented,
     as it was said earlier,[39] you must immediately return
to God and to yourself with a perseverance that merits the
name of heroic virtue, especially in such a case, as St. Francis de Sales describes it.[40] By perseverance you avoid what

---

unfetter and render a heart free, it is abandonment) (bk. 6, Pléiade
ed., 579). Fénelon means "enlarge the heart," which is a common
theme in his letters, inspired by the psalms ("Viam mandatorum
tuorum cucurri, cum dilatasti cor meum" ("I have run the way of thy
commandments, when thou didst enlarge my heart") (Ps. 118:32).

[36] Olphe-Galliard writes "nos" (our) instead of "mes" (my).

[37] Bossuet writes, "Avant qu'il ait eu le temps de s'expliquer
son acte à lui-même, Dieu le voit dans le fond le plus intime du
coeur" (Before one has time to explain to himself his act, God sees it
in the most intimate depths of the heart) (*Instructions sur les états
d'oraison,* bk. 5, chap. 24 [p. 156]).

[38] Olphe-Galliard writes "pendant" (while) instead of "durant"
(during).

[39] Chap. 7, questions 2 and 3.

[40] De Sales calls heroic acts of virtue those consisting in perfect imitation of Christ (*Traité de l'amour de Dieu,* bk. 8, chap. 9, last

the saint reproves in some people: impatience at having
been impatient, vexation at having been vexed, agitation at
having been [149] agitated, discouragement at having been
discouraged.[41] These are endless and wind up disturbing the
inner life.

Q: But finally, if during the most pressing stresses of
        this crucifying state, which is often so obscure and
tangled up that I have no one to consult, what should I do
to reassure and pacify myself?[42]

A: Recall roughly what was just said all along and, in
        order to apply it properly, tell yourself, using a very
natural argument: If I were to find myself in the same inner
state with respect to the world that I usually experience
with respect to God, if all my actual and habitual dispositions with respect to God were about the same with respect
to a profane and heinous object, would I believe that I am
in a good state? What would a confessor think? Wouldn't
he immediately answer me that he finds in me all the symp-
toms of a spoiled, perverted heart that finishes by corrupt-
ing itself with all these most profound feelings, in which he
sees only corruption and sin? [Would he not find] sin in
these fears that ravage me, sin in these doubts that afflict
me, sin in these feelings of melancholy that overwhelm me,
sin in these hopes that reanimate my passion, sin in the
fleeting joys that inflame my passion, sin in a thousand
other feelings that only serve to aggravate my passion in
order to amplify its ferocity? But is more required to progress in the ways of holy love by the actions of grace than to

---

para., Pléiade ed., 739; *Oeuvres,* vol. 5 [vol. 2 of *Traité*]: 88).

[41] Caussade is paraphrasing de Sales: "De la douceur envers
nous-mêmes" (On gentleness towards ourselves) (*Introduction à la vie
dévote,* pt. 3, chap. 9, Pléiade ed., 156–58; *Oeuvres,* 3:166–68).

[42] See Caussade, *Lettres spirituelles,* 1:72f., 100f., which describes the situation for Sr. Marie-Thérèse de Vioménil, who did not
have a good guide to consult at Nancy after Caussade was no longer
confessor of the Visitandines.

[150] become completely perverted through the rapid progress of a profane and heinous love?

O my God! How your direction of souls on the path of inner life is worthy of admiration. You, the author of my nature as well as of grace, change all without destroying anything; for the same grace that changes us, that reforms us by giving you as our unique object, the goal and end of our wishes, of our desires, this grace sanctifies even our passions. From that time onwards, therefore, their most natural movements become in your hands as many instruments of sanctification. But as for us, what astonishing wretchedness! O my God! You are placed in a sort of necessity to work in us in the middle of our great inner darkness, as in hiding and unbeknown to us, so that no vain return of self-love comes to soil the purity of your divine operations.[43]

Q: What do you have to tell them about the extraordinary rebellions of the passions, about the violence of all sorts of temptations?[44]

A: Since this is for these souls a cross still more heavy, a more cruel martyrdom.

---

[43] In Thorold's edition of Caussade's *On Prayer* (his *Instructions spirituelles*), this prayer takes on this form: "O God, how wonderful art thou in thy saints! how profound and incomprehensible are thy effects in them! As author of nature and of grace, thou changest all without destroying anything, for in making the objects of our pursuit to change thou sanctifiest us by our own sufferings, using their most natural movements as so many steps to raise us to the most perfect love; but also what extraordinary unhappiness for us, since it imposes on thee almost a necessity of exercising thy most wonderful operations secretly and unconsciously, amid the darkness of our revolted passions, so that instead of these vain complacencies which would sully thy divine operations, the humility of our feelings helps to keep them in all their purity (bk. 2, dialogue 8 [p. 250]).

[44] See Guilloré, "Sur l'excès des tentations" (On excessive temptations), in *Oeuvres spirituelles,* 516–21.

1. Let them apply in this respect all that we have just said about pure privations.

2. Let them never forget the principle that all we suffer in spite of ourselves is never sinful, but on the contrary fully a source of great merit, [151] perfection, and advancement, because a heart agitated by these continual and[45] violent blows and always held firm by love or fear becomes further rooted in one or the other, like young trees ready to resist the violence of the winds by extending roots deeper into the earth where they were planted.[46]

3. Then they only need invincible patience with total abandonment and should say often, "My God, preserve me from every assent, but concerning the pain, the tearing of the heart, and the holy inner abasement, I accept them without end, without limit, for all the time that it pleases you."[47]

---

[45] The words "continual and" are dropped by Olphe-Galliard.

[46] This comparison is found in Jean-Pierre Camus, who writes: "Qui ne sçait que le pau que l'on veut ficher en terre, s'y enfonce plus il est esbranlé, et que les arbres les plus battus des vents jettent de plus profondes racines dans la terre" (Who does not know that the stake which we want to drive into the earth penetrates all the more when it is shaken and that trees the most buffeted by the wind drive down the deepest roots into the earth) ("Heureux estat, et marque de la faveur de Dieu" [Happy state and mark of God's favor], in *La Luitte spirituelle,* pt. 1, chap. 6 [p. 17]). It is quoted by Marie-Henri Boudon in *Les Saintes Voies de la croix,* bk. 1, chap. 5 (p. 33).

[47] Almost the same words are given by Caussade in a letter (see Le Brun in *Revue d'ascétique et de mystique* 46 [1970]: 343): "My God, preserve me [from every sin, that is to say,] from every assent; but concerning the pain, the tearing of the heart, and the holy ~~inner~~ abasement [where all of that throws me], I accept it without end, without limit, for all the time that it pleases you." (The texts in square brackets are in the letter but not in *Treatise;* the struck-out word is not in the letter.) See the prayer with a similar theme in Caussade, *Lettres spirituelles,* 2:57f. See Francis de Sales, "De l'indifférence que nous devons pratiquer en ce qui regarde notre avancement ès vertus" (On the indifference which we should practice for progress in virtues) (*Traité de l'amour de Dieu,* bk. 9, chap. 7, Pléiade ed., 777–81).

4. The more their rebellions and temptations are violent, strange, or extraordinary, either in[48] themselves or with respect to the persons' character, the more they ought to encourage themselves and entrust themselves to God, because then his permissive will stands out more especially there.

5. Let them often recall in their mind these words of Jesus Christ to St. Paul,[49] when this apostle asked Jesus to deliver him from a temptation that he said pummeled him so much that it humbled him. "Paul, Paul," Jesus replied, "my grace suffices for you, for virtue is perfected in weakness." Why? Because temptation serves to purify self-love [152] and to humble pride.

Q: Can we penetrate the reasons for such a plan by God?

A: His justice, his wisdom, his goodness appear there just as in everything else, for

1. His justice requires that we be punished by what we have sinned with, that these passions, so cherished by us, become our torturers, and that all the voluntary satisfactions of a heinous heart be changed into bitterness;

2. On account of his wise goodness, we are not cured of vices until after we have suffered hundreds of times our

---

[48] Olphe-Galliard reads "par" (by) instead of "en" (in).

[49] "Et ne magnitudo revelationum extollat me, datus est mihi stimulus carnis meæ angelus Satanæ, qui me colaphizet. Propter quod ter Dominum rogavi ut discederet a me: et dixit mihi: Sufficit tibi gratia mea: nam virtus in infirmitate perficitur. Libenter igitur gloriabor in infirmitatibus meis, ut inhabitet in me virtus Christi" ("And lest the greatness of the revelations should exalt me, there was given me a sting of my flesh, an angel of Satan, to buffet [*kolaphízêi*] me. For which thing thrice I besought the Lord, that it might depart from me. And he said to me: My grace is sufficient for thee: for power is made perfect in infirmity. Gladly therefore will I glory in my infirmities, that the power of Christ may dwell in me") (2 Cor. 12:7–9). *Kolaphízein*, whose root *koláptein* means to peck at or to strike or to carve or to chisel, means to buffet, beat, or strike.

weakness and our powerlessness in their regard, so that God alone in this has all the glory and that no one can ever glorify himself except in God.

Those who wish to be further instructed on this subject have only to read what Fr. Surin said in the first volume of *The Spiritual Catechism,*[50] what Fr. Guilloré observed in his *Progress,*[51] and what M. Boudon had to say in his *Ways of the Cross.*[52] We shall find this last work, like the[53] other ones, as filled with the spirit of God and his unction as it appears negligent in its style; but I would willingly say about Boudon with some measure what one of the great geniuses[54] had said about St. Francis de Sales: "What charmed him the most about this great saint was to see a man of great insight, [153] who knew in depth the human heart, never speak except like an artless man who only thinks of edifying." Great God, what self abnegation, what total and heroic forgetfulness of self, a self that continually and fully occupies the attention of all humankind!

---

[50] See especially the chapter entitled "Des peines extraordinaires" (On extraordinary afflictions) in 1:294–312.

[51] "Les Progrès de la vie spirituelle selon les diférents états de l'âme" (The developments of the spiritual life according to the different states of the soul), *Oeuvres spirituelles,* 417–638. This work was recommended by Caussade in his *Lettres spirituelles.*

[52] *Les Saints Voies de la croix.*

[53] Olphe-Galliard writes "tous les" (all) instead of "ces" (these).

[54] Surin is the great genius. Surin writes thus about Francis de Sales: "C'est encore, en leur intérieur, procédant en la dévotion et spiritualité sans affectation de sublimité ou de curiosité, et allant, comme disait le bienheureux François de Sales, à la bonne grosse mode, c'est-à-dire en toute sincérité et naïveté devant Dieu" (Furthermore, within their interior, it is pressing onward in devotion and spirituality without affecting sublimity or curiosity and, as blessed Francis de Sales says, plodding along, i.e., in all sincerity and simplicity before God) (*Catéchisme spirituel,* 1:489f.).

Chapter 12

RECOMMENDATIONS AND CLARIFICATIONS APPROPRIATE FOR ADVANCED PEOPLE WHO HAVE MADE GREAT PROGRESS

Q: Who are these people?

A: Those who, after having undergone trials, are purified like gold in a crucible.[1] But this purification, which is continuously increasing almost infinitely and whose end we shall never see in this life, is still only the ever-growing indifference to all that is not God; and this indifference itself becomes always greater in proportion both to the size of the trials and to the faithfulness in sustaining them with greater submission,[2] with more confidence and abandonment to God, just as was said.[3] [154]

Q: With what do your recommendations and your clarifications deal?[4]

---

[1] A traditional comparison found, for instance, in Wisd. 3:6, where we read, "As gold in the furnace he hath proved them."

[2] Olphe-Galliard drops "with greater submission."

[3] See chap 11, questions 7 and 8.

[4] In this chapter Caussade is emphasizing what Guilloré writes in his "Maxime X: L'esprit de parfait abandon est nécessaire, pour faire régner Dieu sur une âme" (Tenth Maxim: A spirit of perfect abandonment is necessary to have God rule over a soul) (*Maximes spirituelles* [Spiritual maxims], in *Oeuvres spirituelles*, 92–100).

A: With the advantage of the trials already undergone,
        so that we enliven ourselves to undergo new and
greater trials, as it pleases God to purify us more and more
in order to render us more capable of a higher degree of
love and union with the God of every purity, before whom
the angels aren't pure enough, in the language of the Scriptures.[5]

Q: Therefore what is the first advantage of trials?

A: After we have become detached from temporal
        goods, indifference even to spiritual ones is the first
advantage. For our nature finds itself universally so cor-
rupted that spontaneously it corrupts everything. Such are
the ever reviving forces of this damned self-love, which
took birth with us, that no sooner is it detached from one
kind of good than it attaches itself to another with its[6] same
ardor. Without changing its wretched foundation, usually it
only changes object by shifting its affections,[7] its own
whims, from temporal goods to spirituals ones. But because
this new kind of affection [155] appears to be none other
than holy, thus nothing opposes it; we don't even distrust
it. Thus it always continues growing in the heart, often
even becoming very noticeable.[8] In how many people of
piety do we not observe the same attachment to their own
self-will concerning holy things as we see in the worldly

---

[5] "Behold they that serve him are not steadfast, and in his
angels he found wickedness" (Job 4:18).

[6] Olphe-Galliard has "la" (the) instead of "sa" (its).

[7] Olphe-Galliard has the singular, "affection."

[8] Guilloré explains how we can turn trials and tribulations into
attachments in "Sur la défiance de soi-même dans l'amour pour les
croix" (On suspicion of the self in love for crosses), "Les progrès de la
vie spirituelle selon les différents états de l'âme" (Progress in the
spiritual life according to the different states of the soul) (*Oeuvres
spirituelles*, 505–8); and in "Sur l'indifférence dans les vicissitudes des
états intérieurs" (On indifference in the vicissitudes of the interior
states) (ibid., 614–17). Indifference may be the same as abandonment;
on p. 615 he talks about becoming "bête" (mindless).

concerning profane things? Thus, confessors are always trying to break all of the willfulness of [these pious people].[9] How many others are so jealous of all their own practices of devotion, of their own least spiritual comfort whether inner or exterior, that if God permits the least disturbance[10] concerning these practices, they will be as upset, as worried, as anxious, and also as badly disposed as are the worldly over whatever upsets their pleasures. How many pious obstinacies are there in those who alone hardly perceive them and in whose minds all of these are only zeal for salvation and perfection. Such and still more so is the rapid progress of self-love in all the devout who never have learned either to distrust these or to recognize them under the pretext that their purpose[11] is praiseworthy and holy.[12]

Q:　Concerning this point, are there only these visible disorders?

A:　There are an infinity of others even more profound, more refined, less known, and of as many kinds as self-love can have of [156] disordered feelings. Hence we find ambition, avarice, sensuality, envy, spiritual jealousy, and so forth. In a word, I know not how many diverse movements of human passion self-love causes subtly to slip into us all, entering by means of a veritable attachment.

Q:　How therefore can the heart be purified of such an almost imperceptible corruption?

---

[9] Olphe-Galliard has "les" (the) instead of "ses" (these).

[10] Olphe-Galliard has the plural, "disturbances."

[11] The manuscript reads "et" (and); but this is a spelling error, for the meaning is clear: it should be "est" (is).

[12] For an extensive analysis of what Caussade is writing, see Guilloré, "Illusions des vertus" (Illusions of virtue), and "Illusions de la vie spirituelle" (Illusions of the spiritual life), in *Oeuvres spirituelles,* 701–43, 744–811; Francis de Sales, "Du dépouillement parfait de l'âme unie à la volonté de Dieu" (On the perfect renunciation of the soul united to the will of God), in *Traité de l'amour de Dieu,* bk. 9, chap. 16, para. 3 [Pléiade ed., 804–7]; *Oeuvres,* vol. 5 [vol. 2 of *Traité*]: 160–163).

A: If God doesn't put his hand to it in a special way,
         this is impossible. But by means of repeated trials
and of privation of every consolation and perceptible support, he forces us to recognize our veritable attachments of
every stripe, as he forces good people in the world to recognize secret attachments to goods of the earth by the loss
of these very goods. So this is again a blow by which God
forces those of whom we are speaking to know themselves
well and continuously to make these frank acknowledge-
ments, so humbling and sanctifying, in his presence and to
admit that until now all their self-styled piety was merely an
almost disguised spiritualized self-love, and all their best
actions were just like a filthy cloth, according to the expression of the Scriptures.[13] From this arises their longing to
make general confessions, since they are persuaded that they
never [157] have clearly known this chasm of corruption
that they all carry unbeknownst in their hearts. Thus we
continually admire the infinite goodness of God who, in
knowing on the one hand our best disguised spiritual attachments and on the other hand the difficulty of a holy
indifference to all that flatters self-love even spiritually, acts
for spiritual goods as he does for temporal ones, to which
he facilitates indifference either by actual removal or by
instilling secret bitterness into them.

Q: Might you have several principles[14] accessible to ev-
         eryone to support the necessity for this spiritual in-
difference by inner purifications?

A: I have two of them to satisfy your desires. The first
         occupies a prominent place in almost all spiritual
books, but especially in the *Imitation*,[15] which everyone

---

[13] "Et facti sumus ut immundus omnes nos, et quasi pannus
menstruatæ universæ justitiæ nostræ" ("And we are all become as one
unclean, and all our justices as the rag of a menstruous woman") (Isa.
64:6).

[14] Olphe-Galliard has "pratiques" (practices) instead of "principes" (principles).

[15] See "On Disregarding Creatures to Find the Creator," bk.

reads without wanting to probe it deeply, and in which I know that truly spiritual people, as a rule and as if in compendious form, find almost all of what I have already[16] said or what remains for me to say. Here is this principle: We must detach ourselves from all that is not God, in order to attach ourselves only to God. But all the spiritual goods taken together, by the way, no matter how precious and desirable they are, are not God; therefore, we must never attach ourselves to them. We can, we should even, value them, wish for them, ask for them, look for them as [158] the means to unite ourselves to God; but never must we attach our heart to them, for this would be to put them in the place of God and upset all by changing means into an end.

The second principle holds that nothing can be ordered except according to the order of God.[17] But what is the order of God, both in creation and in redemption?

1. the glory that he owes himself and of which he cannot even strip himself
2. the happiness of man which we owe to his pure mercy

We must, therefore, in seeking this happiness and all the means that lead to it, have[18] primarily and principally in view the will of God and his glory, which accords with his will. To upset this order by installing in the foremost place what should only be in the second would be to will to

---

3, chap. 31; and Surin, *Fondements,* bk. 4, chap. 1 (pp. 197–203).

[16] "Already" is missing in the Olphe-Galliard edition.

[17] See "The Mystery of God's Grace," chap. 7 of *Sacrament of the Present Moment,* 42–48. In the French edition the chapter title reads, "Que l'ordre de Dieu fait toute notre sainteté et de la petitesse apparente de cet ordre pour certaines âmes que Dieu sanctifie sans éclat et sans efforts industrieux" (That the plan of God constitutes all of our holiness, and about the apparent smallness of this plan for some souls whom God sanctifies without any show and without active effort) (71–79).

[18] The manuscript has "à voir" (to see), but from the context it is clear that "avoir" (have) is meant.

prefer ourselves over God and never to fulfill his first commandment: You shall love the Lord your God, with all
your mind,[19] with all your heart, with all your might."[20]
Consequently, in the continual quest for spiritual goods, in
their possession, in their privation, I ought to be as fully
submitted to the will of God, as dependent on God, as
resigned, as abandoned to God as I am even concerning
temporal goods. However, on my side, especially concerning spiritual goods, [159] I should do what I ought, what I
can, to acquire them, to keep them, to increase them, or to
retrieve them—but always without those eagernesses, agitations, and worries that come only from self-love and[21] are
its obvious signs, but always in the same way by abandoning success to God, a total abandonment that we cannot
too often exercise during our life.[22] Besides, at death itself
when this abandonment is far more terrible,[23] we must,
however, even though it is happening, abandon ourselves
without reserve to the pure mercy of God with firm hope
not in our miserable deeds, but in the merits of Jesus
Christ.

---

[19] Olphe-Galliard adds "and" here.

[20] With "heart, soul, might" ("Thou shalt love the Lord thy
God with thy whole heart, and with thy whole soul, and with thy
whole strength" [Deut. 6:5]) and with "heart, soul, mind" ("Jesus said
to him: Thou shalt love the Lord thy God with thy whole heart, and
with thy whole soul, and with thy whole mind" [Matt. 22: 37]).

[21] Olphe-Galliard leaves out "that come only from self-love
and."

[22] Fénelon writes: "Le fondement de l'abandon posé, marchez
tranquillement et en confiance. Pourvu que cette disposition de votre
volonté ne soit point changée par des attachements volontaires à
quelque chose contre l'ordre de Dieu, elle subsistera toujours" (Once
the foundation of abandonment is established, proceed peacefully and
confidentially. This disposition of your will should always endure,
provided it is in no way changed by voluntary attachments to something against God's will) ("Discours sur la dissipation et la tristesse"
[Discourse on dissipation and sadness], Pléiade ed. 574).

[23] The manuscript reads "terribles," whereas Olphe-Galliard
shows "terrifiant."

Q: Would you wish to limit God's love to the subordi-
       nation alone of this mixed love?

A: God forbid that I ever give the least attention to acts
       of pure love or its various developments, especially
towards the people of whom I am speaking; although I see
the concerted zeal of all confessors to make them practice
these acts, making even the most unrefined people, the least
learned, and even children do them, under the condition
that this is always done as is customary during the usual act
of contrition, which includes this act of pure love, but
without ever excluding the other great motives, those of
hope and fear. [160]

Q: Would you generally want to encourage everyone to
       practice this indifference towards spiritual goods, as
you have already said?

A: No, without doubt we must always take care to
       whom we speak, for concerning newly converted
sinners and all beginners, even the imperfections of advanced people are a kind of perfection. But to presume that
progress will happen just because we give up every created
thing whether human or divine, things which everyone
understands as true attachments, is absurd. For it is wanting to progress in the love of God while remaining attached
in the heart to what is not God; it is wanting to love God
with all our might, to give him all of our heart, but holding
back what this heart cherishes the most, which are its own
whims in even the most holy things.[24] Likewise God berated his chosen people: "Even in your mortifications and
your fast, your own will is found."[25]

Q: It seems to me, however, that you attribute merit to
       people undergoing trials?

---

[24] See Guilloré, "Les illusions des dépouillements intérieurs"
(Illusions of interior renunciations), in *Oeuvres spirituelles,* 804–11.

[25] "Ecce in die jeiunii vestri invenitur voluntas vestra, et omnes
debitores vestros repetitis" ("Behold, in the day of your fast your own
will is found, and you exact of all your debtors") (Isa. 58:3).

A: [Merit] isn't [due] on account of their diligence,[26]
        but just the opposite, on account of the great sacri-
fice of the same diligence under the most distressing circumstances.

Q: But have you not declared that [161] their inner
        wailing during the most tumultuous feelings from
their privations are of such value in God's eyes?

A: It is, as we can remark, only because they always
        surrendered to every wish of God, which is so true
that if sometimes they happen to willfully fail in perfect
surrender, then

        1. they begin to lose the merit and good effects of their
trials;

        [2.] they commit sins or imperfections in proportion to
the degree of freedom that remains in them during these
stormy states;

        3. even their trials become both stronger and longer.
Why? Because any[27] new faults need new purifications.[28]

Q: What are the advantages of trials for advanced souls
        who have made great progress?

A: There are any number of them and of as many dif-
        ferent kinds as there are in us imperceptible attach-
ments to what isn't God and from which all trials tend to
purify us, in order to dispose us always for a more perfect
union whose degrees run up to[29] infinity.

---

[26] The text reads, "attachments," which Littré defines as "2.
Grande application" . . . "Peut-on avoir plus d'attachement à tous ses
devoirs?—Sévigné" (2. Great diligence . . . Can one have greater
attachment to all his duties?—Sévigné).

[27] Olphe-Galliard gives "les" (the), but the manuscript has
"de" (any).

[28] Guilloré explains that since repeated trials come ultimately
from God, we should submit to them and "adore" them ("Sur la
parfaite soumission aux grandes épreuves" [On prefect surrender to
major trials], in *Oeuvres spirituelles,* 503–5).

[29] Olphe-Galliard has "sont à l'infini" (are infinite), but the

Q: Could you not summarize most of these advantages
       or the chief ones into one advantage? [162]

A: It seems to me that they are summarized in relin-
       quishing proprietary use over the faculties of our
soul.[30] This expression may appear to you a bit mystical,
but I confess that I have been unable to find any alternative
with which to replace it; perhaps, you might be able to do
so after having heard the explanation, which should always
be preceded by correct terminology. Concerning such expressions I made a reflection that doesn't seem inappropriate to me. Most mystical expressions aren't invented indis-
criminately, as expressions in the arts and sciences often are,
because it is inner awareness alone that gives birth to them
when needed. From this it also follows that good souls
who have never read or heard these kinds of expressions
don't fail, however, to find them as needed to explain to us
what is going on in their souls.

       Therefore, pure awareness gives the most appropri-
ate, the most expressive words to each one of us according
to what each one experiences and to the language that each
speaks. The words "proprietary use over the faculties" seem
to me a good way to express one of the most hidden effects
of self-love, which wants to appropriate to itself control
over the faculties of the soul by using them according to its
whims and with a certain independence, even when it
might seem that it is using them only for God, from whom
it has received them, just like one to whom we entrust a[31]
deposit, in truth, to use it for given purposes, but who

---

manuscript prefers "vont à l'infini" (run up to infinity).

[30] Fénelon writes, "Mais, quoiqu'on renonce ainsi à son corps,
il reste de grands obstacles pour renoncer à son esprit" (But although
we renounce our bodies in this way, there remain great obstacles to
the renouncing of our minds) ("Sur le renoncement à soi-même" [On
renunciation of oneself], Pléiade ed., 619). See also Fénelon's "Sur le
détachement de soi-même" (On indifference to oneself) (ibid., 623–28).

[31] Olphe-Galliard has "ce" (this) not "un" (a), as the manuscript prefers.

[163] would always want to decide the how and what of its use, as if he were the absolute master.

Here's what constantly happens to even the most spiritual people. They certainly want to employ only for God the three talents entrusted to them: mind, memory, and will;[32] but they always reserve to themselves the "how" to use them, the "what" to do according to their own will, as if in even these matters they should not be entirely dependent on God. This imperfection is found in all their most holy inner acts, along with such an attachment of the heart that, fully unrecognized as it is, it holds back an infinite number of souls on the beautiful path of perfection. Moreover, when it is recognized, it seems as though we are tearing out their heart every time we speak to them about this renunciation. Such also is one of the last dismantlings of the self.

Q: In what consists this dismantling of the self by the renunciation of the proprietary use over its faculties?

A: It consists in holding ourselves in a continual dependence on God, in even the use of the most holy of our soul's faculties.

Q: In what consists this continual dependence?

A: To listen, to consult, to follow in all our interior operations only the stirrings of grace without ever wanting to anticipate it, or[33] to act in any other way, or to go further than it directs. Such is what God demands from every soul who aspires to perfection, but he asks it only after the other detachments.[34] For as St. Teresa says, we

---

[32] These are the three faculties of the soul. See the parable of the talents (Matt. 25:14–30). Mind, memory, and will are expressions found in John of the Cross. *The Ascent of Mount Carmel,* bk. 2, treats of the purification of the mind, and bk. 3 that of memory and will.

[33] Olphe-Galliard writes "et" (and) instead of "ni" (or).

[34] This is one of the major themes of the *Sacrament of the Present Moment,* where, for example, we read: "The only condition necessary for this state of self-surrender *[l'abandon]* is the present

must not want to fly [164] before we have wings.[35]

Q: Should these souls called to perfection and already
        very advanced wait for an interior urging to carry
out their duties?

A: It would be an error and foolishness to think that
        they should wait. Not only the given duties of state
but also those derived by reason and common sense, each
and all are always signs of God's will that these souls have
to be careful never to miss. This continual dependence on
God and his grace extends to all that is purely free and of
our own choice.

For example, concerning inner exercises carried out
during the day, formerly these people busied themselves
holily with all kinds of deliberate acts, such as fervor for
God, expressed affections, loving conversations; but now
God makes them feel that he is calling them to something
simpler,[36] that he wants a completely different use of their
faculties, and that he wishes them to remain in peace in
direct acts of pure and simple awaiting, which David had so
well expressed with the comparison of a servant maid who
always has her eyes fastened on her mistress in order not to
act on her own but to hold all in readiness and always be

---

moment in which the soul, light as a feather, fluid as water, innocent
as a child, responds to every movement of grace like a floating bal-
loon. Such souls are like molten metal filling whatever vessel God
chooses to pour them into" (22).

[35] *Life*, chap. 31, nos. 17f., and *The Interior Castle*, III: 2, no. 12.

[36] In Fénelon's words, "Il n'est pas permis au chrétien d'atten-
dre que Dieu lui inspire ses actes par inspiration particulière, et il n'a
besoin pour s'y exciter que de la foi qui lui fait connaître la volonté de
Dieu signifiée et déclarée par ses commandements et les exemples de
saints, en supposant toujours le secours de la grâce excitante et préve-
nante" (A Christian is not permitted to expect that God will inspire
his acts by special inspirations, and he only needs to stir up in him
faith that lets him know the will of God manifested and enunciated by
his commandments and the examples of the saints, supposing always
the help of soul-stirring and attentive grace) ("XI Articles d'Issy," in
Fénelon, Pléiade ed., 1535).

disposed to obey at the least wink.[37]

Q: What great good comes to them from these peaceful acts of waiting; and how have the trials contributed to starting them on the way and to know how to hold themselves there?

A: The good that we extract is in truth inexplicable. Why? Because when God sees a soul so dispossessed of all its own wishes, even of the most holy use of its faculties, a soul in which he finds nothing determined by [165] its own choice, but rather a simple desire that he actuates in and with it according to his good pleasure, then he acts without the least obstacle. God follows the full extent of his goodness and wisdom with the most appropriate dispositions for this heart, [which is] so desirous, so upright, and so unaffected, a heart that he finds, by the way, so wary of itself, so filled with confidence and the most perfect abandonment.

But for the soul to get there, all its own wishes, even in the use of its faculties, have to be broken, tamed, and subjugated hundreds of times. The most terrifying emptiness of the mind, after having been sustained for a long time and at different occasions, has to smother or dampen every natural activity; extended inability to execute reflective and sensible acts must put us into the necessity of seeking, recognizing in our inner selves simple direct acts and learning to know to be satisfied with[38] them whenever God wants.[39]

---

[37] "Ecce, sicut oculi servorum in manibus dominorum suorum; sicut oculi ancillæ in manibus dominæ suæ: ita oculi nostri ad dominum Deum nostrum, donec misereatur nostri" ("Behold, as the eyes of servants are on the hands of their masters, as the eyes of the handmaid are on the hands of her mistress: so are our eyes unto the Lord our God, until he have mercy on us") (Ps. 122:2).

[38] Olphe-Galliard gives "ces simples actes" (these simple acts), whereas the manuscript shows "les simples actes directs" (simple direct acts).

[39] See "Perfect Faith," in *Sacrament of the Present Moment,*

Q: On the basis of all that you have said since the be-
     ginning about these simple acts of waiting during
prayer, I would say that these people ought to be in the
prayer of simple recollection during almost the whole day,
[whether their prayer is] active, infused, or mixed.

A: You are correct; this evidently follows. But I add
     that there are hardly any others besides these souls
who know and can accomplish literally the advice of St.
Paul: "You must pray [166] at all times,"[40] advice that is
still more expressly urged upon us by the words of Jesus
Christ, "Pray without ceasing."[41]

Q: Do people following the inner path do within them-
     selves anything else?

A: When God gives them nothing more, they rest there;
     always happy with what God does, and wanting
precisely[42] in themselves only what God wants. When he
stirs them to make reflective acts, to express affections, to
converse within, they do it. When grace stops stirring, they
stop right away, and just as at first, withdraw into themselves with simple recollection accompanied by silent, ardent, and always resigned acts of waiting.

Q: Are they really all faithfully abiding in this renuncia-
     tion by these ongoing acts of waiting, in order to act
only as God wishes?

---

chap. 5 (pp. 28–36).

[40] "Oportet semper orare" ("We ought always to pray") (Luke
18:1).

[41] "Sine intermissione orate" ("Pray without ceasing") (1
Thess. 5:17).

[42] Olphe-Galliard has "spécialement" (especially) instead of
"précisément" (precisely).

A: Oh! this really is necessary, but there are few who
       constantly want to hold themselves[43] thus imprisoned
within themselves, as if bound hand and foot, without any
other desire or movement than what God wants, and who
continually wait for what he will want. In truth, this captivity is so inhibiting that in order to restrain oneself well, all
self-love and all natural activity must beforehand be as if
annihilated by trials and impotencies; and then God must
relieve it with some enticements, without which this interior slavery would be unendurable.[44] [167]

Q: How and why is it that they stray out by backsliding?

A: It comes from the great longing to act within them-
       selves according to their own ideas and whims, ac-
cording to their more sensible, more conscious primitive
ways; but also they are quickly called back by interior remorse, which doesn't let them doubt that at present God
asks of them a use of their faculties quite different from
their earlier uses. Similarly, the venerable Mother de Chantal so often acknowledged this to St. Francis de Sales when
she said that she strongly felt that her imperfections and
infidelities to actual grace held her up a great deal;[45] and

---

[43] Olphe-Galliard has "leur intérieur," the singular, instead of
"leurs intérieurs," the plural, which I have translated by "within themselves."

[44] "Nevertheless, souls find themselves at a loss in this state,
without the help of the insight or discrimination that used to guide
and direct all they did, or of grace, which no longer manifests itself.
But it is in this very loss that they rediscover everything, since that
same grace, taking upon itself a new form, repays them a hundredfold
for what it has taken from them by the perfection of its hidden influence" (*Sacrament of the Present Moment,* 39).

[45] De Maupas du Tour writes the following about Jane de
Chantal: "Il lui semblait quelquefois, que toutes ses facultés et ses
puissances avaient dressé une garnison rebelle en son coeur, pour
l'empêcher de renter ès sacrés cabinets, où elle avoit si savoureusement
pris son repas et son repos, au midi des saintes faveurs de son céleste
Epoux" (Sometimes it seemed to her that all her faculties and all her
powers had constructed in her heart a rebellious garrison to keep her

that she struggled to subjugate her mind to this captivity, to this simplicity of interior acts.

Q: From all that you are saying, wouldn't it seem[46] that we are falling back instead of going forward?

A: Almost all people, even the spiritual, erroneously believe that we advance only insofar as we ourselves with grace do a greater number of perceptible and reflective actions and that we enrich ourselves visibly with graces, favors, and gifts from heaven. The beginnings and the initial advances occur in this fashion; but the great step forward and its development occur in a totally opposite way by the path of renunciation and of death to the whole sensible order in order to live only for God, as *The Imitation of Jesus Christ,* states so well in many passages.[47] Thus by becoming impoverished, we [168] are invisibly enriched with God because we continually unite ourselves more closely[48] to him.

Q: Why do we unite ourselves more closely to God by all these renunciations?

A: [1.] Since God is a unique and simple being, the more we come close to this unity and simplicity by direct actions, which do not at all scatter the soul as reflective actions do, the more there is proportion or, to speak more correctly, the less there is disproportion between God and the creature, which should be united to him.

---

from entering into those sacred rooms where she had with relish feasted and rested in the apogee of the holy favors of her celestial Spouse) (*Vie . . . Jeanne . . . Frémiot,* 421).

[46] The manuscript has "sembleroit" (it would seem), not "semble-t-il" (it seems), as in Olphe-Galliard.

[47] See "On the Royal Road of the Holy Cross," bk. 2, chap. 12 (pp. 72–77). The manuscript reads "en bien des endroits le livre" (in many parts of the book), not "si bien des endroits" (so many parts), which Olphe-Galliard gives.

[48] Olphe-Galliard gives "intensément" (intensively) instead of "étroitement" (tightly).

2. Since God is pure spirit, we can unite ourselves to him only in proportion as we ourselves become pure spirits insofar as it is possible in this life with the special graces that God gives for this purpose. Consequently, the more a soul is divested of the sensible order—what is called nakedness of the spirit—the more its union with God approaches perfection. Why? Because then there is less betwixt, as they say, God and the soul.[49]

Q: Do these souls no longer do those ordinary acts that we call reflective?

A: They do them when they should, but in a totally new way, so profound and so spiritual, so far from the senses that after lengthy conversations with God, these souls would be at a loss to recall a single act. Why? Because all that takes place inside them comes about approximately as St. Francis de Sales [169] tried to explain it in a few words to a soul who was approaching this state; this saint[50] told him: Let all your acts, so to speak, glide, slip by, distilled by the fine point of your spirit. It is thus, he adds, that they will penetrate deeper into the substance of your soul.[51]

---

[49] St. John of the Cross writes, "No creature or knowledge comprehensible to the intellect can serve it as a proximate means for the divine union with God" (*The Ascent of Mount Carmel,* II, 8).

[50] Olphe-Galliard has "le" (the) not "ce" (this).

[51] "Exercice envoyé à Mme de Villesavin" (Exercise sent to Mme de Villesavin), séries 6, opuscule 34, in *Oeuvres,* 26:332f. Caussade often cites this passage (see *Lettres spirituelles,* 1:302; 2:37, 132, 186); but in 1:174 he uses the expression "cime pointe" (uppermost point), perhaps a literal translation of the Latin *apex acies* instead of "fine pointe" (farthermost point). Nyon writes: "Mais ces traits de coeur, ces paroles intérieures doivent être prononcées doucement, et tranquillement . . . elles doivent être distillées, et filées tout bellement en la pointe de l'esprit . . . car ainsi ces sacrées paroles, filées, coulées, et distillées par la pointe de nôtre esprit, le penetreront et detremperont plus intimement et fortement, qu'elles ne feraient si elles étaient dites" (But these movements of the heart, these interior words should

Q: Don't these souls receive more interior consolations?

A: God gives them these more than ever, because he finds them so unattached, so dispossessed of themselves that he sees them in a state ready to receive interior consolations without danger of corruption by any return of self-love or pride. But you must not at all think that these consolations are similar to the earlier ones: they are as different as their state is different from the previous one. All is arranged and adjusted in an admirable way: in the first state, God was giving them sensible consolations, because then they themselves were in the senses, consequently incapable of tasting [any thing] except what is linked to the senses. But now that by[52] dint of walking before God in spirit and in pure faith they are all spiritualized, their consolations are also fully spiritual, divine, and celestial; thus, we call them pure delights of the Spirit and of pure love, because only the pure spirit tastes them and pure love[53] causes them.[54] [170]

---

be pronounced softly and calmly . . . they should be extracted and fully drawn out by the point of the mind . . . for in this way these holy words, drawn out, poured out, and extracted by the point of the mind will penetrate and sink in it more intimately and vigorously than they would do if they were spoken out loud) (*Les reliques,* 78f.). Bossuet writes, quoting Francis de Sales's advice to Jane de Chantal, "[Les actes de piété] concentrer dans le coeur, ou les porter . . . à la cime pointe de l'esprit" ([The acts of piety] concentrated in the heart, or carried . . . to the uppermost point of the mind) (*Instructions,* bk. 8, chap. 39 [p. 329]). Interestingly, the notion of the "point of the mind" comes from St. Augustine's "acies mentis" (see Gilson, *Introduction à l'étude de Saint Augustin,* 56f. n. 1, 284 n. 1, and 288–92).

[52] The manuscript has "qu'à" (that by), but Olphe-Galliard writes only "à" (by).

[53] Olphe-Galliard drops "because only pure spirit that tastes them and pure love."

[54] See what Surin writes in chap. 7, "Du fruit de ces peins, qui est lumière et abondance de biens spirituels" (On the fruit of these trials: light and abundance of spiritual goods) (379–96), in answer to the question: "Quels sont les biens de la volonté, que Dieu met en telles personnes?" (What are the assets of the will that God gives such

Q: How do trials and privations contribute to a change
      in taste?

A: Thus to accommodate our nature, God acts concern-
      ing us nearly as we do in the world concerning an
animal and earthly man who only values, only enjoys the
most coarse sensible pleasures, but in whom we want to
inspire a taste for spiritual pleasures worthy of honest folk,
as they say. In one and in the other, the taste of the soul is
purified, refined both by depriving it fully of its former
satisfactions and giving it bit by bit a new kind.

      O my God, how in everything your guidance is
worthy of respect, adoration, and love!

Q: What is the permanent state of these souls?

A: No permanent state at all can be found here below.
      By the fiat of providence, all is subject to continual
vicissitudes, but after further development, the customary
state of these souls becomes very simplified and spiritualized.

      On the one hand, there is in the mind a certain light
that,[55] fully imperceptible to them in their sensibility, conducts them, directs them in everything; and wherever they
are found, whether in flight from evil or in doing good, it
is a firmer and more[56] constant support than that found in

------

people?). "Ce sont des communications amoureuses avec l'époux
céleste, que ne se peuvent bonnement décrire. Ils ont des ardeurs
incroyables, des délices et des caresses de ce même époux, qui surpas-
sent de beaucoup la portée de nos imaginations et la force même de la
nature" (These are loving communications with the celestial spouse
that cannot be plainly described. They have unbelievable yearnings,
delectations, and caresses from this same spouse, experiences that
greatly surpass the bounds of our imagination and even the power of
nature) (*Catéchisme spirituel*, pt. 4, chap. 7 [p. 391]).

      [55] See Régis Jolivet, *Dieu soleil des esprits. La doctrine Augusti-
nienne de l'illumination*.

      [56] Olphe-Galliard omits "more" (plus).

all their former fervors, [171] tastes, and sensible inclinations, because it is the pure light of faith which never varies like all the others. Through this fully divine light, but without dazzle, God props up their weakness, as by an invisible hand that we perceive when we have been propped up in circumstances almost without knowing how or when.

[On the other hand] in the heart,

1. We find a love very different from the first, for even though greater, it is purer than the first;

[2?] However, by a special benefit of God, it usually remains hidden and unknown to the soul who possess this treasure.

Why? So that the soul[57] has less risk of losing it by acts of thinking, which can little by little lead it to depart from the beloved object by stopping too often and attaching itself to the sweet consolation of its own love,[58] says St. Francis de Sales. Such is the force and the subtlety of this self-love that appropriates all to itself.[59]

Q: But if the soul doesn't recognize it, how can we recognize it in her?

A: By three sure indicators:

1. by her lively fears of not loving God, which sometimes throw her into a kind of despair;

2. by a fierce desire to love God that devours her, although she feels in herself an incapacity to love that tears her apart; these two feelings come from the [172] same principle, since her so-called inability is basically only an insatiable love, which can never love as much as love wants to;

---

[57] The manuscript has "elle," not "il," as Olphe-Galliard shows, and so the reference has to be to the soul, which is feminine in gender.

[58] Olphe-Galliard has "de son premier amour" (its first love) instead of the manuscript's "de son propre amour" (its own love).

[59] Olphe-Galliard has "de" (of), not "et" (and), contrary to the manuscript.

3. because on the one hand we see her always ready to do everything, to suffer everything for God, and on the other hand, although she acts and suffers for God, she always believes that she does nothing or suffers nothing.

In the midst of all this, there is a peace that, by the sheer force of growing and deepening, has become as deep as the unfathomed sea. This is the peace of which St. Paul speaks,[60] which we must no longer look for in feelings because it is above the senses. Where must we look for it? In the depths of the heart, at the center of the soul, or in supreme intelligence, adds the apostle; an unshakable peace [found] not, I say, in the midst of all human upheavals to which we are then almost insensible, but in the midst of all the agitation within us. Why? Because this peace is based

---

[60] St. Francis de Sales describes the spiritual journey of the soul to union with God in "De l'union de l'âme avec son Dieu, que se parfait en l'oraison" (On the union of the soul with its God that is brought to perfection in prayer) (*Traité de l'amour de Dieu,* bk. 7, Pléiade ed., 661–709; *Oeuvres,* vol. 5 [vol. 2 of *Traité*]: 5–57). He describes the struggle for indifference and relates how God leaves sinful desires in us in order to purify us in "De l'amour de soumission par lequel notre volonté s'unit au bon plaisir de Dieu" (On the love of submission by which our will becomes united to the good pleasure of God) (*Traité de l'amour de Dieu,* bk. 9), specifically in the following chapters: "De l'indifférence que nous devons pratiquer en ce qui regarde notre avancement ès vertus" (On the indifference that we should practice for our progress in virtue) (chap. 7); "Comme la pureté de l'indifférence se doit pratiquer ès actions d'amour sacré" (How the purity of indifference should be practiced in acts of sacred love" (chap. 9); "Moyen de connaître le change au sujet de ce saint amour" (Way to know the change from this holy love) (chap. 10); "De la perplexité du coeur qui aime sans savoir qu'il plaît au bien-aimé" (On the perplexity of the heart that loves without knowing whether it is pleasing the beloved) (chap. 11); "Comme entre ces travaux intérieur l'âme ne connaît pas l'amour qu'elle porte à son Dieu et du trépas très aimable de la volonté" (How among these interior toils the soul does not know the love it has for God and of the very loving death of the will) (chap. 12) (Pléiade ed., 777–81, 784–94).

on entire submission, on perfect confidence, on total abandonment to the supreme wishes of a God as merciful as he
is powerful.[61]

---

[61] "Et pax Dei, quæ exsuperat omnem sensum, custodiat corda
vestra, et intelligentias vestras in Christo Iesu" ("And the peace of
God, which surpasseth all understanding, keep your hearts and minds
in Christ Jesus") (Phil. 4:7).

Chapter 13

RECAPITULATION OF ALL THAT HAS BEEN SAID

Q: What is the paramount aim of what has been written here and what should its conclusion be? [173]

A: The paramount aim is to make the direct and intimate acts of the heart well known, and that for five important reasons:

1. The origin and source of all deliberate and expressed acts, either from the mouth or from purely interior words, lie there in the heart, for everything springs from the free but simple movements of the heart; nothing can come out of it in any way whatsoever unless it is first conceived. Therefore, it is in their earliest stages, if we can speak in this fashion, that we must look on these direct acts, although often we cannot give birth to them, so to speak, in any way at all by reflective acts.[1]

---

[1] This paragraph clearly shows the similarity and difference between Caussade and Bossuet. Caussade holds to what Bossuet writes: "Quels sont les actes du coeur" and "Comment David les explique" (What are the acts of the heart and How David explains them) (*Instrucions,* bk. 5, chaps. 23–24 [pp. 155–57]), where Bossuet argues that God speaks to us in silence in the very depths of our hearts and hears what we are to say before we even express our thoughts interiorly. But for Bossuet the heart is really the will, the blind spiritual appetitive faculty of the soul. Intelligence plays a key role in our inner lives, for the intellect, the other faculty of the soul, presents to the will the object that attracts it and deliberates whether

2. We should all apply ourselves principally to these intimate acts, which ought to animate all our prayers and without which prayer would be no more than a vain sounding of words or a purely mental game.

3. No one should become discouraged with his prayer even if it is the least of all, which, according to the views of Msgr. de Meaux [Bossuet], is vocal prayer;[2] no one should believe herself idle as long as her mind or heart abides in her[3] intimate acts.

4. I have constantly pointed out that with respect to the prayer of simple recollection, a person ceases to fight against it when, from an exact knowledge of direct acts, he or she clearly understood that we are never without acts during this prayer, although they are not at all reflective [174] or expressed in any way.[4]

---

one should follow the impulses of the will. Thus, Bossuet calls reflection (deliberation) the eye (134) or the force (133) of the soul; reflection (deliberation) should guide us in our spiritual life. But Caussade, who follows a Fénelonian tack, holds our reflections (deliberations) in great suspicion and urges us to follow the spontaneous movements coming up from within us, in order to keep selfish thinking from poisoning the inspirations that God gives us.

[2] Bossuet writes: "Les actes . . . les plus impurs . . . sont ceux qu'on reduit en formule et qu'on fait comme on les trouve dans les livers sous ce titre: acte de contrition, acte d'offrande et ainsi des autres" (The most impure . . . acts . . . are those that we reduce into a formula and recite as we find them in books entitled: act of contrition, offering act, and so on for others) (*Instructions,* bk. 5, chap. 18 [p. 155]). Interestingly, earlier Bossuet writes: "Au contraire regulièrement parlant, comme un peché commis avec reflexion a plus de malice, il semble aussi qu'un acte vertueux produit avec reflexion et avec une connoisance plus expresse ait plus de bonté" (On the contrary, properly speaking, just as a sin committed with deliberation has more malice, so it also seems that a virtuous act done with deliberation and with more explicit knowledge has greater good) (ibid., bk. 5, chap. 16 [p. 147]).

[3] Olphe-Galliard substituted "des" (the) for "ses" (her).

[4] Bossuet writes: "Le langage du coeur, sur tout dans l'acte d'amour, qui ne se peut ni ne se veut expliquer à Dieu que par luy-

5. This same knowledge could serve those who, in order to acquire[5] infused recollection, would have enough courage to subjugate themselves

a. to constant practice of the four kinds of purity,[6] which are the remote dispositions for this double prayer, and

[b.] to the exercise of attentive pauses, which are the proximate directions.

Q: What practical conclusion should follow?

A: It is fully expressed in the following dispositions:

1. Let all apply themselves with care to their usual prayer, since on the one hand there cannot be attentive pauses without prayer and, on the other hand, none ought to give up their prayer, except insofar as God himself withdraws them little by little when it pleases him, and in the way he wants.

2. While continuing their prayer in this way, they should let these pauses be more or less frequent and long, depending on how it pleases God to speak, to communicate himself, to make himself felt within the self.

---

mesme. On ne luy dit qu'on l'aime qu'en aimant, et le coeur alors parle à Dieu seul. Si l'on vient et jusqu'où l'on vient à la perfection d'un tel acte pendant cette vie, et si l'on en peut venir jusqu'au point de faire entierement cesser au-dedans de soy toute image et toute parole, je le laisse à décider aux parfaits spirituels" (The language of the heart, especially in acts of love, can and wants to communicate with God only through itself. We tell him we love him only in loving him, and then the heart speaks with God alone. If we achieve and up to the point where we achieve the perfection of such an act during this life and if we can arrive at the point where we fully cease to entertain every image and every word within ourselves—I let the totally adept spirituals decide about it) (*Instructions,* bk. 5, chap. 20 [p. 152]); see above, chap. 6, ques. 7.

[5] The manuscript has "acquerir" (acquire), but Olphe-Galliard writes "accueillir" (receive).

[6] Purity of conscience, heart, mind, and action.

3. Because God usually only communicates in proportion to the purity of the soul, let them apply themselves therefore to acquire the four kinds of purity.

4. In proportion to these proximate and remote dispositions, they will enter into and be established in recollection of whatever kind it might be. It is precisely then that those to whom God has given this grace can apply themselves to the three recommendations just given, [175] each according to his or her actual state as either beginner, progressing, or advanced.

[5] In addition I beg certain individuals

a. not to consider fully lost for them the time that I used both to give a rough idea of their prayer and to parry those who attack it only because they lack knowledge of it, since basically all this only tends to anticipate the specious doubts that could come to trouble these people inopportunely;

b. Moreover, I implore them not to be at all surprised to discover so little instruction for themselves and[7] comfort in this book except towards the end, because I have limited myself to speak only, on the one hand, of the usual simple recollection and, on the other hand, to people at the lowest degree of this prayer. Why? Because I often found that, lacking a firm enough practice of purity of conscience, heart, mind, or action, most of these good souls hardly ever move beyond the lowest degree of simple recollection, the kind we call mixed; that is to say, partly acquired, partly infused, but almost always practiced with a great deal of imperfection[8] and [176] sometimes so feebly that to maintain it they need to return to their first discursive acts, to their old affections formerly expressed and developed interiorly.

---

[7] Olphe-Galliard substituted "ou" (or) for "et" (and).

[8] In the singular, not the plural as Olphe-Galliard gives.

Q: In spite of all your warnings, which, so it seems, go
       very far, can it not truly happen that someone mis-
uses this treatise?

A: Didn't we say and show in the beginning[9] that there
       isn't anything that we don't abuse and, furthermore,
that if in matters of devotion and piety we must remove
all[10] that has so often been misused, there would remain
almost nothing; and, moreover, that we would no longer
speak about anything, not even preach,[11] except about what
is purely necessary? But let what I have written receive the
same reception as a sermon: isn't it true that after a solid
sermon dealing with nonessential matters but including
topics as delicate as they are useful, there can be some
minds (and[12] they are found everywhere) who take things
somewhat the wrong way? In these circumstances, the usual
rejoinder is that the preacher explained himself fairly clearly; too bad for evil minds who will want to make bad use
of what was said; good people will profit from the preaching. However, there is a great deal of difference between
words that fly by so quickly and a written piece that remains under our eyes. Let us apply the principle that leads
people of good sense to speak thus [177] in matters of
preaching, by comparing here, as we do in everything, the
good of the thing with its shortcomings; that is, the profit
for which we can hope—the great number who can profit
from it—to the badly founded fears with respect to a very
small number. Moreover, I cannot conceive how anyone in
this small band of idiots and weak-minded [readers] could
misuse it or any part of it. By the way, aren't there everywhere confessors and directors for these kinds of people,
who usually (we must render them this justice) are fairly
docile through timidity or ignorance?

----

[9] Chap. 3, ques. 1.

[10] Olphe-Galliard drops "tout" (all).

[11] Olphe-Galliard adds here to the text "si ce n'est" (if this is
not).

[12] Olphe-Galliard drops "et" (and).

Q: Won't someone perhaps ask why you didn't in the beginning dwell extensively on the fear of self-delusion?

A: The reason is that I preferred to apply my principles for[13] everyone, to warn people rather than to waste time dwelling on a fear that the whole world recognizes and that often produces effects totally contrary to those we had in view.[14]

Q: What are these principles and means?

A: [1.] First of all, to cut out everything that is extraordinary and that could have even the appearance of it, because the Gospel teaches me that all that elevates the spirit of man humbles him before God[15] and that the most humbling prayer of whatever kind it may be is always the best, were it even vocal.[16] [178]

2. Because self-love and pride are the true sources of every self-delusion and because we observe how they are in everything and everywhere, I did not cease to pursue these two monsters right into their innermost lairs. There's where I tried to cut the roots of every self-delusion, of every disorder, of every imperfection.

Q: After all that you come to add, I have only one question; let me ask it. Everywhere[17] there are minds who, unwilling to deepen anything, are satisfied with staying on the surface of things; they reject everything on the most trivial pretexts. Aren't there also those so biased that they hardly see the demonstrations that go against their old ideas and deeply rooted convictions? Aren't there those [who], rather than admitting humbly before God and tell-

---

[13] Olphe-Galliard writes "Par" (by) instead of "Pour" (for).

[14] Note that François Guilloré, whom Caussade draws on, spent time discussing the danger of self-delusions in the spiritual life (see his *Illusions de la vie spirituelle*).

[15] Matt. 19:30, Mark 10:31, and Luke 13:30.

[16] E.g., the prayer of the publican; see Luke 18:13.

[17] Olphe-Galliard writes "Parmi [tant]" (among so many) instead of "Partout les" (everywhere).

ing themselves in their own hearts that they have badly
understood, badly judged, perhaps badly spoken since they
are insufficiently informed, only split hairs, wrangle about
everything, so as to preserve a vain pretext in order to
continue to censure what they had censured before? Aren't
there those who believe themselves perfectly informed
about all that concerns Christian piety, so that at the instant
when they hear what they haven't yet read or thought,
conclude that it is a novelty, [179] that such are chimeras
or errors?[18] Finally, aren't there those who, by a zeal much
more cautious than penetrating, sometimes mingle the true
with the false and then combat the truth with all the fervor
of their good intentions?[19] How can we answer such a
variety of different[20] mental makeups?

A: By silence and prayer.

Great God, who for purposes unknown to us have
from all eternity orchestrated a collection of small circumstances that all together have contributed to the production
of this little book, do not allow [the wise] or [the devout]
to have[21] any reason to upbraid themselves at death's door

---

[18] See above chap. 3: "Abuses and Errors to Fear from This
Prayer." Caussade is attacking his critics, especially the Jansenists.

[19] Might not Caussade be criticizing Bossuet and revealing his
true views concerning Bossuet's attacks on Fénelon?

[20] Olphe-Galliard drops "differents."

[21] Olphe-Galliard transcribes this passage thus: "Les uns ni les
autres ayons" [instead of "les unes" (les personnes sages) "ni les autres" (les dévotes) "ayent"] sujet de se reprocher au lit de la mort
d'avoir jamais entrepris de vous fermer l'entré de je ne scay combien
de coeur." The version that is published by Olphe-Galliard after the
text of the *Instructions spirituelles* as part of "Manière courte et facile
pour faire l'oraison en foi et de simple présence de Dieu par Monseigneur Bossuet, évêque de Meaux" (A short and simple way to practice
the prayer of faith and of simple presence of God by Msgr. Bossuet,
bishop of Meaux) (361–71) has here: "Ne permettez pas que certains
esprits, dont les uns se rangent parmi les savants, les autres parmi le
spirituels, puissent jamais être accusé à votre redoutable tribunal
d'avoir contribué en aucune sorte à vous fermer l'entrée de je sais

for ever having undertaken to block you from the entrance to hearts—how many they are I don't know—because you wanted to enter by a way they didn't like and by a door that was perhaps unknown to them. I am not asking enough. Great God, also make all of us become as small as children, as Jesus Christ commands,[22] [and grant that] these, once entering by this little door, may soon call thither your good servants, your humble servants, with greater power and effectiveness than I would ever know how to bring about. Amen, Jesus.[23]

---

combien de coeurs" (367). In the Thorold edition this reads: "Do not permit certain spirits, some of whom are among the scholars and others among the spiritual, to be accused before thy dread Tribunal of having helped in any way towards closing the way to thee to number-less hearts" (286; 272f. in the 2nd ed. revised of 1949).

[22] Matt. 18:3.

[23] A slightly modified version of this prayer concludes the "Manière courte et facile pour faire l'oraison en foi et de simple pré-sence de Dieu par Monseigneur Bossuet [?], évêque de Meaux" (A short and simple way to practice the prayer of faith and of simple presence of God by Msgr. Bossuet, bishop of Meaux). This "short and simple way" is published at the end of Caussade's *Instructions spirituel-les* in Olphe-Galliard's edition of Caussade's *Traité sur l'oraison du coeur, Instructions spirituelles* on pp. 361–71; in the English translation of 1931, it appears on pp. 279–86 and in the English edition of 1949 on pp. 266–73; but it is not found in the manuscript version of the "Manière courte" preserved at Nancy and published by Le Brun in *Opuscule spirituels de Bossuet,* 51–55. Pierre de Clorivière's version of the "Moyen court et facile" (Short and simple way) in his "Règlement dressé par M. Bossuet pour ceux qui sont dans cet état d'oraison" (Rule established by Msgr. Bossuet for those who are in this state of prayer) omits the concluding prayer (*Considérations sur l'exercice de la prière et de l'oraison,* no. 31, [pp. 148–53]).

BIBLIOGRAPHY

Álvarez, Baltasar. *See* La Puente.

Anné Sainte des religieuses de la Visitation Sainte-Marie. 12 vols., with a table in 12:809. Annecy: Ch. Bardet and Lyon: P.-N. Josserad, 1867–71.

Articles d'Issy. See Fénelon, *Oeuvres.*

Augustine, St. *Augustine of Hippo: Selected Writings.* Ed. Mary T. Clark. Ramsey: Paulist Press, 1984.

———. *City of God.* Trans. Marcus Dods. New York: Random House; The Modern Library, 1950.

———. *Confessions.* 3 vols. Oxford: Clarendon Press, 1992.

   Vol. 1: Latin text; vols. 2–3: commentary. English translation by Henry Chadwick (Oxford: Oxford University Press; World's Classics paperback, 1992). French translation with Latin text in *Bibliothèque augustinienne,* nos. 13 and 14, vol. 13. (Paris: Desclée de Brouwer, 1962).

———. *De trinitate libri XV* (libri I–XII). In *Opera,* pt. 16, i. Corpus Christianorum, series latina, vol. 50. Turnhout: Brepols, 1968.

———. *Enarrationes in psalmos I–L.* In *Opera,* pt. 10, 1. Corpus Christianorum, series latina, vol. 38. Turnhout: Brepols, 1956.

———. "Quæstiones XVI in Matthæum." In *Opera,* pt. 12, 3, pp. 124–32. Corpus Christianorum, series latina, vol. 44. B. Turnhout: Brepols, 1980.

———. *Sermones.* In *Opera,* pt. 11, 1, pp, 501–6. Corpus Christianorum, series latina, vol. 41. Turnhout: Brepols, 1961.

Baiole, André. *De la vie intérieure.* Paris: N. Boin, 1649.

Baron, Roger. "L'Influence de Hugues de Saint-Victor." *Recherches de théologie ancienne et médiévale* 22 (1955): 64–71.

————. *Science et sagesse chez Hugues de Saint-Victor*. Paris: Lethielleux, 1957.

Bellere du Tronchay, de. *For biography see* Maillard, Jean, *Le Triomph de la pauvreté*.

Bérulle, Pierre de. *Oeuvres complètes*. Paris: J.-A. Migne, 1856.

Bible, The Holy. Rockford: Tan Books and Publishers, 1989; photographic reproduction of Baltimore: John Murphy Co., 1899.

> This is the Douay-Rheims Bible (OT Douay, 1609, and NT Rheims, 1582) as revised and compared with the Latin Vulgate by Bishop Richard Challoner in 1749–52; I have used this edition for the English translations of the Vulgate.

Biblia sacra juxta Vulgatam clementinam, nova editio. 8th ed. Madrid: Biblioteca de Autores Christianos, 1985.

> Even though this edition does give the new and old version of the Psalms, it is not a faithful reproduction of the post-Tridentine Vulgate.

Boland, André, S.J. "Le Père Jean-Pierre de Caussade, auteur mystique." *Nouvelle revue de théologie* 107 (1985): 238–54.

————. *Dictionnaire de spiritualité*, s.v. "Présent (Moment)." Vol. 12, pt. 2, cols. 2136–68.

Bonaventure, St. *See also* Le Roux, *Traités spirituels*.

Bonaventure, St. *Itinerarium mentis in Deum*, in *Itinéraire de l'esprit vers Dieu*. 6th ed. Paris: Libraire Philosophique J. Vrin, 1990.

————. *Opera omnia*. 5 vols. Lyon: Phil. Borde, Laur. Arnaud, Petri Borde, 1668.

————. *The Soul's Journey into God; The Tree of Life; The Life of Saint Francis*. Ramsey: Paulist Press, 1978.

Bossuet, Jacques-Bénigne. *Instruction sur les états d'oraison*. 2nd ed. Paris: Anisson, 1697.

> References are given to this edition; this second edition has twenty more pages than the first edition of the same date; otherwise it is identical.

Boudon, Henri-Marie, archdeacon of Evreux (1624–1702). *Dieu seul, ou l'association pour l'intérest de Dieu seul*. Paris: F. Lambert, 1663.

————. *Oeuvres complètes*. Paris: Migne, 1856.

———. *Les Saintes Voies de la croix*. Paris: Estienne Michallet, 1687.

    The copy of this edition preserved at Les Fontaines at Chantilly came from the Monastère de la Visitation Sainte Maire de Dole.

Bremond, Henri. *Bossuet, maître d'oraison: Instructions spirituelles en forme de dialogues sur les divers états d'oraison suivant la doctrine de M. Bossuet, par le père Caussade de la Compagnie de Jésus, docteur en théologie*. New edition in accord with the original edition of 1741, with an introduction and notes by Henri Bremond. Paris: Bloud et Gay, 1931.

———. *Histoire littéraire du sentiment religieux en France*. 11 vols. and index. Paris: Bloud et Gay, 1916–1932; photo ed., Paris: Armond Colin, 1967–71. This edition lacks pts. 2 and 3 of vol. 3 (i.e., pp. 281–698).

Camus, Jean-Pierre. *L'Esprit de saint François de Sales*. Paris: Gaume Frères, 1840.

    This is a faithful representation of the original edition; the edition by Pierre Collot (2nd ed. revised and corrected [Paris: Jacques Estienne, 1731]) abridges and changes the original edition.

———. *La Luitte spirituelle, ou encouragement à une âne tentée de l'esprit de blaspheme, et d'infidelité*. Paris: Sebastien Huré, 1631.

Cassian. *Conférences*. Mahwah: Paulist Press, 1985.

    Also found in Owen Chadwick, *Western Asceticism*, 190–289. Philadelphia; The Westminster Press, 1958.

Catherine of Siena, St. *The Dialogue*. Ramsey: Paulist Press, 1980.

———. *Le Dialogue*. Trans. and ed. Lucienne Portier. Paris: Editions du Cerf, 1992.

———. *Lettres*. Trans. E. Cartier. Paris: Editions P. Téqui, 1976; reproduced in Paris: Poussielgue, 1886.

———. *Les Oraisons*. Trans. and ed. Lucienne Portier. Paris: Editions du Cerf, 1992.

Caussade, Jean Pierre. *L'Abandon à le providence divine*. Paris: Desclée de Brouwer, 1966.

    The English translations made before 1966 (e.g., that of John Beevers) are based on the editions of Fr. Henri Ramière, which were published during the second half of the nineteenth century. Unfortunately, Ramière's editions differ significantly from the manuscript on which he worked. Olphe-Galliard's edition, which follows the manuscript and is much more reliable than Ramière's, is published in English as *The Sacrament of the Present Moment,* trans. Kitty Muggeridge (New York: Harper and Row, 1982; first published at Glasgow: William Collins Sons & Co., 1981). A study in *Bulletin de littérature écclésiastique* of L'Institut catholique de Toulouse (82 [January 1981]: 25–54) argues convincingly that chap. 1 of *L'Abandon* is a letter of Caussade but that the rest of the treatise is by Mme Guyon.

———. *Instructions spirituelles en forme de dialogues sur les divers états d'oraison suivant la doctrine de M. Bossuet, évêque de Meaux.* Perpignan: Jean-Baptiste Reynier, 1741; republished at Avignon: Sequin, 1825.

This work was actually published under the name of Paul-Gabriel Antoine; Henri Bremond published it under the title *Bossuet, maître d'oraison* (Paris: Bloud et Gay, 1931); a truncated edition of only the second part was published in Perpignan in 1758, then Ludovic de Besse published it in 1891. Canon Bussenot reproduced this edition in 1892 and 1895; thereafter it included Olphe-Galliard's edition. The 1931 English translation is not truncated: Jean Pierre de Caussade, *On Prayer: Spiritual Instructions on the Various States of Prayer according to the Doctrine of Bossuet, Bishop of Meaux,* trans. Algar Thorold with introduction by John Chapman, abbot of Downside (London: Burns Oates and Washbourne, 1931; 2nd rev. ed., 1949).

———. *Lettres spirituelles.* Ed. Michel Olphe-Galliard. Paris: Desclée de Brouwer, vol. 1 in 1962 and vol. 2 in 1964.

———. *Traité sur l'oraison du coeur, Instructions spirituelles.* Ed. Michel Olphe-Galliard, Collection Christus, no. 49. Paris: Desclée de Brouwer, 1981.

———. "Texte inédits du père de Caussade publiés par Jacques Le Brun." *Revue d'ascétique et de mystique* 46 (1970): 99–114, 219–30, 321–54, 429–48; 47 (1971): 75–88; publication of MS 1092 of Bibliothèque Publique de Nancy.

———. MS letters found by Fr. Paul Veyron, S.J., from Dijon, a photocopy of which can be found at the Bibliothèque des Fontaines in Chantilly.

———. "Traité sur l'oraison du coeur." MS 12° 202 at the Bibliothèque des Fontaines in Chantilly.

Cavallera, F. "Caussade, auteur des *Instructions spirituelles.*" *Revue d'ascétique et de mystique* 12 (1931): 179f.

Cayré, Fulbert. *Initiation à la philosophie de saint Augustin.* Paris: Desclée de Brouwer, 1947.

———. *Les Sources de l'amour divin. La divine présence d'après saint Augustin.* Paris: Desclée de Brouwer, 1933.

Certeau, Michel de, "L'Illettré éclairé dans l'histoire de la lettre de Surin sur le Jeune Homme du Coche (1630)." *Revue d'ascétique et de mystique* 44 (1968): 369–412.

Champion, Pierre. *La Vie du Père Jean Rigoleu de la Compagnie de Jésus avec ses traitez de dévotion, et ses lettres spirituelles.* 3rd ed. revised and enlarged, with biog. Paris: Imbert de Bats, 1698.

Champion, Pierre. *La Vie et la doctrine spirituelle du père L. Lallemant.* Paris: Estienne Michallet, 1694.

Chaugy, Françoise-Madeleine de, Mère. "Mémoires sur la vie et les oeuvres de sainte Jeanne-Françoise Frémyot de Chantal." Vol. 1 of *Sainte Jeanne . . . de Chantal. Sa vie et ses oeuvres,* q.v.

Cherel, Albert. *Fénelon au XVIIIe siècle en France (1715–1820), son prestige, son influence.* Paris: Hachette, 1917; reprinted at Geneva: Slatkine Reprints, 1970.

Clorivière, Pierre de. *Considérations sur l'exercice de la prière et de l'oraison.* Ed. André Rayez. Paris: Desclée de Brouwer, 1961.

Cognet, Louis. *Crépuscule des mystiques. Le conflit Fénelon-Bossuet.* Paris: Desclée de Brouwer; new edition by Armogathe, 1991.

———. "Bérulle et la théologie de l'Incarnation." *Revue du XVII siècle,* no. 29 (October, 1955).

Colliander, Tito. *Way of the Ascetics.* San Francisco: Harper & Row, 1982.

Combès, Gustave. *La Charité d'après saint Augustin.* Paris: Desclée de Brouwer, 1934.

Crasset, Jean. *Vie de Madame Heylot.* Paris: Estienne Michalet, 1683.

Crouslé, L. *Fénelon et Bossuet, étude morale et littéraire.* 2 vols. Paris: Champion, 1894–95.

Daubenton, Guillaume. *La Vie du bienheureux Jean-François Regis.* Paris: Nicolas Leclerc, 1716.

De Maupas du Tour, Msgr. Henri. *See* Maupas du Tour, Msgr. Henri de.

D'Istria, Madeleine Huillet. *Le Père de Caussade et la querelle du pur amour.* Paris: Aubier, 1964.

Dubay, Thomas. *Fire Within.* San Francisco: Ignatius Press, 1989.

Dudon, Paul. "Les Leçons d'oraison du père Balthazar Alvarez (1573–1578)." *Revue d'ascétique et de mystique* 2 (1921): 36–57.

———. "Note sur les éditions du P. de Caussade." *Revue d'ascétique et de mystique* 11 (1930): 63–71.

Evagrius Ponticus. *The Praktikos-Chapters on Prayer.* Ed. John Eudes Bamberger. Spencer, Mass.: Cistercian Publications, 1970.

Fénelon, François de Salignac. *Articles d'Issy.* In *Oeuvres* (Pléiade ed.), 1:1543–38.

———. *Letters of Love and Counsel.* Trans. and ed. John McEwen, with intro. by Thomas Merton. New York: Harcourt, Brace & World, 1964.

———. *Oeuvres spirituelles.* Vol. 1. of *Oeuvres.* Ed. and annotated by Jacques Le Brun. Paris: Gallimard, Bibliothèque de la Pléiade, 1983.

This work, which will be cited as Pléiade, includes the following:

1. *Lettres et opuscules spirituels,* 555–777, 1415–69 (the best critical edition)

2. *Explication des maximes des saints sur la vie intérieure,* 999–1095 and 1530–1607

3. *Réponse . . . à . . . [la] rélation sur le quiétisme,* 1097–99 and 1607–23

Francis de Sales, St. *Correspondance. Les lettres d'amitié spirituelle.* Ed. André Ravier. Paris: Desclée de Brouwer, 1980.

———. *Les Epistres du bienheureux Messire François de Sales, évesque et Prince de Genève.* Ed. Jane de Chantal and Louis de Sales. Lyon: Vincent de Coeursilly, 1662; the 1758 edition was modified by Corru.

———. *Introduction à la vie dévote.* Last edition reviewed, corrected, and enlarged by the author while preaching in Paris and published by Henrion from the only known copy preserved at the Abbey of Belmont. Tours: Mame, 1930; republished by Club du Livre Religieux in 1956.

————. *Introduction à la vie dévote.* In *Oeuvres,* Pléiade ed., 3:3–317. English translation by John K Ryan. Garden City: Image Books, 1955.

————. *Oeuvres.* Paris: Gallimard, Bibliothèque de la Pléiade, 1969.

This work, which will be cited as Pléiade, includes *Entretiens spirituels,* 973–1347, and *Traité de l'amour de Dieu,* 319–972. In both cases the best critical editions are from Pléiade.

————. *Oeuvres de saint François de Sales, evêque de Genève et docteur de l'Eglise.* Complete ed. after the autographs and the original editions, . . . published . . . under the care of the Religieuses de la Visitation du 1ᵉʳ Monastère d'Annecy. 27 vols. Annecy: J Niérat, et al., 1892–1964).

Vol. 26, the last volume of text, appeared in 1932; vol. 27 (1964) contains indices; vols. 11–21 (1900–1923) contain his extant correspondence of about 2,100 letters, about 10 percent of his actual correspondence. I cite this standard edition as *Oeuvres;* but for *Traité de l'amour de Dieu* (herein vols. 4 and 5 or vols. 1 and 2 of *Traité*) and for *Entretiens,* one should use the Pléiade edition.

François de Sales and Jeanne de Chantal: Letters of Spiritual Direction. Mahwah: Paulist Press, 1988.

Gagey, Jacques. "*Le Traité,* où l'on découvre la vraie science de la perfection du salut et la tradition spirituelle caussadienne. Histoire critique et théologie." 3 vols. Doctoral dissertation presented at the Pontifical Gregorian University in Rome, 1993–94.

Gilson, Etienne. *Introduction à l'étude de saint Augustin.* 3rd ed. Paris: Vrin, 1949.

Gondal, Marie-Louise. *Madame Guyon.* Paris: Beauchesne, 1989.

Gosselin, "Analyse raisonnée de la controverse du quiétisme." In *Oeuvres de Fénelon.* Vol 4, pp. lxxvii–cxxviii and ccxxix–ccxxxiv (additions and corrections). Versailles: J. A. Lebel, 1820.

Guibert, Joseph de, S.J. *The Jesuits, Their Spiritual Doctrine and Practice.* Chicago: Loyola University Press, 1964; St. Louis: The Institute of Jesuit Sources, 1972. A translation of *La Spiritualité de la Compagnie de Jésus* (Rome: Historical Institute of the Society of Jesus, 1953).

Guillaumont, Antoine. "Les Sens des noms de coeur dans l'anti-quité." In *Le Coeur,* no. 10, pp. 41–81. Paris: Les Etudes carmélitaines, 1950.

Guilloré, François. *Oeuvres spirituelles.* Paris: Estenne Michallet, 1684.

> Contained in this volume are "Les Progrès de la vie spirituelle selon les diférents états de l'âme," 417–638 (1st ed. at Paris: Estienne Michallet, 1675); "Des illusions des austérités," 644–51; "Les Illusions des prières vocales et des pratiques," 670–75; "Les Illusions de la vie spirituelle," 701–8.

Guyon, Jeanne Marie Bouvier de la Mothe. *Les Opuscules spirituels.* Hildesheim: Georg Olms, 1978; photoedition of Cologne: Pierre Poiret, 1720.

> 1. *Moyen court,* 1–78
>
> 2. *Les Torrents,* 129–276.

———. *Récits de captivité inédit.* Paris: Editions Jérôme Millon, 1992.

———. "La Vie de Madame Guyon écrite par elle-même." Ed. Jean Bruno. In *Les Cahiers de la Tour Saint-Jacques,* 6:v–144. Paris: H. Roudil.

Hand, Thomas A. *St. Augustine on Prayer.* Westminster: Newman Press, 1963.

Heylot, Claude. *For biography see* Crasset, *Vie de Madame Heylot.*

Heylot, Claude, *Oeuvres spirituelles.* Paris: J.-B. Coignard, 1710.

Hillenaar, Henk. *Fénelon et les jésuites.* The Hague: Martinus Nij-hoff, 1967.

Hugh of Balma. *Mystica theologia.*

> This work is published in St. Bonaventure, *Opera om-nia* (Lyon: Phil. Borde, Laur. Arnaud, Petri Borde, 1668), tome 7 (in the fifth bound volume), pp. 657c2–687c1. It is also published under title of *Théologie mystique,* vols. 1 and 2, in *Sources chrétiennes,* no. 408–9 (Paris: Editions du Cerf, 1995–96).

Hugh of Saint Victor. *See also* Baron, Roger, *Science et sagesse.*

Hugh of Saint Victor. *De arrha animæ* (Treatise on the foretastes of the soul joined to God). In Patrologiæ cursus latinæ, ed. J.-P. Migne, vol. 176.

Ignatius of Loyola, St. *Exercitia spiritualia.* Paris: Imprimerie Royale, 1643.

    For an English translation see *The Spiritual Exercises of Saint Ignatius,* trans. with commentary by George E. Ganss, S.J. (Saint Louis: The Institute of Jesuit Sources, 1992).

Jane de Chantal, St. *See also* Chaugy, "Mémoires sur la vie et les oeuvres."

Jane Frances Frémyot de Chantal, St. *Doctrine spirituelle de . . . Chantal.* Paris: Monastère de la Visitation, 1980; reprint of second edition of 1928 compiled by Denys Mézard.

————. *Les Épistres spirituelles de la Mère Jeanne-Françoise Frémiot . . . fidèlemment reueillies par les religieuses du monastère d'Annes-sy.* Ed. Mother Marie-Aimée de Blomay. Lyon: Vincent de Coeursillys, 1644, 1666; 8th ed. Paris: Siméon Piget, 1667.

————. "Petit traité sur l'oraison." In *Oeuvres* ("Oeuvres Diverses II"), 3:260–96; or *Doctrine spirituelle,* 187–240.

————. *Réponses de notre très honorée et digne Mère Jeanne-Françoise Frémiot, sur les règles, constitutions et coutumes de nostre ordre de la Visitation.* Paris, 1665.

————. *Vive Jésus réponses . . . sur les règles, constitutions, et coustu-mier.* 2nd ed. Paris: n. p., 1665.

Sainte Jeanne-Françoise Frémyot de Chantal. Sa vie et ses oeuvres.

    Authoritative edition published under the care of the religious of the first monastery of La Visitation Sainte-Marie d'Annecy. 8 vols. Paris: Plon, 1874–79.

John of the Cross. *The Collected Works.* Trans. with intro. by Kieran Kavanaugh and Otilio Rodriguez. ICS Publications: Washington D.C., 1973.

————. *Les oeuvres spirituelles . . . nouvellement revues et très-exacte-ment corrigées sur l'original par le R. P. Cyprien de la Nativité de la Vierge.* Paris: Veuve Pierre Chevalier, 1652.

    This volume also contains a theological clarification of the mystical phrases used by St. John of the Cross, pre-pared by Fr. Nicolas de Jésus Maria, lecturer in theology at the College of Salamanca. It features as well notes and commentary to provide a greater understanding of the mystical expressions and the doctrine found in this volume, prepared by Fr. Jacques de Jésus, prior of the Monastère des Carmes Deschaussez at Toledo and translated from the

Spanish by M. R. G. C. D. R. The entire work was translated into French by Fr. Cyprien of the Nativity of the Virgin.

Jolivet, Régis. *Dieu soleil des esprits. La doctrine augustinienne de l'illumination.* Paris: Desclée de Brouwer, 1933.

Kempis, Thomas à. *De imitatione Christi libri quatuor,* ed. P. A. Fleury (Turin: A. Mame and Sons, 1925).
———. *The Imitation of Christ.* South Bend: Greenlawn Press, 1990; Knox/Oakley translation of 1959).

La Puente, Louis. *La Vie du père Baltasar Alvares.* Paris: Charles Chastellain, 1618.

La Rivière, Louis de. *Vie de l'illustrissime et révérendissime François de Sales.* Lyon: P. Rigaud, 1625.

Lafuma, Louis. "L'Ordre de l'esprit et l'ordre du coeur selon Pascal." *Recherches de science religieuse* 46 (1958): 416–20.

Lallemant, Louis. *See also* Champion, *La Vie et la doctrine spirituelle.*

Lallemant, Louis. *Doctrine spirituelle.* Paris: Estienne Michallet, 1694.
This work was reedited by François Courel, S.J. (Paris: Desclée de Brouwer, 1979; 3rd ed. in Collection Christus, no. 3). Citations in this book will be made from the 1979 edition.

Languet, Jean-Joseph. *Traité de la confiance en la miséricorde de Dieu.* Paris: Viva Raymond Mixers, 1720.
———. *La Vie de la Vénérable Mère Marguerite-Marie [Alacoque].* Paris: Ve Mixers et J.-B. Garnier, 1729.

Laporte, Jean. *Le Coeur et la raison selon Pascal.* Paris: Editions Elzévir, 1950, reprinted from an article appearing in *Revue philosophique,* 1927.

Le Brun, Jacques. *See also* Caussade, "Texte inédits."

Le Brun, Jacques. "Caussade." In Josef Sudbrack and James Walsh. *Grosse Gestalten christlicher Spiritualität,* 310–321. Würzburg: Echter, 1969.
———. "Entre la mystique et la morale." *Dix-huitième siècle* 8 (1976): 46ff.
———. *Les Opuscules spirituels de Bossuet. Recherches sur les traditions nancéiennes.* In *Annales de l'Est,* no. 38. Nancy: Presses Universitaires de Nancy, 1970.

———. "Quelques documents relatifs au père de Caussade conservés aux Archives de Meurthe-et-Moselle." *Revue d'ascétique et de mystique* 40 (1964): 477–80.

Le Coeur. In *Les Etudes carmélitaines.* 29th year. Paris: Desclée de Brouwer, 1950.

Le Roux, François. *Traités spirituels tirés de St. Bonaventure pour l'instruction des religieux, et de toutes sortes de personnes, qui veulent se régler et faire du progrès dans la piété.* Collected, translated, and organized by the author. 2 vols. Paris: Edme Couterot, 1693.

Leclerq, Joseph. "Jansénisme et doctrine de la prière chez Pierre Nicole." *Revue diocésaine de Tournai* 4 (1951): 97–116.

Louf, André. *Tuning In to Grace: The Quest for God.* Kalamazoo: Cistercian Publications, 1992.

Maillard, Jean. *Le Triomphe de la pauvreté et des humiliations, ou la vie de Mlle de Bellère du Tronchay, appelée communément soeur Louise, avec ses lettres.* Paris: G. Martin, 1732.

Maupas du Tour, Henri de, *La Vie de la vénérable Jeanne Françoise Frémiot, fondatrice, première Mère et religieuse de l'ordre de la Visitation de sainte Marie.* Paris: Siméon Piget, 1644; 3rd ed., Paris: Simeon Piget, 1645.

Mézard, Denys. *See* Jane de Chantal, *Doctrine spirituelle.*

Morel, Robert. *De l'espérance chrétienne et de la confiance en Dieu.* Paris: Vincent and Lottin, 1728.

Nicole, Pierre. *See also* Leclercq, "Jansénisme et doctrine de la prière."

Nicole, Pierre. *Imaginaires et les visionnaires.* Liège: Adolphe Beyer, 1692.

———. *Réfutation des principales erreurs des quiétistes contenues dans les livres censurés par Msgr. l'archevêque de Paris du 16 octobre 1694.* Paris: E. Josset, 1695.

———. *Traité de l'oraison, divisé en sept livres.* 3rd ed. Lyon: C. de la Roche et Claude Rey, 1686.

Nyon, Jean. *Reliques du B. François de Sales.* Lyon: Vincent de Coeursilly, 1626.

Olphe-Galliard, Michel. *La Théologie mystique en France au XVIII siècle.* Paris: Beauchesne, 1984.

———. *Traité sur l'oraison du coeur* et *Instructions spirituelles.* Collection Christus, no. 49. Paris: Desclée de Brouwer; Montréal: Bellarmin, 1979.

———. "Le J.-P. de Caussade, directeur d'âmes." *Revue d'ascétique et de mystique,* vol. 19 (1938).

Pascal, Blaise. *Pensées.* In *Oeuvres complètes.* Ed. Louis Lafuma, 493–649. Paris: Seuil, 1963.

Pope, Hugh. *The Teaching of St. Augustine on Prayer and the Contemplative Life.* London: Burns Oates and Washbourne, 1935.

Poulin, Augustin-François. *Des grâces d'oraison. Traité de théologie mystique.* 11th ed. Paris: Beauchesne, 1931.

Pseudo-Dionysius. *The Complete Works.* Mahwah: Paulist Press, 1987.

Raimondo da Capua. *La Vie miraculeuse de la seraphique et devote Ste. Catherine de Siene.* Lyon: Pierre Rigaud, 1615.

    The copy of this edition preserved at Les Fontaines at Chantilly came from the Monastère de la Visitation Sainte Maire de Reims. This work is available in an English translation: *The Life of Catherine of Siena,* trans. with intro. and notes by Conleth Kearns, O.P. (Dublin: Dominican Publications, and Wilmington: Michael Glazier, Inc., 1980).

Ratzinger, Joseph. *Lettre aux évêques de l'Eglise catholique sur quelques aspect de la méditation chrétienne.* Paris: Tequi, 1989.

Raymond De Capoue. *See* Raimondo da Capua.

Renty, M. de. *See* Saint-Jure, *La Vie de Monsieur de Renty.*

Ricard, Robert. "La Folle du logis." *Vie et langage,* no. 100 (July 1960), 387–89.

———. "La loca de la casa." *Mélanges de la casa de Velasquez,* 3:487–91. Paris-Madrid, 1967.

Rigoleu, Jean (1595–1658). *See also* Champion, *La Vie du Père Jean Rigoleu.*

Rigoleu, Jean. *L'Oraison sans illusion: contre les erreurs de la fausse contemplation.* Paris: Estienne Michellet, 1687.

    This is Treatise 2 and 3 of 1686 ed. of *La Vie . . . Rigoleu,* but the definitive edition to use is that of 1698, given above under Champion, Pierre.

Saint-Jure, Jean-Baptiste. *La Vie de Monsieur de Renty.* Paris: P. Le Petit, 1651.

Schmittlein, Raymond. *L'Aspect politique du différend Bossuet-Fénelon.* Bade: Art et Science Bade, 1954.

Scupoli, Lorenzo. *The Spiritual Combat, and a Treatise on Peace of Soul.* Rockford: Tan Books and Publishers, 1990, a photographic reproduction of the Paulist Press edition.

Surin, Jean-Joseph. "Addition à la *Doctrine spirituelle* du P. Louis Lallemant." In Champion, *La Vie et la doctrine spirituelle du Père L. Lallemant,* 492ff.

———. *Catéchisme spirituel.* 2nd ed. Paris: Claude Cramoisy, 1663.

———. *Correspondence.* Paris: Desclée de Brouwer, 1966.

———. *Dialogues spirituels, où la perfection chrétienne est expliquée pour toutes sortes de personnes.* 2 vols. Avignon: Les Frères Delorme, 1721.

———. *Les Fondements de la vie spirituelle tirés du livre de l'Imitation de Jésus-Christ.* Paris: Editions Spes, 1930, based on the original seventeenth-century edition.

———. *Guide spirituel.* Paris: Desclée de Brouwer, 1963, based on a seventeenth-century manuscript and a work that surely circulated fairly widely in manuscript form.

———. *Lettres spirituelles.* 2 vols. Avignon: Les Frères Delorme, 1721

———. *Les Secrets de la vie spirituelle enseignées par . . . et par un berger à un bon religieux en forme de conférence spirituelle. . . . II partie par le R. P. Surin de la même Compagnie.* Pages 133ff. Paris: Sebastien Huré, 1661.

Suzuki, Shunryu. *Zen Mind, Beginner's Mind.* New York: Weatherhill, 1977.

Tanner, Norman P., G. Alberigo, et al. *Decrees of the Ecumenical Councils.* 2 vols. Washington D.C.: Georgetown University Press, 1990.

Teresa of Avila. *The Collected Works.* Trans. Kieran Kavanaugh and Otilio Rodriguez. 3 vols. ICS Publications: Washington D.C., 1976–1985.

Thomas Aquinas, St. *Summa theologica.*

Underhill, Evelyn. *Mysticism: A Study in the Nature and Development of Man's Spiritual Consciousness.* Cleveland: World Publishing Co., 1955.

Vincent, Monique. *Saint Augustin, maître de prière d'après les Enarrationes in Psalmos.* Collection Théologie Historique, no. 84. Paris: Beauchesne, 1990.